Bruce Nauman — Raw Materials

Tate Publishing

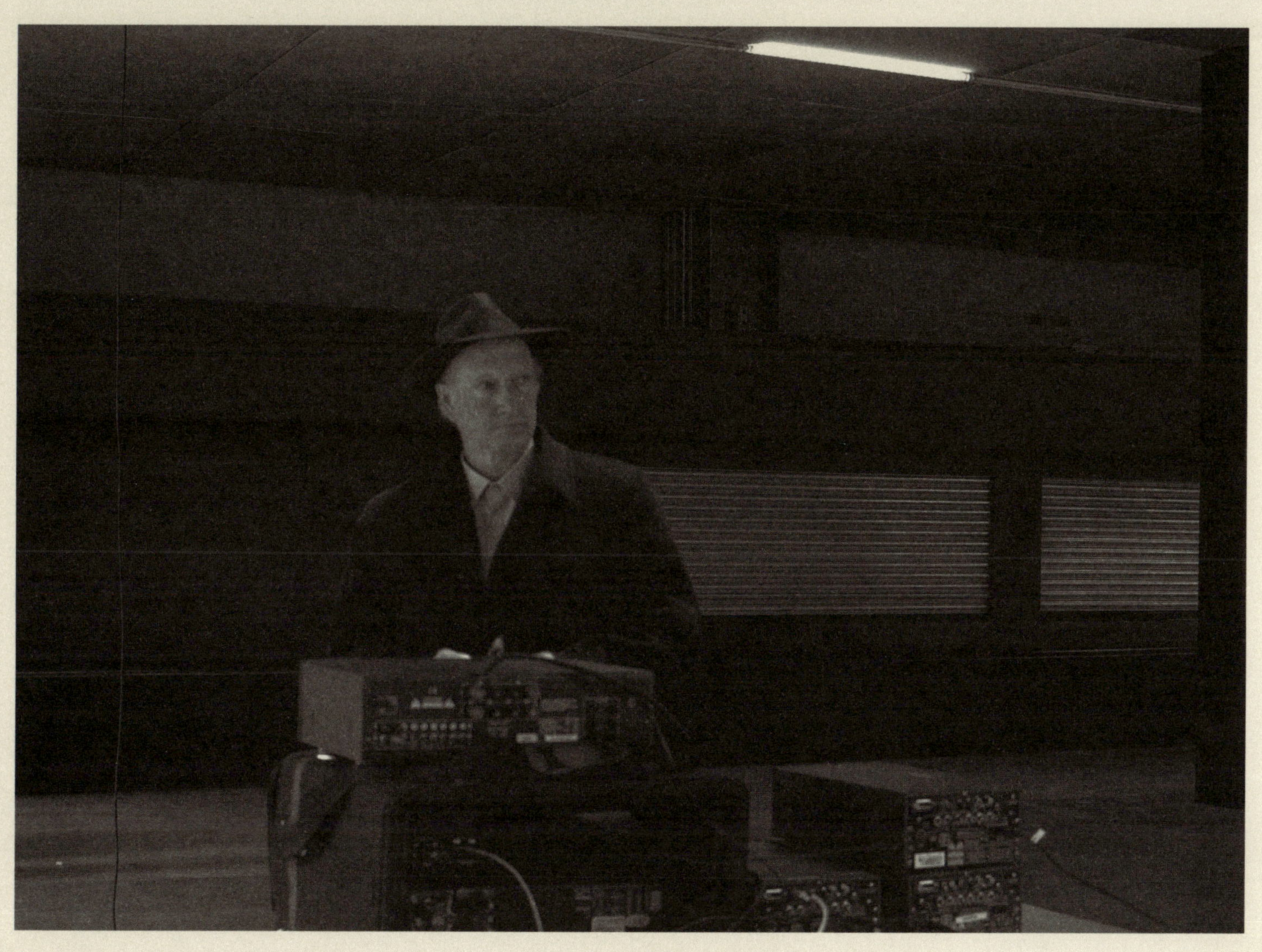

Bruce Nauman at Tate Modern, April 2004

The Unilever Series
An annual art commission sponsored by Unilever

Published by order of the Tate Trustees
on the occasion of the exhibition at Tate Modern, London
12 October 2004 – 28 March 2005

This exhibition is the fifth commission in The Unilever Series

Published 2004 by Tate Publishing,
a division of Tate Enterprises Ltd,
Millbank, London SW1P 4RG
www.tate.org.uk/publishing

British Library Cataloguing in Publication Data
A catalogue record for this book is available
from the British Library

ISBN 1 85437 559 8 (pbk)
ISBN 1 85437 602 0 (hbk)

Distributed in the United States and Canada by
Harry N. Abrams, Inc., New York

Library of Congress Cataloging in Publication Data
Library of Congress Control Number 2004111327

Designed by Cartlidge Levene
Printed and bound in Belgium by Die Keure

Cover: Bruce Nauman Thank You 1992 (detail)
Ydessa Hendeles Art Foundation

Contents Page

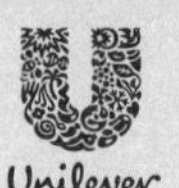

Sponsor's Foreword

The Unilever Series has gone from strength to strength since its inception in 2000, with each successive commission finding breathtaking new ways to transform the vast space of the Turbine Hall. In this, the fifth year of The Unilever Series, the internationally renowned artist Bruce Nauman has explored a fresh dimension: sound. In the same way that Anish Kapoor's Marsyas and Olafur Eliasson's The Weather Project filled the Turbine Hall visually, Nauman's Raw Materials has filled it aurally. We congratulate him on his magnificent work.

Unilever is proud to be a founder sponsor of Tate Modern. The Unilever Series reflects Unilever's passion for creativity, innovation and our new corporate mission – to add vitality to life. To us, vitality is about more than health and well-being; it's about enjoyment, stimulation and quality of life in its broadest sense. The Unilever Series is the epitome of that mission, bringing inspirational art to millions of people each year. In recognition of this we have strengthened our commitment to Tate Modern by extending The Unilever Series until 2008, so that millions more can be moved and challenged in the coming years.

Patrick Cescau
Chairman, Unilever

Since Tate Modern opened in 2000, the Turbine Hall has become one of the world's most celebrated museum spaces. It is a great honour that Bruce Nauman has produced Raw Materials, an ambitious new work, for the fifth commission in The Unilever Series. Emerging in the mid-1960s, Nauman has remained one of the most enigmatic, groundbreaking and engaging artists of our times. Although widely considered a sculptor, his work has consistently evaded any confinement to sculptural conventions, and he has used a broad range of materials, including video, neon, photography, prints, architectural installation and sound. While Nauman has explored certain themes throughout his career, he can be relied upon to surprise and challenge his audience. With characteristic sleight of hand and play on language, Raw Materials addresses itself to volume, and in the process challenges our common understanding of sculpture. The Turbine Hall is empty but its entire space has, paradoxically, been filled with acoustic material. There are no sculptural elements in the conventional sense, only twenty-two voices played through speakers located throughout the Turbine Hall, which the artist has neither gone to great lengths to hide nor to make visible. Each audio track is a text related to one of Nauman's works in which language is explored, interrogated and tested to its breaking point, just as he has done with the sculptural and linguistic possibilities of the word 'volume'. Even though the vastness of the Turbine Hall seems untouched, Nauman's work is utterly specific to the qualities of the space, which is, to a great extent, defined by the insistent background hum of the building. Like a great cathedral, the Turbine Hall has a unique sonority – a combination of its awesome architecture, drone and visitors' behaviour.

Nauman's brilliance as an artist is the ability to always bring the underlying ambiguities and contradictions of his subject-matter to the surface. We cannot thank him enough for the privilege of working on this extraordinary commission that transforms our perception of the Turbine Hall as a sonic space. Employing the simplest of means to convey such a vastly complex set of ideas has made this a rewarding process for everyone involved. Sheena Wagstaff, Tate Modern's Head of Exhibitions and Displays, started initial discussions with the artist, and in the past year Nauman has worked closely with Emma Dexter, Senior Curator at Tate Modern, who has curated this project and catalogue with familiar dedication and professionalism. Her essay for the catalogue illuminates how the artist's past practice has fed into this particular commission. My thanks go to her and to Ben Borthwick, who has provided exceptional organisational and administrative support for the project, as well as writing invaluable catalogue entries that trace the disparate sources of this work. The various tests and the final installation were expertly managed by Phil Monk, whose work with Fergus Rougier of Sound Directions and the team at Marquee Audio was instrumental in realising the project. Our efforts have been augmented by the unstinting support of Angela Westwater and her staff at Sperone Westwater Gallery, as well as Juliet Myers at Nauman's studio. The delicate job of mastering audio that was, in certain instances, recorded on primitive video technology and of giving it clarity was handled by Dennis Diamond of Video D Studios in New York.

We would also like to thank everyone whose efforts are realised in this catalogue, in particular Michael Auping for contributing such a comprehensive survey of Nauman's career, John Jervis and Sarah Tucker for steering it through the editorial and production processes with such energy, Cliff Lauson for his research in all areas, Alessandra Serri for sourcing the images, Tate photographers Andrew Dunkley and Marcus Leith, and Hector Pottie of Cartlidge Levene for his elegant design.

A work of this complexity and importance necessitates dedicated input from across Tate, particularly from Press and Marketing: Nadine Thompson, Ruth Findlay, Jennifer Lea, Caroline Priest; Development: Nicky White, Amanda Cropper and Camilla Miesegaes; Education and Interpretation: Dominic Willsdon, Stuart Comer and Jane Burton; Digital Programmes: Jemima Rellie, Will Renny and Kelli Dipple; Events: Brad Macdonald, Emily Paget and Denise Yeats; and at Tate Modern: Steven Mellor, Dennis Ahern and Adrian Hardwicke. As a courtesy we would also like to acknowledge and thank all the owners of those works, from both public and private collections, that have provided the inspiration or the source text for Raw Materials – many have been dedicated supporters of Nauman's work from the earliest years.

Finally, we would like to offer our most sincere gratitude to Unilever and its Chairman Patrick Cescau. This commitment to Tate Modern was established by Niall FitzGerald, Unilever Chairman between 1996–2004, whose vision helped bring the unique contributions of the artists commissioned in the first five years of The Unilever Series to a vast, diverse public. Without this level of support, projects of this ambition and scale would not be possible. After an astonishing series of commissions, we are delighted that this collaboration has already been extended for a further three years.

Vicente Todolí
Director, Tate Modern

Metacommunicator

Michael Auping

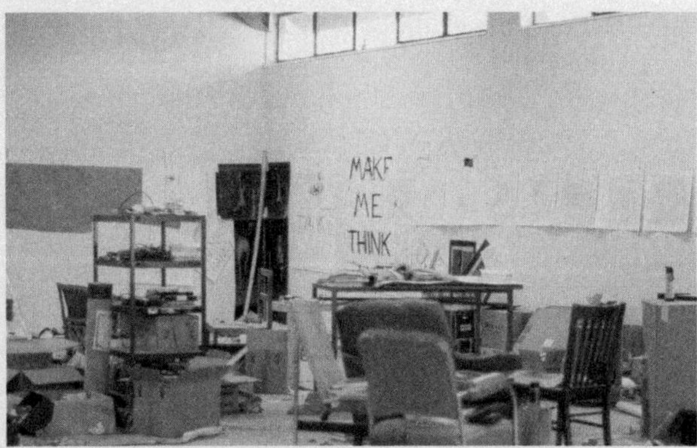

Fig.1
View of Bruce Nauman's studio, 1993

Sculpture is a pretty big area. There aren't a lot of limitations that you don't impose yourself … The biggest problem is deciding what not to use, and then not using too much of what you do. It seems to revolve around how much to give and how much not to give. I'm interested in the tension between these two decisions – using a little bit of a lot of things. Bruce Nauman[1]

I always listen to what I can leave out. Miles Davis[2]

One of the central questions that Bruce Nauman has consistently posed to himself is, how much information should be offered, and in what form? For Nauman, this is not just a question concerning art, but communication in general. If, as they say, relationships are based on communication, Nauman will be the first to ask, what constitutes communication, and what are the boundaries of its form? To a certain degree, all artists ask this question, but few stretch the boundaries as elastically as Nauman. Throughout his career, he has intrigued and frustrated his audience in equal parts by speaking minimally in a variety of forms and 'tongues'. The result is a powerful, if at times disquieting, form of communication.

Nauman, who began making art in the mid-1960s, witnessed the powerful rise of Minimalism. One of the early chroniclers of that movement, Rosalind Krauss, described it as a type of formalism so austere as to be analogous with 'inert matter – with things untouched by thought or unmediated by personality'.[3] Nauman absorbed the deadpan drama of 'less is more', but his eventual contribution was to shape Minimalism's iconic (platonic) form into something more mutative and psychological. His work has become the quintessential example of the famous 1969 exhibition title that in many ways defined his generation: When Attitudes Become Form.[4]

Nauman's awareness of Minimalism notwithstanding, his early work emerged at a time when a great deal was occurring in the art world, much of it 'minimal', but equally distinctive was the fact that it was occurring in a remarkably wide range of forms and media. What would eventually be called post-Minimalism was an explosion of experimental, often deconstructive, work in film, video, sculpture, performance, music, dance, Conceptual art and photography. Nauman is unusual in his ability to synthesise this diverse range of media into his artistic practice. Since his earliest work of 1965, he has worked in freestanding sculpture, drawing, site-specific installation, sound pieces, neon, photography, film, video, performance and text/language, the last being a particularly important but often under-recognised aspect of his output.

Nauman's inclination to cross-wire disciplines surfaced early in his education. Before he was an artist, he briefly fashioned himself as a mathematician. 'Toward the end of high school', he recalled recently:

I had a very good physics teacher and then a math teacher who offered to work with some of us on calculus, which was not offered, but was needed for the more interesting physics. So when I got to the University I got into some more advanced courses. While I found that I didn't have a great passion for the kind of physics that was being done, or at least the way it was being taught there, the theoretical math that was going on was of interest and I stuck with that for a while ... I always liked the structural aspects of mathematics. It's a rigorous language that stays vital by creating problems that then carry the language farther.

Nauman's mathematical interests took him toward topology, which Webster's defines as 'The study of those properties of geometric figures that remain unchanged even when under distortion, so long as no surfaces are torn, as with a Möbius strip.' The classic example of this kind of transference is between a doughnut and a coffee cup. The theoretical exercise involves imagining that both objects are made of a substance like putty. We can take either item and transform it into the other by stretching and squeezing, without tearing the material or sticking together bits that were previously separate. It follows that there is no topological difference between the two. Nauman would eventually approach the making of art in topological terms, in the sense that his work consists of twisting without tearing one idea or form into a number of different media and disciplines.

At the University of Wisconsin, Nauman began to study music (in particular, the works of Beethoven, Webern, Berg and Schoenberg) and for a time worked as a jazz bassist. 'At some point', he explains:

I started to slip into the music department. Again, I was interested in music theory and composition rather than having to practice, and that didn't go over too well. What was interesting was that I had the same feeling for music that I had for mathematics and eventually for art. For me a lot of it had to do with the rearrangement of conditions within a discipline; seeing if you could find the edge of the structure. The decision to become an artist comes out of this somehow, but is still inexplicable to me.

Nauman's roaming did not stop there. He also took a class in the philosophy department, and through his ongoing studies in mathematics and logic became especially interested in Ludwig Wittgenstein. Wittgenstein's research centred on the nature of language and its relation to the world, continuously pushing at the edges of language and the limits of philosophy. In Tractatus Logico-Philosophicus (1921) he wrote, 'The boundaries of my language mean the boundaries of my world.'[5] Wittgenstein's writings are the work of a lexical minimalist, characterised by rigorous brevity. The Tractatus consists of seven brief propositions, each – save the last – followed by many further propositions (numbered in decimal system) that elucidate and develop what has gone before. His 'lectures', given to small groups of devotees, involved periods of intense concentration during which he 'thought aloud', asking a barrage of questions until a problem had been solved, or proved unsolvable or nonsensical. 'I liked the clarity of his process', Nauman recalls, 'and the fact that he developed an argument to the point of logical absurdity – the point where logic and language break down.'

One of Nauman's earliest works, CODIFICATION 1966, is a text piece that in its terse style echoes Wittgenstein. Written during the year that he graduated with an MFA from the University of California, Davis, it is a rudimentary lexical map of subjects that the young artist was interested in investigating. Like a researcher identifying problems, Nauman wrote:

CODIFICATION, 1966

1. Personal appearance and skin
2. Gestures
3. Ordinary actions such as those concerned with eating and drinking
4. Traces of activity such as footprints and material objects
5. Simple sounds – spoken and written words
   Metacommunication messages

Feedback
Analogic and digital codification

Over the next four decades, each of these themes would play an interchangeable role in what Nauman would summarise as 'Metacommunication messages'. Like the anthropologist and researcher Gregory Bateson, who published influential studies in communication theory and perception, Nauman used a word not found in Webster's to describe a complex condition. The combining of two words, *meta* ('between', 'among') and *communication* ('the act of transmitting; a giving or exchanging of information, signals, or messages'), suggests the existence of porous boundaries within a kind of communication that can take place 'between signals'. In other words, communication that in gestalt terms is greater than the sum of its parts. The type of messaging in which Nauman engaged in the late 1960s, addressing directly or obliquely the subjects/analogies laid out in CODIFICATION, sometimes forged and often tested the relationship between words, forms and their meanings.

Nauman's initial approach was through humour, using a deadpan documentary style of photography in Eleven Color Photographs 1966–7 to create a series of visual/verbal puns in which common statements were materialised: a photograph of two feet covered in clay (Feet of Clay); a photograph of Nauman

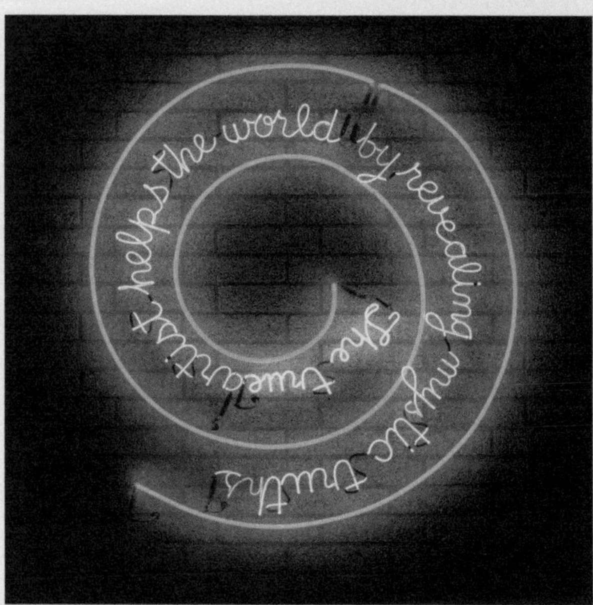

Fig.2
The True Artist Helps the World by Revealing Mystic Truths (Window or Wall Sign) 1967. Neon tubing with clear glass tubing suspension frame, 149.9 x 139.7 x 5.1. Collection Kröller Müller, Otterlo

polishing the red letters H.O.T. (*Waxing Hot*); and another in which he spreads jam on letters cut out of bread (*Eating My Words*). One of the most interesting photographs in the series is an image of Nauman's arms tied behind his back, entitled *Bound to Fail*.

Bound to Fail refers to the dilemma of the artist and his ambiguous role as messenger in modern society, and was quickly followed by one of Nauman's most celebrated word sculptures. When he rented a vacant grocery store in San Francisco's Mission District for a studio in 1967, he inherited an old neon beer sign. With its droning buzz and its radiant words, the sign inspired Nauman to experiment with another materialisation of language. In this case, he probed the boundaries between public messaging and private thinking. In bright blue cursive script that spirals out from a centre, Nauman's sign reads, 'The true artist helps the world by revealing mystic truths' (fig.2). What initially reads as deadpan humour, on further reflection turns out to be more complicated. In *The True Artist*, the business of advertising and the high-minded business of art are wickedly confused, and as he has so often done throughout his career, Nauman articulates a position carefully balanced between sense and possible nonsense. In the 1960s, the glow of a neon sign in a storefront window was not unusual. Markets, liquor stores and bars all employed them, most often to advertise a form of alcoholic beverage. Nauman replaced a beer sign with a deeply philosophical message, the kind of idealistic statement one might make after drinking more than a few beers.

Recalling Wittgenstein's conjectural lecture statements, Nauman explains, 'I was just wondering out loud. I needed to see it visually to test if I believed it.' The fact that he chose a statement that could not be proven was part of the point. 'When you're starting out, you're naturally asking a lot of questions, and some of them are very tough. The things that you can't answer are sometimes the things you should be putting out there.'

The True Artist was in fact an opening question or series of questions in an ongoing dialogue that Nauman has continually conducted with his audience. Exactly what is the role of an artist? What do we expect an artist to communicate – redemption, comfort, private-autobiographical expressions, entertainment, platonic form? For better or worse, he offers us none of these. What he does do is play on these expectations. Nauman's art is one of imbalance, constantly shifting the rules of engagement, inducing us to think about how we construct our image of the world and our image of ourselves. In Nauman's world, these differences often create a dysfunctional relationship.

In this sense, Nauman is not the subject of his art. We are the subject. Nauman is the ghost in the machine, and few artists use absence to such great effect. *CODIFICATION #4* reads, 'Traces of activity such as footprints ...'. A footprint is a negative positive, an absence that communicates the existence of form. In 1966, when performance and Body art were beginning to emerge, often focusing on autobiographical narratives, Nauman used his body as a template, which resulted in hollow self-portraits in which the sculpture would consist of an empty cast of fragments of the artist's body.

Even when he stepped in front of his own camera, Nauman would perform a type of self-effacement. CODIFICATION #1 – 'Personal appearance and skin' – would be explored in Art Make-Up 1967, in which he demonstrates that the flip side of 'personal appearance' is non-appearance. In the video he is shown using his face and upper torso as a canvas for applying successive layers of coloured makeup, literally masking himself and making himself up at the same time. In this sense, he turns Robert Rauschenberg's famous Erased de Kooning 1953 back on himself. As Nauman puts it, 'You are not getting what you are not getting.'

In 'Notes and Projects', published in the December 1970 issue of Artforum, one of the most interesting notations reads, 'Withdrawal as an Artform.' As Nauman remembers it, 'I got interested in how much information you could take away from a situation and still have it be effective.' In most cases, however, there was still room for language. Indeed, the more the artist took away, the more language seemed to insinuate itself into the work – a way of withdrawing and speaking directly to his audience at the same time.

Nonetheless, Nauman has always defined himself as a sculptor, and as such, spatial issues are paramount in his thinking. He was one of the pioneers in the late 1960s and early 1970s of what came to be loosely known as 'Installation Art'. This involved creating a physical structure within a room to alter the viewer's perception of the space, or using existing architecture to contain the viewer, literally placing him or her inside the sculpture. Within this genre, Nauman's installations are distinguished by their austerity, as well as by their psychological underpinnings.

In one of his most powerful installations, Get Out of My Mind, Get Out of This Room 1968, language became a way of communicating with his audience, but at the same time, he aggressively withdrew. The work consisted of an empty room with speakers hidden in the walls. In this case, Nauman felt the need to vocalise his language, directing the viewer, who had no idea where the voice was coming from, to 'Get out of my mind, get out of this room'. The standard narrative of activity and expectation was shattered. The artist is given a room, makes a work of art for that room, invites us into the room, and then implores us to get out. The work acknowledges the ambiguous, darkly comic relationship between artist and audience, and the tension that exists when private and public spaces overlap.

The premise is almost comical, but the effect is insidious. Here language, in its spoken incarnation, achieves a graphic and mental effect that resonates both attraction and repulsion. The pacing and different emphasis of Nauman's vocalisations are emotional, poetic, deadpan, dramatic, even musical at times. 'Music plays a role in a lot of my work', Nauman has said. 'Even when there is no music.' In recording Get Out of My Mind, Get Out of This Room, he used different intonations, as he remembers, 'yelling, imploring, hissing, etc.', in an effort to communicate the sense of urgency of the message. Such verbal statements have been interpreted as 'commands' and a heavy-handed, authoritarian means of manipulating the viewer. This first-layer response is only half of the equation, however. In fact, Nauman's voice acknowledges the viewer in a highly intimate way. He has transformed the room into a metaphor of his mind, and we are standing directly inside it. We are the subject of the artist's mind, and his disembodied voice resonates as if his mind were in direct contact with us. The result is a strangely intimate melding of mind, language and sculpture.

In Get Out of My Mind both artist and audience are caught in a dynamic of exposure and withdrawal, a dynamic that Nauman would explore in subsequent works. 'When you are alone, you accept the space by filling it with your presence', he would say in a 1979 Vanguard interview, but 'as soon as someone else comes into view, you withdraw and protect yourself.'[6] False Silence 1975 consists of a long, narrow corridor that draws the viewer in with bright lights emanating midway down the passage (figs.50–1). The illumination leads to triangular rooms – one on each side – that are small, sharp-cornered dead ends, initially as seductive as false escapes are in reality. When filled with other people, these spaces begin to evoke what is perhaps an innate fear of intimacy with strangers, the claustrophobic walls feeling tighter, like a crowded elevator. When you are alone, Nauman's voice becomes audible:

YOU CAN'T REACH ME. YOU CAN'T HURT ME
I CAN SUCK YOU DRY

YOU CAN'T HURT ME
YOU CAN'T HELP ME
SHUFFLE THE PAGES
FIND ME A LINE
ARAPAHOE, ARAPAHOE
WHERE DID YOU GO
I BLINK MY EYES
TO KEEP THE TIME

At a certain point, the hypnotic effect of the voice allows the language to detach itself from the sender. Is Nauman talking to us, or are we talking to ourselves? The title False Silence may be a reference to John Cage, whose work inspired Nauman early in his career, and whose concerts may have included silent

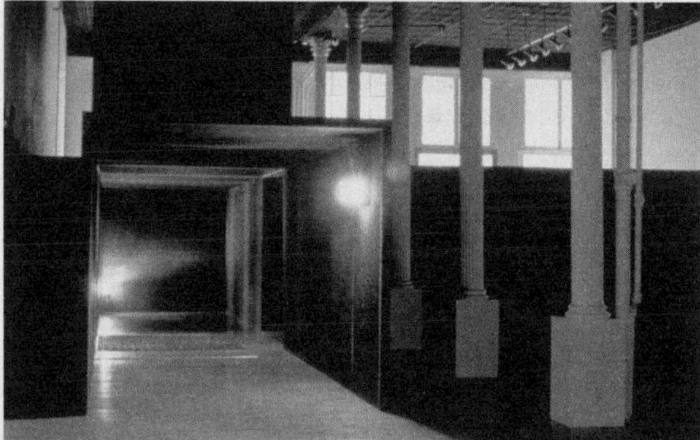

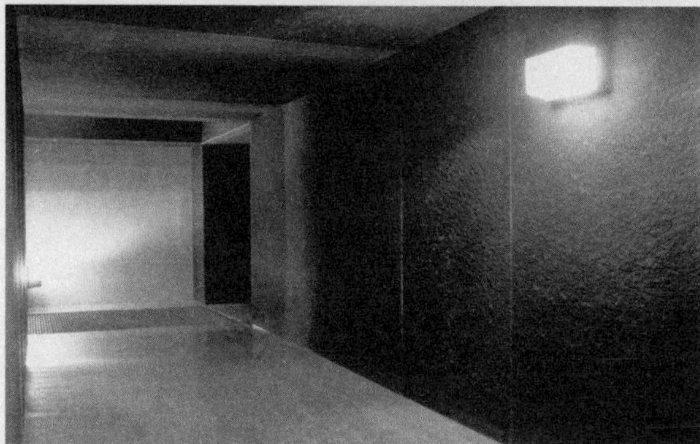

Figs.3 & 4
Room with My Soul Left Out, Room That Does Not Care 1984. Celotex, steel grate, yellow lights, 1,036.3 x 1,463 x 929.6. Installed at Leo Castelli Gallery, New York, 1984. Collection of the artist

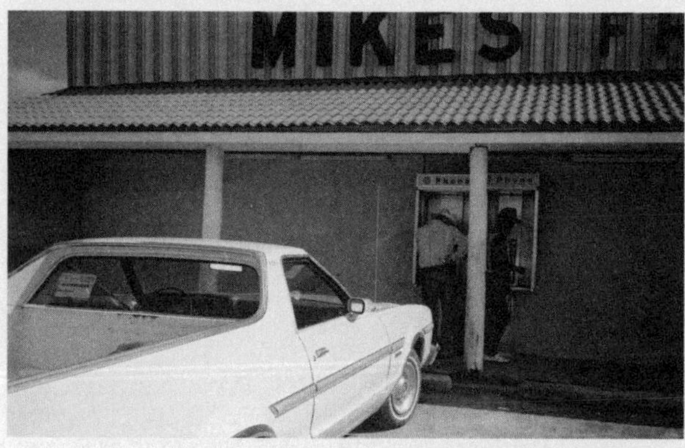

Fig.5
Bruce Nauman at a telephone booth, July 1991

musicians but certainly not genuine silence. Nauman adds a psychological dimension. 'There is no silence', he has said. 'Your mind makes noise.'

In a 1984 installation, Nauman built an elaborate structure identified by only a few words, yet these words fill the piece with emptiness, if not pathos: Room with My Soul Left Out, Room that Does Not Care (figs.3–4). The multi-level installation consists of three intersecting black Celotex tunnels (two horizontal and one vertical). Where the three tubes meet, the floor is covered with a grating, through which it is possible to look into a vertical shaft continuing down into the basement. The tunnels are lit with a yellow light that is dimmed by the surrounding black walls. The effect is that of a distant light at the end of long tunnels.

Again, private and public space become strangely confused. The experience involves a shifting between introspection and voyeurism. At times, the sound of people walking and whispering in different parts of the installation is apparent, and the temptation to eavesdrop irresistible. Then it becomes obvious that the opposite is also true. While there are powerful moments of being alone, there is also the sense of watching and being watched. Standing where the three passageways come together, one feels conspicuously exposed, since people can look in from different directions. The term 'alone in a crowd' comes to mind. Nauman compares the experience to what he calls the 'telephone booth syndrome': in order to make a private telephone call, Nauman points out, 'one has to step into a booth, which means one stands out uncomfortably, because of the separation from the crowd outside'.[7]

The development of these environments coincided with Nauman's interest in Frederick Perls's Gestalt psychology, and his theories of perceptual organisation geared towards understanding the structure of the human personality and how it functions within an environmental field. Nauman explains:

> *What interested me was the idea that you go to your resistances, to whatever physical or social situation in your life or your work causes you problems. In other words, you don't try to avoid the resistance. You go straight to it, try to analyse the parts that make you uncomfortable. You can get at those things physically and then certain mental blocks will be released, or you can get at them mentally, using language, and then certain physical blocks will be released – or at least you will react physically to certain disruptions in the mental pattern. I've always thought that was an interesting approach, even if you think about it in terms of sculpture.*

Between 1971 and 1975, Nauman created a number of works in which language is combined with different environments to create rooms that offer a resistance to perceptual patterning, in the form of uncomfortably proportioned and strangely lit corridors and rooms. Anyone who has ever experienced one of these installations remembers the experience of talking oneself through it. Nauman makes things more complicated by providing language in the form of written texts accompanying the installation that simultaneously stimulate and irritate the relation between mind and environment. In some cases these writings inspired the making of a particular space, and in others the space called for the language. Regardless, the result is an experience that takes place between the language and the space.

In 1971 Nauman constructed an austere and awkwardly configured space based on irregular corner and wall relationships. Originally titled Installation with Yellow Lights but renamed Left or Standing, Standing or Left Standing, it took the form of a trapezoidal room lit with bright yellow fluorescent light and flanked by two wedge-shaped rooms that were illuminated with clean white gallery lighting (see figs.67–72). There were only two parallel walls in the entire configuration, and making sense of the architecture was exacerbated by the lighting: adjusting from cool white to fluorescent yellow creates shadowy purple after-images.

A third element in this disjunctive gestalt was language. When he was asked to make a poster for the exhibition, Nauman recalls that he 'couldn't imagine what particular image could represent this space. There wasn't any part that summed it up. There wasn't an image that could give you that underlying sense that you were maybe in the wrong place.' So he resorted once again to language. Rather than making a poster, he wrote a prose text, which was distributed as a broadsheet with the sculpture, and later shown on a monitor:

Left or Standing

His precision and accuracy
suggesting clean cuts, leaving
a vacancy, a slight physical
depression as though I had been
in a vaguely uncomfortable place
for a not long but undeterminable
period; not waiting.

Standing or Left Standing

His preciseness and acuity left
small cuts on the tips of my
fingers or across the backs of
my hands without any need to
sit or otherwise withdraw.

The text has a strange and somewhat strained relationship to the space. Using a minimum of words, it in no way attempts to describe the physical character of the rooms. Yet it evokes a mental condition that seems to parallel it. The text and the space touch each other through strangely discursive analogies in which reasoning and consciousness blur with disconnectedness and unconscious feeling. Seeing the text on a monitor before walking into the space is particularly effective because the language provides an internal dissonance that anticipates the low levels of anxieties and subtle discomfort evoked in the space. A word comes into focus on the video screen, and then lingers in the back of the mind while one walks through a room that does not seem to be a room at all, but a moment on the way to somewhere else. Since there is nothing specific to focus on, deciding where to walk or stand becomes an exaggerated condition. The title/repeat title suggests a sense of location that is neither deliberate nor accidental: 'as though I had been in a vaguely uncomfortable place for a not long but undeterminable period; not waiting'. As a sculpture constructed both physically and linguistically, Left or Standing taps that slightly anxious pivot point between the physical and the mental that does not make sense but is not nonsense. Nor is it surreal; 'sub-real' would be a more accurate description – an experience that takes place below normal channels of communication.

Nauman's reference in his text to skin ('small cuts on the tips of my fingers') is another way in which he destabilises boundaries. Willem de Kooning, the Abstract Expressionist whom Nauman greatly admired as a graduate student, once said, 'I think one could spend one's life having this desire to be in and outside at the same time.'[8] De Kooning also remarked that flesh was the reason why oil painting was invented, and he began his famous series of Woman paintings with the image of a mouth, an area of the body that is inside and outside at the same time. Skin is often referred to in Nauman's work, whether in relation to the human body, architecture or sculpture. Nauman has often probed those boundaries, physically and metaphorically, deliberately confusing the two. The surface of his cast sculptures shows the rough interior of the moulds that made them, while the exteriors of his corridors expose the two-by-fours and unpainted drywall that are typically hidden inside such sculptural installations.

Nauman uses architecture as a metaphor for the human body, containers to be turned inside out. His 1973 installation Flayed Earth/Flayed Self (Skin/Sink) (figs.6–7), for example, consists of long lines of masking tape spiralling out from the centre of a rectangular floor onto the walls. Crossing the borders between walls and floor, the taped lines give the subtle illusion of cutting through the box-like space, flaying it into a spiral. Another physically austere installation, it incorporates one of his longest pieces of prose writing, and like the masking tape that suggests both a contraction and expansion of the room, the text spirals in and out of mental and sculptural conditions:

... The problem is to divide your
skin into six equal parts
lines starting at your feet and
ending at your head (five lines to make six
equal surface areas) to twist and spiral

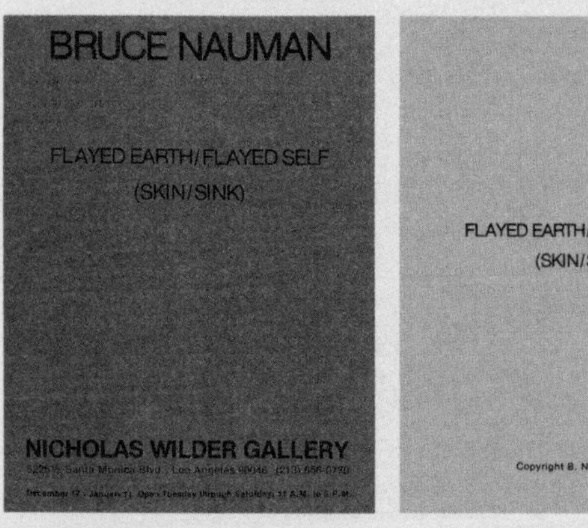

BRUCE NAUMAN

FLAYED EARTH/FLAYED SELF
(SKIN/SINK)

NICHOLAS WILDER GALLERY

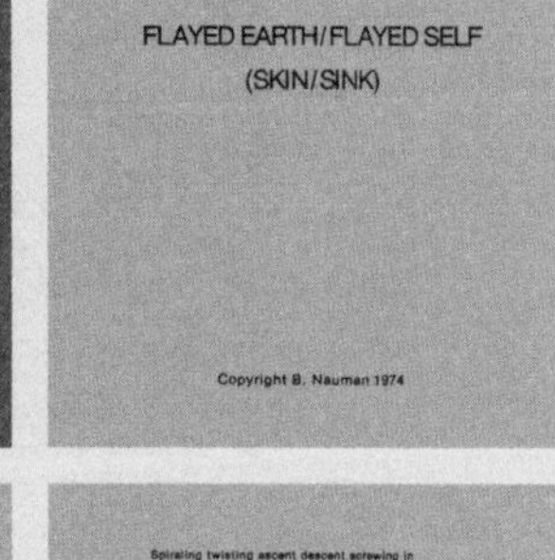

FLAYED EARTH/FLAYED SELF
(SKIN/SINK)

Copyright B. Nauman 1974

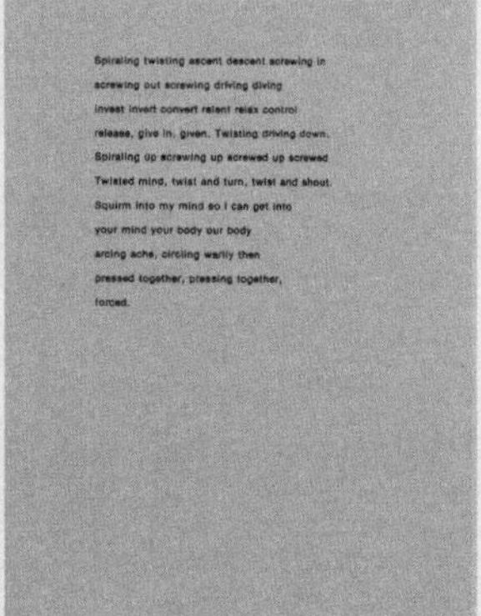

Peeling skin peeling earth - peeled earth
raw earth, peeled skin
The problem is to divide your
skin into six equal parts
lines starting at your feet and
ending at your head (five lines to make six
equal surface areas) to twist and spiral
into the ground, your skin peeling off
stretching and expanding to cover the surface
of the earth indicated by the spiraling
waves generated by the spiraling twisting
screwing descent and investiture (investment
or investing) of the earth by your swelling body.

Spiraling twisting ascent descent screwing in
screwing out screwing driving diving
invest invert convert relent relax control
release, give in, given. Twisting driving down.
Spiraling up screwing up screwed up screwed
Twisted mind, twist and turn, twist and shout.
Squirm into my mind so I can get into
your mind your body our body
arcing ache, circling warily then
pressed together, pressing together,
forced.

Fig.6
Flayed Earth/Flayed Self (Skin/Sink) 1973.
Text. Collection of the artist

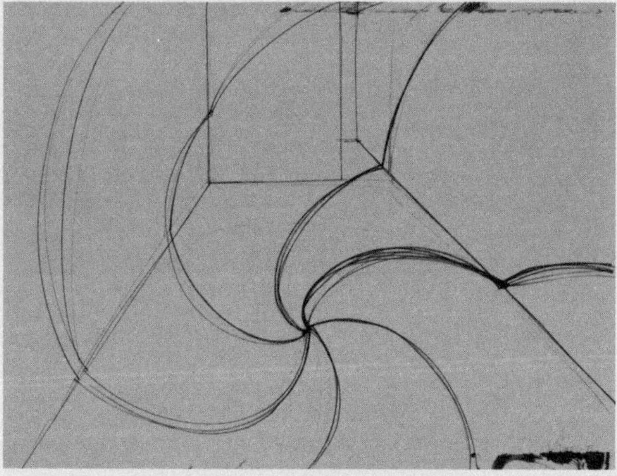

Fig.7
Untitled (Drawing for Flayed Earth/Flayed Self: Skin/Sink) 1973. Pencil, felt pen and ink, 56.5 x 102.
Zurich, Crex Collection

into the ground, your skin peeling off
stretching and expanding to cover the surface
of the earth indicated by the spiraling
waves generated by the spiraling twisting ...

The text accompanying the piece carries much of the sculpture's energy, and again brings into play questions of attachment and withdrawal, and of boundaries between the mental and the physical, in this case with an erotic dimension. At one moment the artist recedes: 'I AM AN IMPLODING LIGHT BULB'. As he pulls himself inward, he draws us in: 'Squirm into my mind so I can get into your mind your body our body ...'.

In Nauman's art, a need to withdraw is inextricably tied to a need to connect, to cross the boundary between self-protection and an opening up. In this regard, some of his texts seem powerfully honest and self-confessional. The text for the sculptural installation Consummate Mask of Rock 1975 was initially titled The Mask to Cover the Need for Human Companionship (see figs.73–7). The installation revolves around the subject of relationships: one formal and material, the other psychological and linguistic. The former involves the use of stone to unsettle the viewer's relationship to the room. Sandstone blocks of different sizes (14- and 15-inch cubes) are arranged in pairs around the perimeter of a large room. At first glance, the arrangement suggests a mathematical or musical system of positioning. The diagonal configurations of the scattered pairs and the variation in heights of the stones, however, disturb the serene cubical character of the room. The diagonal placement of each stone within a pair suggests shifting perspectives and ambiguous movement, as if the paired stones are coming together and falling away at the same time. It is not difficult to see the stones as a surrogate group of people, particularly after reading Nauman's text, which uses words to explore the uneven way in which people relate. Here the artist is communicating in a clearly analogical way.

In an act of Wittgensteinian rigour, Consummate Mask of Rock begins with a series of statements about human companionship based on different combinations of seventeen words, among them *mask*, *fidelity*, *truth*, *cover*, *pain*, *desire*, *need*. As he had done in the Art Make-Up films, Nauman uses the mask as a symbol of communication between people.

14. This is the need for pain that contorts my mask conveying the message of truth and fidelity to life.
15. This is the truth that distorts my need for human companionship.
16. This is the distortion of truth masked by my painful need.

17. This is the mask of my painful need distressed by truth and human companionship.
18. This is my painless mask that fails to touch my face but floats before the surface of my skin my eyes my teeth my tongue.

Each statement has a penetrating truthfulness. A few of the statements are in capital letters, presumably indicating their importance to the artist. 'COVER REVOKED' speaks of the need to unmask, to reveal oneself as part of the process of communication and relationship. 'PEOPLE DIE OF EXPOSURE' underscores the innate need to withdraw. 'THE CONSUMING TASK OF HUMAN COMPANIONSHIP IS FALSE' throws an existential wrench into the entire project. Is Nauman saying that in the end we are all alone, or that the process of communicating is flawed to the point of absurdity? His use of stone in conjunction with this text underscores the cold, inert, stoic quality of the final statement.

World Peace 1996, whose title evokes the possibility of global understanding, began as a text and evolved into a video performance (fig.106). In many ways, video is the perfect metacommunication device for Nauman; a medium that delivers image, language, speech/sound, and can be arranged in a space to create a field of senders and receivers. In Nauman's hands, the video monitor, like the neon sign, can be both a private and public form of communication. In fact, the title is an ironic nod to the global-political misunderstanding between leaders of nations and the often-evoked maxim made famous in Stuart Rosenberg's 1967 film Cool Hand Luke: 'What we have here is failure to communicate.' Five radically enlarged images of talking heads are projected onto the walls of a room. A group of actors performs the same set of phrases based on different combinations of the verbs *talk* and *listen*, and the pronouns *I, you, me, them*: 'I'll talk to you. You'll listen to me. You'll talk to me. I'll listen to you ... They'll talk to you. You'll listen to them. I'll talk to them. They'll listen to me', and so on. Although we don't respond, we are at the centre of a three-way conversation that loops into a kind of controlled chaos.

In World Peace, words are once again vocalised and given identities through the different appearances, mannerisms (one signs rather than speaks), and intonations, from threatening to pleading. The poet Robert Duncan has observed, 'None of us really understand the subtle complexities of how we communicate, how we reach each other with words. There is a lot of energy – visual and physical – that takes place around language that makes language move in different directions.'[9] In other words, what you say is a function of how you say it. This energy comes into play in World Peace, where the same words display almost graphic differences, like colours filling the space.

As World Peace unfolds, voices begin to overlap and compete for attention. What initially appears as a polite systematic means towards communication – I, you and they each taking turns at talking and listening – evolves into something more violent. The suggestion is that communication is, in the end, a primitive form of action and only truly takes place between the boundary of decorum and violence. This boundary is clearly crossed in the artist's 1986 video Violent Incident, in which a man and a woman prepare for a peaceful dinner and end up in a brawl, and where interchange is synonymous with physical trespassing. Nauman describes Violent Incident:

I started with a scenario, a sequence of events which was this: Two people come to a table that's set for dinner with plates, cocktails, flowers. The man holds the woman's chair for her as she sits down. But as she sits down, he pulls the chair out from under her and she falls on the floor. He turns around to pick up the chair and as he bends over, she's standing up, and she gooses him. He turns around and yells at her – calls her names. She grabs the cocktail glass and throws the drink in his face. He slaps her, she knees him in the groin and, as he's doubling over, he grabs a knife from the table. They struggle and both of them end up on the floor. Now this action takes all of about eighteen seconds. But then it's repeated three more times: the man and woman exchange roles, then the scene is played by two men, and then by two women.[10]

One of the classic symbols of violent and darkly comic communication is the cartoon pairing of the cat and the mouse, which is at the centre of Nauman's recent marathon video installation Mapping the Studio I (Fat Chance John Cage) 2001 (fig.8). In the summer of 2000, his studio in northern New Mexico was being overrun by field mice, an influx great enough to keep his live-in cat busier than usual. Over a period of months, the artist set up an infra-red video camera in seven locations in the studio and recorded the nightly comings and goings of the cat and the mice, among other things. The results are seven large video projections arranged to approximate the layout of the artist's two-thousand-square-foot studio. Mapping is a game of cat and mouse, not only between the animal protagonists, but once again between Nauman and his audience. In Get Out of My Mind, Get Out of This Room, he invited us in and then told us to get out. In Mapping, he invites us in and then leaves. A subtly repeated motif that appears throughout the tape and the journal is 'Bruce walking out of room ... '. The thematic motif of exposure and withdrawal remains.

We are left with the cat and the mice, and once we recognise their presence, we are set up to participate in another drama of pursuit, withdrawal and exposure. Our interest in the relationship between the cat and the mice revolves around implied violence. Do we cheer for the mice or the cat, or do we just want to see a kill? In fact, over six hours there is little killing to be had. Sometimes the cat is aware of the mice. Sometimes he

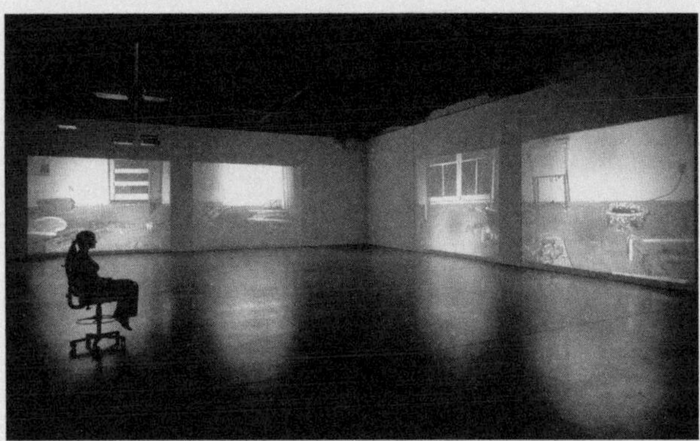

Fig.8
Mapping the Studio I (Fat Chance John Cage) 2001. Video installation. Installed Dia Center for the Arts, 2002. Collection Lannan Foundation; long-term loan to Dia Art Foundation, New York

appears to ignore them. The animals seem to pass their time throughout this video as if they are living parallel lives. When they do cross paths, you sense in them a recognition that the game is back on. It doesn't take long before one starts to think of the cat and the mice (mouse/muse?) as surrogates for the artist and his pursuit of art. In one sequence, the cat enters the studio from a small outer office, where Nauman himself would enter. The cat's careful gait and watchful, bright eyes indicate that he is clearly on to something. Like the cat, the artist is a predator living for the chase, regardless or in spite of the reward. It's hard not to be reminded of George Herriman's subversive cartoon strip 'Krazy Kat', which revolves around the unlikely story of a large black cat that has inexplicably fallen madly in love with a wisecracking mouse who does not return his affections but instead sends bricks flying at the cat's head, which the cat interprets as flirtation. As Nauman says, 'Communication is a funny thing.' In some ways, it is the mice that mimic Nauman's trafficking between exposure and withdrawal. Not wanting to be in the unprotected areas of the studio, they stick close to the wall; their movements literally map the perimeter of the studio, as Nauman – through this studio documentary – explores the perimeters of his artistic practice, if not himself.

Most of the time, however, Mapping presents a strangely plaintive space where the cat and mice go about their business, navigating a field of tools, furniture and debris. In this landscape of leftover and partially made ideas in the form of creative detritus, it is difficult to discern what is art, what is about to be art, or what is just garbage. Because the artist was using the studio during the day, while recording at night, the scene changes in subtle, at times ironic, ways. One frame shows a group of chairs stacked with video equipment. We see it gradually disappearing as Nauman puts the equipment to use over the following months. The presence of the artist at work is thus signalled by things that disappear rather than things that are made. The entire piece is full of this kind of emptiness. Again, Nauman's ability to create a strange kind of disaffection comes into play. One can't help but think about Room with My Soul Left Out, Room That Does Not Care. In this case, however, the studio offers a haunting self-portrait, or double self-portrait; a video map of the artist's studio, it is also a late-life map of Nauman's career, containing many of the polarities that the artist has juggled throughout his forty years of art-making: presence and absence, private activity versus public exposure, pursuit and entrapment, the boundaries between interiors and exteriors.

One of the best aspects of Mapping the Studio is the soundtrack (CODIFICATION #5: Simple sounds). Ambient noise is used to underscore the spooky quality of the eerily lit studio space. A low buzz (the heating fans) is interrupted throughout the piece by the sounds of dogs, horses, distant coyotes and traffic, and occasionally the whine of the cat, which sounds less like a cat than a distant human wail. As the sounds penetrate the walls, doors and screens of the studio, the building and its passageways suggest an uncanny sculptural form that speaks to us in many tongues.

Given this reflective mood, it is not surprising that Nauman would now turn his attention back to language, which offers a different kind of map. For him, language is analogous to drawing, a kind of thinking form. With it he has mapped many of the themes that run through his work in all its different forms. Moreover, language offers the artist a means of withdrawing while also communicating with his audience directly, even intimately. As in *Mapping*, Nauman is nowhere and everywhere in the Turbine Hall. Here the matrix that the 1966 *CODIFICATION* provided has expanded to an immense lexical field, where a seemingly endless space collides with waves of language in a grand metacommunication.

Notes

1 Unless otherwise noted, quotations from the artist are taken from numerous conversations with the author from 1998 to 2004.

2 Quoted in Jon Pareles, 'Miles Davis, Trumpeter, Dies; Jazz Genius, 65, Defined Cool', *New York Times*, 29 September 1991.

3 Rosalind E. Krauss, *Passages in Modern Sculpture*, New York 1977, p.249.

4 Harald Szeemann organised the landmark exhibition *When Attitudes Become Form* in 1969 at the Kunsthalle Bern in Bern, Switzerland.

5 Ludwig Wittgenstein, Proposition 5.6, *Tractatus Logico-Philosophicus*, 1921.

6 In Ian Wallace and Russell Keziere, 'Bruce Nauman Interviewed', *Vanguard*, vol.8, no.1, February 1979, p.16.

7 Quoted in Coosje van Bruggen, *Bruce Nauman*, New York 1988, p.21.

8 Willem de Kooning in an interview with David Sylvester, 1963. Reprinted in Clifford Ross (ed.), *Abstract Expressionism: Creators and Critics*, New York 1990, p.46.

9 Robert Duncan in conversation with the author, May 1983.

10 In Joan Simon, 'Breaking the Silence: An Interview with Bruce Nauman', January 1987. Reprinted in *Please Pay Attention Please: Bruce Nauman's Words*, ed. Janet Kraynak, Cambridge, Massachusetts, and London 2003, p.333.

Raw Materials
Emma Dexter

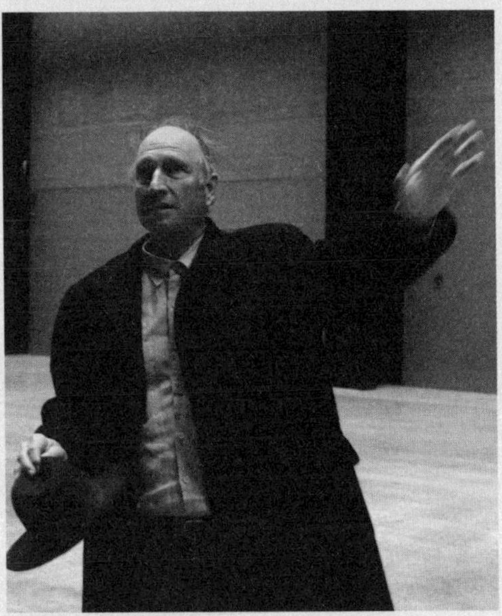
Fig.9
Bruce Nauman in the Turbine Hall, Tate Modern, April 2004

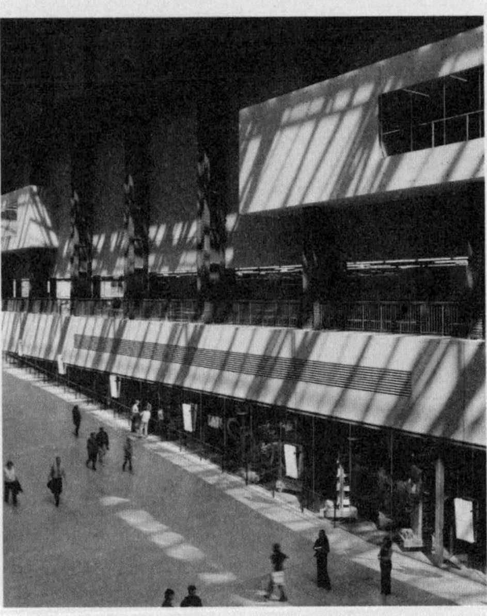
Fig.10
The Turbine Hall, Tate Modern, June 2004

Yes, the words I heard, and heard distinctly, having quite a sensitive ear, were heard a first time, then a second, and often even a third, as pure sounds, free of all meaning, and this is probably one of the reasons why conversation was unspeakably painful to me. And the words I uttered myself, and which must nearly always have gone with an effort of the intelligence, were often to me as the buzzing of an insect. And this is perhaps one of the reasons I was so untalkative, I mean this trouble I had in understanding not only what others said to me, but also what I said to them. It is true that in the end, by dint of patience, we made ourselves understood, but understood with regard to what, I ask of you, and to what purpose? Molloy, in Samuel Beckett, Molloy, Malone Dies, The Unnamable, London 1959, p.50.

An engagement with language and space runs like a continuous thread throughout Bruce Nauman's oeuvre, brought into focus as much by the artist's interest in new music and literature, and in phenomenology and behaviourism, as by Conceptual or post-Minimal art strategies. Working during the 1960s with an extremely heterodox range of materials, including photography, neon and fibreglass, Nauman increasingly moved away from traditional object-making. Non-objectified materials such as space, the body and speech became important, contributing to Nauman's key role as one of a group of artists, including Gordon Matta-Clark and Robert Smithson, who shattered the more rigid norms of Minimalism in the late 1960s and early 1970s. Nothing was off limits in terms of what he experimented with and the influences he absorbed, which were as likely to be literary, musical and philosophical as artistic.[1]

Early in his career, under the influence of his teacher William T. Wiley, Nauman developed the notion of 'seeing with the dumb eye'.[2] By this he meant unlearning all accepted notions of what art is or can be, developing a form of innocence that overturns any idea of correct procedure, and exploring the use of language, the body and behaviour as material. As a result, Nauman doggedly challenged the artistic conventions of his day: 'To every rule, I also try to find the opposite, to reverse it.'[3] This included finding even repetitive and easily overlooked aspects of human behaviour worthy subjects of scrutiny – Beckett's obsessive character, Molloy, was a source of literary inspiration: 'They're all human activities, no matter how limited, strange, or pointless, they're worthy of being examined carefully.'[4] Even in his very early sculptures, Nauman not only took an iconoclastic approach to his choice of materials, but also challenged the whole business of object-making by focusing on process, by finding ambiguity stimulating, and by rethinking questions of completion, finish and failure. He admired the way in which Wittgenstein incorporated failure as part of his process, how he would follow 'an idea until he could say either that it worked or that life doesn't work this way and we have to start over. He would not throw away the failed argument, but would include it in his book.'[5] Nauman's practice therefore has something of the character of scientific enquiry, an open-ended investigative activity in which the stuff of the world – materials, the body, language and emotions – are explored, tested and reconfigured in order to reach a greater understanding of humanity and our place within the world. His investigations are philosophical as well as practical; he has said that he is not interested in 'adding to a collection of things that are art', but in 'investigating the possibilities of what art may be'.[6] It is also his belief that activity in the studio is the core of the art-making process, a view that designates art as an activity rather than a product.[7]

For Raw Materials, Nauman has filled the Turbine Hall with voices, in some places distinctly audible, in others indistinct. Directional wall-mounted speakers allow the creation of bands of audio clarity that criss-cross the width of the space, between which are areas of barely audible or inaudible sound. In the background an ambient drone fills the whole space, merging seamlessly with the pre-existing hum of the building. It was this original hum that suggested the approach that Nauman should take: 'What edged me towards an audio environment was the turbine drone and how it varied as I moved from place to place.'[8] It is that ambient drone that gave rise to the title Raw Materials, which refers back to a video of 1990, Raw Material – MMMM, in which the artist hums 'Mmmm' continuously (fig.108). This sound, which more closely resembles a howling wind than any human utterance when heard in the Turbine Hall, becomes an abstraction of the human voice. The wording of the title also illustrates Nauman's close attention to language, for it performs several functions: it suggests the relationship between individual texts as components and the overall schema as a plurality; it references the notion that pre-existing works can function as *raw materials* for this new piece, which are then *cooked* in this new configuration; and it refers to the fact that Nauman has used the Turbine Hall in its naked or *raw* state. The word 'material' also raises one of the paradoxes of the work, which is that the chief elements from which it is composed – sound, speech and space – are all intangible and supposedly immaterial, yet the work materialises speech and space together into one entity. As Joan Simon has observed, Nauman treats 'linguistic fragments and material issues as interchangeable'.[9] It is this consistent interweaving of the linguistic and the material in Nauman's work that is revisited in Raw Materials.

The installation consists of twenty-two spoken and sung texts culled from Nauman's existing oeuvre, originally presented in a wide range of media from drawings and prints to neon works, installations and videos. This allows him the opportunity to revisit important works, and in particular texts that have played a significant role in his development as an artist. In other cases, it offers the chance to revisit works that may never, in some senses, have been 'completed', such as the text You May Not Want To Be Here, which was recorded for the first time this year, but originally appeared in 1968 on the sculpture First Poem Piece (figs.18–19). Raw Materials therefore has the aspect of a re-view – it brings to the fore a common currency of language and speech that has always been present in the artist's work, but it draws attention to the words themselves in new and surprising ways. Stripping the audio component from the visual element of video, presenting texts in a solely spatial and aural dimension, provides the opportunity for different nuances, readings and understandings of the works themselves, and makes something entirely new from that reworked material. Nevertheless, each text and each utterance heard as part of Raw Materials has an echo elsewhere in the past, in another pre-existing manifestation or version.[10]

Other artists have used the Turbine Hall as a gallery – a place in which to display fabricated objects or to create fictional environments. But Nauman has accepted the Turbine Hall exactly as it is; he has chosen to display nothing, add no imagery, and conceal nothing of the ordinary workings and functions of the space. The decision to accept the extraneous and distracting elements of the space allows the Turbine Hall (one of the most important social spaces in London) to act as a cypher for the social realm (of which language is such an important part) as well as revealing an acceptance of the vernacular role and function of the building. This decision also denies artifice, concealment or any other form of easy distraction – no more stuff to fill up the world. And finally it forces visitors to look at the space anew, to become conscious of it, and conscious of themselves within it: to see and be aware of the space as if for the very first time. The use of language and space in Raw Materials goes back to Nauman's investigation of first principles; he takes nothing for granted and uses materials (language and space) that are everywhere and invisible.

From the late 1960s into the first half of the 1970s, Nauman created numerous empty or semi-empty spaces, including cages and corridors. Some of these were accompanied by a related text, some included video or closed-circuit TV. A riposte to the object-making of Minimalism, they are hard to categorise, for, as Nauman himself observed when analysing the difference between his generation and immediate predecessors such as Donald Judd or Robert Morris, 'We might wake up one day and make something which was *itself* – whether it was abstract or figurative did not matter'.[11] Resolutely themselves, these empty rooms/spaces reveal Nauman's anti-formalist tendencies. As he has said, he is concerned with 'Making the thing itself less important to look at'.[12] In addition, Nauman's spaces reflect his phenomenological, psychological and political concerns. They are claustrophobic and disconcerting: corridors that are too narrow for comfort, unusually shaped, lit by harsh and hostile lighting, combined with enigmatic texts or deliberately disorienting closed-circuit TV monitoring.[13]

In these spaces, Nauman was particularly interested in controlling the behaviour of the visitor or spectator. Rather than allowing a form of free play, he limited potential movement and closely delineated the experience visitors were to have. Heightening a sense of self-consciousness on the part of visitors and establishing them as participants and contributors to the ultimate meaning of the work was key: 'When you are alone, you accept the space by filling it with your presence', but 'as soon as someone else comes into view, you withdraw and protect yourself'.[14] These empty rooms therefore act as theatrical stages combined with laboratory labyrinths for behavioural studies. The mere act of 'physically entering the piece gives another kind of information – emotional, physical, psychological'.[15]

In the original installation of Get Out of My Mind, Get Out of This Room 1968 (one of the texts re-presented in Raw Materials), visitors entered a small, apparently empty chamber where they were assaulted by a recording of the artist screaming, growling, whispering the words of the title. As Nauman says 'it's so angry it scares people'.[16] But the arrival of the visitor is required to make sense of the piece – as a text composed entirely of an instruction, it needs the viewer to act as addressee and receiver of the command. This work also highlights Nauman's use of language to express emotional and psychological states – a fact that distinguishes his approach from other Conceptual artists, who were often more interested in what Robert Storr describes as 'post-Structuralist gambits that toy with the discrepancy between things or thoughts and the names they are given'.[17] Get Out of My Mind, Get Out of This Room acts as a prototype for the installation that Nauman has created thirty-six years later in the Turbine Hall.

In another work, Installation with Yellow Lights 1971 (later retitled Left or Standing, Standing or Left Standing; see figs.67–72), Nauman created a trapezoidal space dominated by harsh yellow fluorescent light. This space was accompanied by a text that was sent out as the exhibition announcement and stacked outside the installation. The relationship between the text and the space is 'not parallel but skewed',[18] creating a vague and unspecific sense of anxiety: 'Perhaps the space was insufficient ... [I]n a way [the text is] a poem that stands by itself, next to the space, without describing it. The writing is about language; it includes a kind of anxiety that the space seemed to generate.'[19] The text is typical of Nauman's writing: precise yet enigmatic, deliberate, thoughtful and ultimately obtuse. The mood is one of social unease combined with the notion of the suppressed violence inherent in language and social interaction: 'His preciseness and acuity left small cuts on the tips of my fingers or across the backs of my hands without any need to sit or otherwise withdraw.' As Nauman commented to Coosje van Bruggen, he was seeking 'an art that puts you on an edge: it forces you into a heightened awareness of yourself and the situation. Often without you knowing what it is that you're confronting and/or experiencing. All you know is that you're being pushed into a place that you're not used to and that there's an anxiety involved in that.'[20]

False Silence 1975 is a large architectural installation comprising a narrow corridor that opens at its centre onto two triangular rooms. A spoken text is broadcast from speakers installed on the outside of the walls (figs.50–1). The text, written and recorded by Nauman himself in 1975, and selected here for Raw Materials, was re-recorded with a female voice in 2000 when the work was recreated. It has a Beckettian aspect: the words of an observer and consumer who claims to emit no excreta of any kind – 'I don't speak, make no other sounds, you can't hear my heart, my footsteps' – yet paradoxically we are listening to her voice. This disembodied voice boasts of its inviolability and articulates a fear of the social, of exchange of bodily fluids, ideas, touch:

No expression, no communication of any kind,
An observer, a consumer, a user only
My body absorbs all communications, emotions, sucks up heat and cold
Super reptilian soaking up all knowledge, compactor of all information

Of course the ultimate empty space for Nauman is his studio – a place where he is confronted with *horror vacui*. Each empty room created by Nauman, including the cavernous space of the Turbine Hall, is merely an echo of that original space, which Nauman has designated as the meeting place for psychological and material process.[21]

Language has been a key element in Nauman's practice since his earliest works. He has a profound understanding of its importance: 'Language is a very powerful tool ... It is considered more significant now than at any other time in history and it is given more importance than any of our faculties.'[22] Looking at the texts Nauman has selected for the Turbine Hall and which are symptomatic of his writing in general, certain qualities emerge: the language is plain, everyday almost; it has an internal playfulness and complexity due to the use of rhymes and its singsong musicality, yet actual meaning remains obscure. Even in the most basic texts the meaning becomes twisted and reversed due to the ferocity of the delivery – hence Thank You Thank You transmutes from a polite greeting to an insult and back again. The texts often break down into a range of linguistic and logical functions: commands, exhortations, statements, lists, jokes, instructions, propositions, deductions. They demonstrate Nauman's interest in the extreme shifts of meaning that can be achieved by removing one or two words from a given phrase, as he has said: 'I think it is almost like reading Robbe-Grillet: you come to a point where he has repeated what he said earlier, but it means something altogether different, because even though he has changed only two words, they have changed the whole meaning.'[23] Nauman uses a vast battery of devices to play with language, to twist and bend it just as if it were a piece of steel: syllogisms, linguistic games, puns, repetition, syntactic slippage, changes of word order are all deployed: 'I think the point where language starts to break down as a useful tool for communication is the same edge where poetry and art occur.'[24]

Janet Kraynak in her excellent essay 'Bruce Nauman's Words' makes the cogent suggestion that we look at Nauman's use of language in particular relation to Mikhail Bakhtin's concept of the 'utterance'. The utterance can take many forms, both verbal and written, and is part of Bakhtin's wider theory of 'dialogue'– a metalanguage in which context and situation as well as the subjectivity of the speaker and listener are integral parts.[25] The notion of the utterance therefore stresses the subjectivity of language, the importance of context, particularly the fact that each utterance comes in relation to what Bakhtin described as 'a very complexly organised chain of other utterances'.[26] Inherent in this theory of language is the sense that every utterance is by necessity a response to something already said. As he says: 'Any speaker is himself a respondent to a greater or lesser degree. He is not, after all, the first speaker, the one who disturbs the eternal silence of the universe.'[27] Seen in this way, Nauman's filling of the container of the Turbine Hall with the human voice acts as a metaphor for the existence of language within the world and within history.

The concept of metalanguage and the connections that language creates through time and space are reinforced in <u>Raw Materials</u> through works such as <u>100 Live and Die</u>, in which multiple voices chant Nauman's horrifying yet humorous summation of human life and death: 'Live and Die/Die and Die/Shit and Die/Piss and Die ... '. The effect of multiple voices chanting the text not only reinforces its universal applicability, but also brings into focus the role of the social in Bakhtin's theory. Communality and shared experience are further underlined by the shifts in <u>Good Boy Bad Boy</u> from the first-person singular ('I was a bad girl') to the first-person plural ('We were bad girls'). <u>Good Boy Bad Boy</u> depends upon the paradox that, while its constituent parts suggest versions and varieties of subjectivity, nevertheless the form and uniformity of the delivery and the text insist on a shared and inevitable trajectory. This is repeatedly summarised in the text by the use of demonstratives such as 'This' or 'That' to conclude each segment of the text. The chilling final phrases have a ghastly finality and authority:

I don't want to die,
You don't want to die,
We don't want to die,
This is fear of death.

Kraynak also highlights 'the performativity of language' based on the speech-act theories of J.L. Austin. She explains how some utterances contain an action in themselves, or what Austin called 'illocutionary' performatives.[28] The very act of saying them performs the function they describe. Nauman's <u>Thank You Thank You</u>, which is the first audio element that visitors encounter as they enter the Turbine Hall, works in this way. Thus speech and action are inextricably entwined; words do not only signify but perform as well. As such, the binaries of mind/body, words/action described by the Cartesian philosophical model start to break down. This understanding of the performative qualities of language depends on the development of past uses or iterations of a word to develop an agreed meaning for the word. In this way all speech is linked inextricably to earlier utterances, and derives its function from them.

While Kraynak is at pains to stress the performative quality inherent in language in whatever form it takes, when confronted with Nauman's <u>Raw Materials</u> we realise that the entire experience is intrinsically a performance. Language is spoken (not written) by a disparate range of voices: male, female, child, Portuguese, professional actor, amateur, and on various occasions the artist himself, with variations of pitch, intonation, speed, accent, volume, and ranging in expression from whispering to shouting, singing and chanting. All of these variations strongly contribute to reinforcing the subjective nature of performance, as well as underlining its inherent repeatability, in other ways, with other actors, in other places. Of course its iterative qualities are further underlined by the fact that the texts themselves are played on continuous loops, and Nauman's preoccupation with repetition means that each text contains numerous iterations within it. His placement of twenty-two endlessly looped texts within the Turbine Hall suggests that speech and language are part of a vast continuum, something that has no beginning or end, which is beyond our understanding of history, and which brings the universal and the human into collision.

Kraynak refers to Judith Butler's notion of performance and ritual as having a 'condensed historicity'.[29] This means that each utterance is linked with all past and future uses; due to its repeatability in time, it is therefore not limited in its operation to any particular moment and, as Judith Butler describes it, 'it is never merely a single moment. The moment in ritual is a condensed historicity; it exceeds itself in past and future directions, an effect of prior and future invocations that constitute and escape the instance of utterance.'[30] Via the technology of recording in <u>Raw Materials</u> we receive an endlessly repeatable series of performed utterances, an enactment that connects us specifically to Nauman's past work, but more crucially connects to a continuum of all past and future voices in the world.

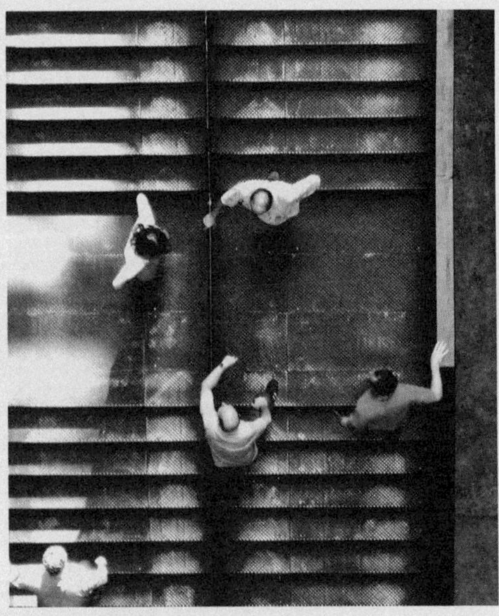

Fig.11
The Turbine Hall, Tate Modern, June 2004

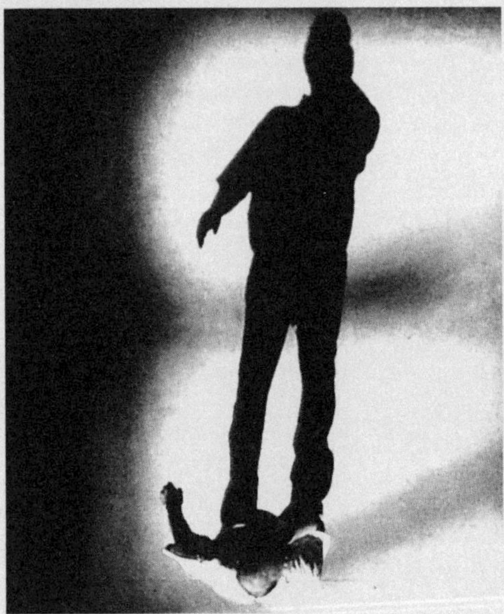

Fig.12
Bruce Nauman in the Turbine Hall, Tate Modern, June 2004

In Raw Materials Nauman has 'spatialized' language,[31] using the Turbine Hall as a container that draws attention to the ultimate strangeness of something so familiar to all of us: speech.

The work that visitors encounter at the eastern end of the Turbine Hall is World Peace.[32] Nauman has described the placement of this work at the end as providing a 'resting place' – a space for contemplation.[33] The text of World Peace underlines the notion that the meaning of Raw Materials is concerned with communication: the utterance that implies a listener, the imperfections of the process, the inherent and inevitable failures in understanding. It also relies on that melding of word and action earlier described as a speech-act (as they say the word 'talk', they are indeed talking; as we hear the word 'listen', we are indeed listening), as well as ironically enacting a slippage and failure in that very notion. For, as the voices endlessly repeat their commitment to dialogue, they fail to utter anything that actually constitutes any meaning beyond the purely solipsistic:

I'll talk to you
You'll listen to me
You'll talk to me
I'll listen to you

The insistent presence of time is another element that relates to the performative and durational qualities of Raw Materials. In reference to making the video work Good Boy Bad Boy 1985 (figs.82–93, 95–6), Nauman talked about the influence of Warhol's films, and how their durational character evoked the sense that they were always there, whether you were watching them or not. This connects with John Cage, Philip Glass and La Monte Young creating music that was also 'something that was there'.[34] Nauman has said that he liked that way of 'structuring time'.[35] In making Good Boy Bad Boy he had been interested in the content and the image, but he was also 'filling a space and taking up time'.[36] Raw Materials fills up the Turbine Hall with language, both spatially and temporally.

As time is integral to any understanding of the nature of language, and performance is an intrinsically repeatable ritual, Raw Materials brings together space, time and language in one single work, ultimately probing the nature of existence. Whatever the medium, as Robert Storr has observed, Nauman's works all ask the same question: 'How does being resonate in language?'[37]

In 'The Task of the Translator' (1923), Walter Benjamin quotes Mallarmé on the implications of the plurality of languages: 'The imperfection of languages consists in their plurality; the supreme language is lacking ... the immortal word still remains silent; the diversity of idioms on earth prevents anyone uttering the words which otherwise, at a single stroke, would materialise as truth.'[38] This provides a platonic twist to our understanding of Raw Materials. It reminds us of the inherent imperfections of language and human communication, and how those very imperfections connect language with the universal and thereby with time itself. If, according to Bakhtin, each ordinary utterance is linked inextricably with all past and future utterances, so Raw Materials can move, with components such as No No No No, from the apparent simplicity of an ordinary 'No' to a connection with every 'No' ever uttered or likely to be uttered in the future, thereby becoming a 'No' that reverberates at the very edge of our universe. The effect of Raw Materials is to suggest the weight of the entire history of human speech, transforming the Turbine Hall into a Tower of Babel, a metaphorical container for that endless babble of words.

Notes

1 Samuel Beckett, Alain Robbe-Grillet, Ludwig Wittgenstein, Meredith Monk and Steve Reich were all important early influences. See Bruce Nauman, ed. Joan Simon, exh. cat., Walker Art Center, Minneapolis 1994, particularly 'Surveying Nauman' by Neal Benezra and 'Beyond Words' by Robert Storr, as well as Gijs van Tuyl's 'Human Condition/Human Body' for a discussion of Nauman and Beckett in Bruce Nauman: Image/Text 1966–1996, exh. cat., Hayward Gallery, London 1998.

2 Storr 1994, p.50. Nauman also suggests another point of departure for this attitude: 'Wiley and I had friends involved in the San Francisco Zen Center. A collection of talks by Suzuki Roshi – the abbot – called Zen Mind, Beginner's Mind exemplifies this way of being. Our friends Dan and Louise were being married by Suzuki at the Zen Center at Tasahara and at the time of the ceremony both my son, who was around two, and Suzuki had disappeared. After quite some searching they were found back behind the zendo throwing rocks in the creek – one of my favourite zen stories.' Bruce Nauman, August 2004.

3 From Chris Dercon, Keep Taking It Apart: A Conversation with Bruce Nauman, July 1986. Reprinted in Please Pay Attention Please: Bruce Nauman's Words, ed. Janet Kraynak, London 2003, p.313.

4 Quoted in Benezra 1994, p.25.

5 Ibid., p.21.

6 Coosje van Bruggen, Bruce Nauman, New York 1988, p.7.

7 Benezra 1994, p.22.

8 From a conversation with the artist, August 2004.

9 From the introduction to 'Breaking the Silence: An Interview with Bruce Nauman', reprinted in Kraynak 2003, p.317.

10 The catalogue entries at the end of this publication list the original works and closely related works together in 'families'.

11 Van Bruggen 1988, p.8.

12 Benezra 1994, p.16.

13 For example Corridor Installation (Nick Wilder Installation) 1980, no.172 in Simon 1994, p.241.

14 Van Bruggen 1988, p.193.

15 From the 1982 interview with Bob Smith, reprinted in Kraynak 2003, p.297.

16 From Joan Simon, 'Breaking the Silence: An Interview with Bruce Nauman', reprinted in Kraynak 2003, p.335.

17 Storr 1994, p.62.

18 Van Bruggen 1988, p.193.

19 Ibid.

20 Ibid., p.194.

21 Storr 1994, p.62.

22 Kraynak 2003, p.35.

23 Storr 1994, p.54.

24 Ibid., p.55.

25 Kraynak 2003, p.4.

26 Ibid.

27 Ibid.

28 Ibid., p.13.

29 Ibid., p.18.

30 Ibid., p.42.

31 Janet Kraynak coins this phrase when discussing the installation Consummate Mask of Rock, but it is a phrase which perfectly encapsulates the nature of Raw Materials. Kraynak 2003, p.33.

32 I have chosen to use the word 'visitor' rather than 'viewer' for those coming to the Turbine Hall to experience Nauman's work. Not only is there little to see, but the term 'viewer' suggests a unitary sensory experience, when in fact visitors to Raw Materials are exposed to multiple experiential stimuli. I also like the spatial and temporal implications of the word 'visitor', suggesting a subject specifically located in space and time.

33 In a sense, Raw Materials is circular. As visitors reach the eastern end of the space, they do not exit, but revisit the work again, encountering its constituent audio elements in a different order. There is no prescribed starting point or end point to the work.

34 From the 1986 interview by Chris Dercon, reprinted in Kraynak 2003, p.306.

35 Ibid.

36 Ibid.

37 Storr 1994, p.62.

38 Walter Benjamin, Selected Writings, vol.1, Cambridge, Massachusetts 1996, p.263.

Raw Materials Turbine Hall Layout

West Entrance

1	1	Thank You Thank You
2	2	You May Not Want To Be Here
3	3	Work Work
4	4	Pete and Repeat/Dark and Stormy Night
5	6	No No No No — New Museum/Walter
7	7	100 Live and Die
8	8	False Silence
Bridge		
9	9	OK OK OK (Below Bridge)
		North Entrance
10		Think Think Think (Above Bridge)
11	11	The True Artist Is An Amazing Luminous Fountain
12	12	Get Out of My Mind, Get Out of This Room
13	13	Left or Standing/Standing or Left Standing
14	14	Consummate Mask of Rock
15	15	Anthro/Socio
16	17	Good Boy Bad Boy — Tucker/Joan
18	18	Shit In Your Hat — Head On A Chair
19	20	World Peace — Bernard/mei mei
	21	Raw Material — MMMM (Ambient sound throughout Turbine Hall)

Raw Materials Audio Texts — Page

Thank You Thank You

Thank you thank you thank you thank you thank you thank
you thank you thank you thank you thank you thank you
thank you thank you thank you thank you thank you thank
you thank you thank you thank you thank you thank you
thank you thank you thank you thank you thank you thank
you thank you thank you thank you thank you thank you
thank you thank you thank you thank you thank you thank
you thank you thank you thank you thank you thank you
thank you thank you thank you thank you thank you thank
you thank you thank you thank you thank you thank you
thank you thank you thank you thank you thank you thank
you thank you thank you thank you thank you thank you
thank you thank you thank you thank you thank you thank
you thank you thank you thank you thank you thank you
thank you thank you thank you thank you thank you thank
you thank you thank you thank you thank you thank you
thank you thank you thank you thank you thank you thank
you thank you thank you thank you thank you thank you
thank you thank you thank you thank you thank you thank
you thank you thank you thank you thank you thank you
thank you thank you thank you thank you thank you thank
you thank you thank you thank you thank you thank you
thank you thank you thank you thank you thank you thank
you thank you thank you thank you thank you thank you
thank you thank you thank you thank you thank you ...

You May Not Want To Be Here

You may not want to be here
You may want to be here
You want to be here
You want to be
You may want to be
You may not want to be
You may not want
You may want
You may be
You may not be
You may not be here
You may be here
You may not want to hear
You may want to hear
You want to hear
You may not hear
You may hear
You hear

Work Work

Work work ...

Pete and Repeat

Pete and Repeat were sitting on a fence. Pete fell off. Who was left? Repeat. Pete and Repeat were sitting on a fence. Pete fell off. Who was left? Repeat. Pete and Repeat were sitting on a fence. Pete fell off. Who was left? Repeat. Pete and Repeat were sitting on a fence. Pete fell off. Who was left? Repeat. Pete and Repeat were sitting on a fence. Pete fell off. Who was left? Repeat. Pete and Repeat were sitting on a fence. Pete fell off. Who was left? Repeat. Pete and Repeat were sitting on a fence. Pete fell off. Who was left? Repeat. Pete and Repeat were sitting on a fence. Pete fell off. Who was left? Repeat. Pete and Repeat were sitting on a fence. Pete fell off. Who was left? Repeat. Pete and Repeat were sitting on a fence. Pete fell off. Who was left? Repeat. Pete and Repeat were sitting on a fence. Pete fell off. Who was left? Repeat. Pete and Repeat were sitting on a fence. Pete fell off. Who was left? Repeat. Pete and Repeat were sitting on a fence. Pete fell off. Who was left? Repeat. Pete and Repeat were sitting on a fence. Pete fell off. Who was left? Repeat. Pete and Repeat were sitting on a fence. Pete fell off. Who was left? Repeat. Pete and Repeat were sitting on a fence. Pete fell off. Who was left? Repeat. Pete and Repeat were sitting on a fence ...

Dark and Stormy Night

It was a dark and stormy night. Three men were sitting around a campfire. One of the men said, 'Tell us a story, Jack.' And Jack said, 'It was a dark and stormy night. Three men were sitting around a campfire. One of the men said, 'Tell us a story, Jack.' And Jack said, 'It was a dark and stormy night. Three men were sitting around a campfire. One of the men said, 'Tell us a story, Jack.' And Jack said, 'It was a dark and stormy night. Three men were sitting around a campfire. One of the men said, 'Tell us a story, Jack.' And Jack said, 'It was a dark and stormy night. Three men were sitting around a campfire. One of the men said, 'Tell us a story, Jack.' And Jack said, 'It was a dark and stormy night. Three men were sitting around a campfire. One of the men said, 'Tell us a story, Jack.' And Jack said, 'It was a dark and stormy night. Three men were sitting around a campfire. One of the men said, 'Tell us a story, Jack.' And Jack said, 'It was a dark and stormy night. Three men were sitting around a campfire. One of the men said, 'Tell us a story, Jack.' And Jack said, 'It was a dark and stormy night. Three men were sitting around a campfire. One of the men said, 'Tell us a story, Jack.' And Jack said, 'It was a dark and stormy night. Three men were sitting around a campfire. One of the men said, 'Tell us a story, Jack.' And Jack said, 'It was a dark and stormy night' ...

No No No No — New Museum

No no no no no no no no no no no no no no no no no no no no
no no no no no no no no no no no no no no no no no no no no
no no no no no no no no no no no no no no no no no no no no
no no no no no no no no no no no no no no no no no no no no
no no no no no no no no no no no no no no no no no no no no
no no no no no no no no no no no no no no no no no no no no
no no no no no no no no no no no no no no no no no no no no
no no no no no no no no no no no no no no no no no no no no
no no no no no no no no no no no no no no no no no no no no
no no no no no no no no no no no no no no no no no no no no
no no no no no no no no no no no no no no no no no no no no
no no no no no no no no no no no no no no no no no no no no
no no no no no no no no no no no no no no no no no no no no
no no no no no no no no no no no no no no no no no no no no
no no no no no no no no no no no no no no no no no no no no
no no no no no no no no no no no no no no no no no no no no
no no no no no no no no no no no no no no no no no no no no
no no no no no no no no no no no no no no no no no no no no
no no no no no no no no no no no no no no no no no no no no
no no no no no no no no no no no no no no no no no no no no
no no no no no no no no no no no no no no no no no no no no
no no no no no no no no no no no no no no no no no no no no
no no no no no no no no no no no no no no no no no no no no
no no no no no no no no no no no no no no no no no no no no
no no no no no no no no no no no no no no no no no no no ...

No No No No — Walter

No no no no no no no no no no no no no no no no no no no no
no no no no no no no no no no no no no no no no no no no no
no no no no no no no no no no no no no no no no no no no no
no no no no no no no no no no no no no no no no no no no no
no no no no no no no no no no no no no no no no no no no no
no no no no no no no no no no no no no no no no no no no no
no no no no no no no no no no no no no no no no no no no no
no no no no no no no no no no no no no no no no no no no no
no no no no no no no no no no no no no no no no no no no no
no no no no no no no no no no no no no no no no no no no no
no no no no no no no no no no no no no no no no no no no no
no no no no no no no no no no no no no no no no no no no no
no no no no no no no no no no no no no no no no no no no no
no no no no no no no no no no no no no no no no no no no no
no no no no no no no no no no no no no no no no no no no no
no no no no no no no no no no no no no no no no no no no no
no no no no no no no no no no no no no no no no no no no no
no no no no no no no no no no no no no no no no no no no no
no no no no no no no no no no no no no no no no no no no no
no no no no no no no no no no no no no no no no no no no no
no no no no no no no no no no no no no no no no no no no no
no no no no no no no no no no no no no no no no no no no no
no no no no no no no no no no no no no no no no no no no no
no no no no no no no no no no no no no no no no no no no no
no no no no no no no no no no no no no no no no no no no ...

100 Live and Die

Live and Die
Die and Die
Shit and Die
Piss and Die
Eat and Die
Sleep and Die
Love and Die
Hate and Die
Fuck and Die
Speak and Die
Lie and Die
Hear and Die
Cry and Die
Kiss and Die
Rage and Die
Laugh and Die
Touch and Die
Feel and Die
Fear and Die
Sick and Die
Well and Die
Black and Die
White and Die
Red and Die
Yellow and Die

Live and Live
Die and Live
Shit and Live
Piss and Live
Eat and Live
Sleep and Live
Love and Live
Hate and Live
Fuck and Live
Speak and Live
Lie and Live
Hear and Live
Cry and Live
Kiss and Live
Rage and Live
Laugh and Live
Touch and Live
Feel and Live
Fear and Live
Sick and Live
Well and Live
Black and Live
White and Live
Red and Live
Yellow and Live

Sing and Die
Scream and Die
Young and Die
Old and Die
Cut and Die
Run and Die
Stay and Die
Play and Die
Kill and Die
Suck and Die
Come and Die
Go and Die
Know and Die
Tell and Die
Smell and Die
Fall and Die
Rise and Die
Stand and Die
Sit and Die
Spit and Die
Try and Die
Fail and Die
Smile and Die
Think and Die
Pay and Die

Sing and Live
Scream and Live
Young and Live
Old and Live
Cut and Live
Run and Live
Stay and Live
Play and Live
Kill and Live
Suck and Live
Come and Live
Go and Live
Know and Live
Tell and Live
Smell and Live
Fall and Live
Rise and Live
Stand and Live
Sit and Live
Spit and Live
Try and Live
Fail and Live
Smile and Live
Think and Live
Pay and Live

False Silence

I don't sweat
I have no odor
I inhale, don't exhale
No urine
I don't defecate: no excretions of any kind
I consume only
Oxygen, all foods, any form
I see, hear
I don't speak, make no other sounds, you can't hear my heart, my footsteps
No expression, no communication of any kind
An observer, a consumer, a user only
My body absorbs all communications, emotions, sucks up heat and cold
Super reptilian soaking up all knowledge, compactor of all information
Not growing
I feel don't touch
I have no control over the kinds and qualities of thoughts
I collect, I can't process
I can't react to or act on sensation
No emotional response to situations

There is no reaction of instinct to physical or mental threats
You can't reach me, you can't hurt me
I can suck you dry
You can't hurt me
You can't help me
Shuffle the pages
Find me a line
Arapahoe, Arapahoe
Where did you go
I blink my eyes
To keep the time

<u>OK OK OK</u>

OK OK OK OK OK OK OK OK OK OK OK OK OK OK OK OK
OK OK OK OK OK OK OK OK OK OK OK OK OK OK OK OK
OK OK OK OK OK OK OK OK OK OK OK OK OK OK OK OK
OK OK OK OK OK OK OK OK OK OK OK OK OK OK OK OK
OK OK OK OK OK OK OK OK OK OK OK OK OK OK OK OK
OK OK OK OK OK OK OK OK OK OK OK OK OK OK OK OK
OK OK OK OK OK OK OK OK OK OK OK OK OK OK OK OK
OK OK OK OK OK OK OK OK OK OK OK OK OK OK OK OK
OK OK OK OK OK OK OK OK OK OK OK OK OK OK OK OK
OK OK OK OK OK OK OK OK OK OK OK OK OK OK OK OK
OK OK OK OK OK OK OK OK OK OK OK OK OK OK OK OK
OK OK OK OK OK OK OK OK OK OK OK OK OK OK OK OK
OK OK OK OK OK OK OK OK OK OK OK OK OK OK OK OK
OK OK OK OK OK OK OK OK OK OK OK OK OK OK OK OK
OK OK OK OK OK OK OK OK OK OK OK OK OK OK OK OK
OK OK OK OK OK OK OK OK OK OK OK OK OK OK OK OK
OK OK OK OK OK OK OK OK OK OK OK OK OK OK OK OK
OK OK OK OK OK OK OK OK OK OK OK OK OK OK OK OK
OK OK OK OK OK OK OK OK OK OK OK OK OK OK OK OK
OK OK OK OK OK OK OK OK OK OK OK OK OK OK OK OK
OK OK OK OK OK OK OK OK OK OK OK OK OK OK OK OK
OK OK OK OK OK OK OK OK OK OK OK OK OK OK OK OK
OK OK OK OK OK OK OK OK OK OK OK OK OK OK OK OK
OK OK OK OK OK OK OK OK OK OK OK OK OK OK OK ...

Think Think Think

Think think ...

The True Artist Is An Amazing Luminous Fountain

O verdadeiro artista é uma maravilhosa fonte luminosa.
O verdadeiro artista é uma assombrosa fonte luminosa.
O verdadeiro artista é uma maravilhosa fonte luminosa.
O verdadeiro artista é uma assombrosa fonte luminosa.
O verdadeiro artista é uma maravilhosa fonte luminosa.
O verdadeiro artista é uma assombrosa fonte luminosa.
O verdadeiro artista é uma maravilhosa fonte luminosa.
O verdadeiro artista é uma assombrosa fonte luminosa.
O verdadeiro artista é uma maravilhosa fonte luminosa.
O verdadeiro artista é uma assombrosa fonte luminosa.
O verdadeiro artista é uma maravilhosa fonte luminosa.
O verdadeiro artista é uma assombrosa fonte luminosa.
O verdadeiro artista é uma maravilhosa fonte luminosa.
O verdadeiro artista é uma assombrosa fonte luminosa.
O verdadeiro artista é uma maravilhosa fonte luminosa.
O verdadeiro artista é uma assombrosa fonte luminosa.
O verdadeiro artista é uma maravilhosa fonte luminosa.
O verdadeiro artista é uma assombrosa fonte luminosa.
O verdadeiro artista é uma maravilhosa fonte luminosa.
O verdadeiro artista é uma assombrosa fonte luminosa.
O verdadeiro artista é uma maravilhosa fonte luminosa.
O verdadeiro artista é uma assombrosa fonte luminosa.
O verdadeiro artista é uma maravilhosa fonte luminosa.
O verdadeiro artista é uma assombrosa fonte luminosa.
O verdadeiro artista é uma maravilhosa fonte luminosa ...

Get Out of My Mind, Get Out of This Room

Get out of my mind, get out of this room, get out of my mind,
get out of this room, get out of my mind, get out of this room,
get out of my mind, get out of this room, get out of my mind,
get out of this room, get out of my mind, get out of this room,
get out of my mind, get out of this room, get out of my mind,
get out of this room, get out of my mind, get out of this room,
get out of my mind, get out of this room, get out of my mind,
get out of this room, get out of my mind, get out of this room,
get out of my mind, get out of this room, get out of my mind,
get out of this room, get out of my mind, get out of this room,
get out of my mind, get out of this room, get out of my mind,
get out of this room, get out of my mind, get out of this room,
get out of my mind, get out of this room, get out of my mind,
get out of this room, get out of my mind, get out of this room,
get out of my mind, get out of this room, get out of my mind,
get out of this room, get out of my mind, get out of this room,
get out of my mind, get out of this room, get out of my mind,
get out of this room, get out of my mind, get out of this room,
get out of my mind, get out of this room, get out of my mind,
get out of this room, get out of my mind, get out of this room,
get out of my mind, get out of this room, get out of my mind,
get out of this room, get out of my mind, get out of this room,
get out of my mind, get out of this room, get out of my mind,
get out of this room, get out of my mind, get out of this room,
get out of my mind, get out of this room, get out of my mind ...

Left or Standing

Left or Standing.
His precision and accuracy
suggesting clean cuts, leaving
a vacancy, a slight physical
depression as though I had been
in a vaguely uncomfortable place
for a not long but undeterminable
period; not waiting.

Standing or Left Standing

Standing or Left Standing. His preciseness and acuity left small cuts on the tips of my fingers or across the backs of my hands without any need to sit or otherwise withdraw.

Consummate Mask of Rock

1. mask
2. fidelity
3. truth
4. life
5. cover
6. pain
7. desire
8. need
9. human companionship
10. nothing
11. COVER REVOKED
12. infidelity
13. painless
14. musk/skum
15. people
16. die
17. exposure.

1. This is my mask of fidelity to truth and life.
2. This is to cover the mask of pain and desire.
3. This is to mask the cover of need for human companionship.
4. This is to mask the cover.
5. This is to cover the mask.
6. This is the need of cover.
7. This is the need of the mask.
8. This is the mask of cover of need.
   Nothing and no
9. No thing and no mask can cover the lack, alas.
10. Lack after nothing before cover revoked.
11. Lack before cover
    paper covers rock
    rock breaks mask
    alas, alack.
12. Nothing to cover.
13. This is the mask to cover my infidelity to truth.
    (This is my cover.)
14. This is the need for pain that contorts my mask conveying
    the message of truth and fidelity to life.
15. This is the truth that distorts my need for human
    companionship.
16. This is the distortion of truth masked by my painful need.
17. This is the mask of my painful need distressed by truth and
    human companionship.

18. This is my painless mask that fails to touch my face but floats before the surface of my skin my eyes my teeth my tongue.
19. Desire is my mask.
    (Musk of desire)
20. Rescind desire
    cover revoked
    desire revoked
    cover rescinded.
21. PEOPLE DIE OF EXPOSURE.

CONSUMMATION/CONSUMNATION/TASK

(passive) paper covers rock
(active – threatening) scissors cuts paper
(active – violent) rock breaks scissors

1. mask
2. cover
3. diminish
4. desire
5. need for human companionship
6. lack

desire covers mask
need for human companionship masks desire
mask diminishes need for human companionship
need for human companionship diminishes cover
desire consumes human companionship
cover lacks desire

THIS IS THE COVER THAT DESIRES THE MASK
OF LACK THAT CONSUMES THE NEED FOR
HUMAN COMPANIONSHIP.
THIS IS THE COVER THAT DESPISES THE TASK
OF THE NEED OF HUMAN COMP.
THIS IS THE TASK OF CONSUMING HUMAN COMP.

1. some kind of fact
2. some kind of fiction.
3. the way we behaved in the past
4. what we believe to be the case now
5. the consuming task of human companionship
6. the consummate mask of rock

<u>Consummate Mask of Rock</u> continued

(1.) Fiction erodes fact.
(2.) Fact becomes the way we have behaved in the past.
(3.) The way we have behaved in the past congeals into the consummate mask of rock.
(4.) The way we have behaved in the past contributes to the consuming task of human companionship.
(5.) The consuming task of human comp. erodes the consummate mask of rock. However (2.) Fact becomes the way we have behaved in the past may be substituted into (3.) and (4.) so that
(6.) Fact congeals into the consummate mask of rock. But (5.) the consuming task of human comp. erodes the consummate mask of rock or the consuming task of human comp. erodes fact, then from (1.) it follows that THE CONSUMING TASK OF HUMAN COMPANIONSHIP IS FALSE

THE CONSUMMATE MASK OF ROCK HAVING DRIVEN THE WEDGE OF DESIRE THAT DISTINGUISHED TRUTH AND FALSITY LIES COVERED BY PAPER.

1. (This young man, taken to task so often, now finds is his only sexual relief.)
2. (This young man, so often taken to task, now finds it his only sexual fulfillment.)
3. (This man, so often taken to task as a child ...)
4. (This man, often taken to task, now finds it satisfies (arouses) his sexual desires(needs).)
5. This man, so often taken as a child, now wears the consummate mask of rock and uses it to drive his wedge of desire into the ever squeezing gap between truth and falsity.
6. This man, so often taken as a child, now uses his consummate mask of his rock to drive his wedge of his desire into his ever squeezing (his) gap between his truth, his falsity.
7. (This) man, (so often) taken as (a) child, finding his consummate mask of rock covered by paper, he finding his wedge being squeezed (from) between his desired truth (truth desired) and his desireless falsity (falsity desireless), he unable to arouse his satisfaction, he unable to desire his needs, he proceeds into the gap of his fulfillment his relief lacking the task of human companionship.

Moral
Paper cut from rock, releases rock to crush scissors.
Rock freed from restrictions of paper/scissors/rock, lacking context proceeds.

Anthro/Socio

Feed Me
Eat Me
Anthropology

Feed Me
Eat Me
Anthropology

Feed Me
Eat Me
Anthropology

Feed Me
Eat Me
Anthropology

Feed Me
Eat Me
Anthropology

Feed Me
Eat Me
Anthropology

Feed Me
Eat Me
Anthropology

Feed Me
Eat Me
Anthropology

Feed Me
Eat Me
Anthropology

Feed Me
Eat Me
Anthropology

Feed Me
Eat Me
Anthropology

Feed Me
Eat Me
Anthropology

Feed Me
Eat Me
Anthropology

Feed Me
Eat Me
Anthropology

Feed Me
Eat Me
Anthropology

Feed Me
Eat Me
Anthropology

Feed Me
Eat Me
Anthropology

Feed Me
Eat Me
Anthropology ...

Good Boy Bad Boy — Tucker/Joan

I was a good boy,
You were a good boy,
We were good boys,
That was good.
I was a good girl,
You were a good girl,
We were good girls,
That was good.
I was a bad boy,
You were a bad boy,
We were bad boys,
That was bad.
I was a bad girl,
You were a bad girl,
We were bad girls,
That was bad.
I am a virtuous man,
You are a virtuous man,
We are virtuous men,
This is virtue.
I am a virtuous woman,
You are a virtuous woman,
We are virtuous women,
This is virtue.
I am an evil man,
You are an evil man,
We are evil men,
This is evil.
I am an evil woman,
You are an evil woman,
We are evil women,
This is evil.
I'm alive,
You're alive,
We're alive,
This is our life.
I live the good life,
You live the good life,
We live the good life,
This is the good life.
I have work,
You have work,
We have work,
This is work.
I play,
You play,
We play,
This is play.
I'm having fun,
You're having fun,

We're having fun,
This is fun.
I'm bored,
You're bored,
We're bored,
Life is boring.
I'm boring,
You're boring,
We're boring,
This is boring.
I have sex,
You have sex,
We have sex,
This is sex.
I love,
You love,
We love,
This is our love.
I hate,
You hate,
We hate,
This is hating.
I like to eat,
You like to eat,
We like to eat,
This is eating.
I like to drink,
You like to drink,
We like to drink,
This is drinking.
I like to shit,
You like to shit,
We like to shit,
This is shitting.
I piss,
You piss,
We piss,
This is piss.
I like to sleep,
You like to sleep,
We like to sleep,
Sleep well.
I pay,
You pay,
We pay,
This is payment.
I don't want to die,
You don't want to die,
We don't want to die,
This is fear of death.

Shit In Your Hat — Head On A Chair

Put your hat on the table. Put your head on your hat. Put your hand on your head with your head on your hat. Put your hat in your lap. Put your hand on your hat, your hat in your lap. Drop your hat. Put your hand in your lap. Put your head on your hand, your hand in your lap. Put your hand in your lap. Put your hat in your hand in your lap. Put your head on your lap, your hand in your lap. Put your hat on your face. Put your hand in your lap, your hat on your face. Put your hands on your face, your hat on your head. Put your hands in your lap, your hat on your head. Sit on your hat, your hands on your head. Shit in your hat. Show me your hat. Put your hat on your head. Put your head on the table. Put your hat on the table ...

World Peace — Bernard/mei mei

I'll talk
You'll listen

I'll talk
They'll listen

You'll talk
They'll listen

We'll talk
They'll listen

You'll talk
They'll listen

I'll talk
They'll listen

I'll talk
You'll listen

You'll talk
I'll listen

They'll talk
I'll listen

They'll talk
You'll listen

They'll talk
We'll listen

They'll talk
You'll listen

They'll talk
I'll listen

You'll talk
I'll listen

You'll talk to me
I'll listen to you

They'll talk to me
I'll listen to them

They'll talk to you
You'll listen to them

They'll talk to us
We'll listen to them

They'll talk to you
You'll listen to them

They'll talk to me
I'll listen to them

You'll talk to me
I'll listen to you

I'll talk to you
You'll listen to me

I'll talk to them
They'll listen to me

You'll talk to them
They'll listen to you

We'll talk to them
They'll listen to us

You'll talk to them
They'll listen to you

I'll talk to them
They'll listen to me

I'll talk to you
You'll listen to me

Raw Material — MMMM

Mmmmm mmmmm ...

Raw Materials Images — Page

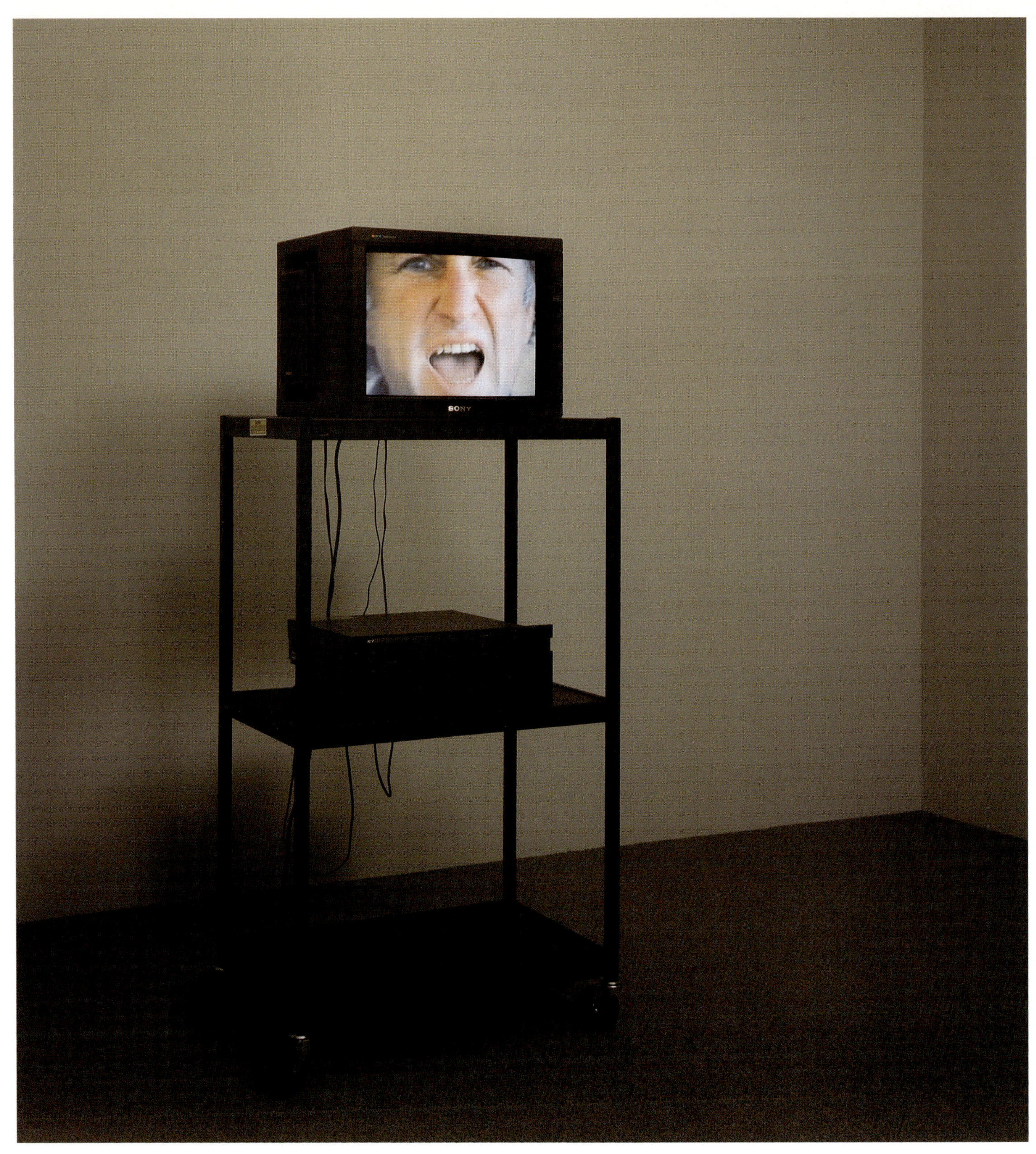

Thank You Thank You (Fig.13)

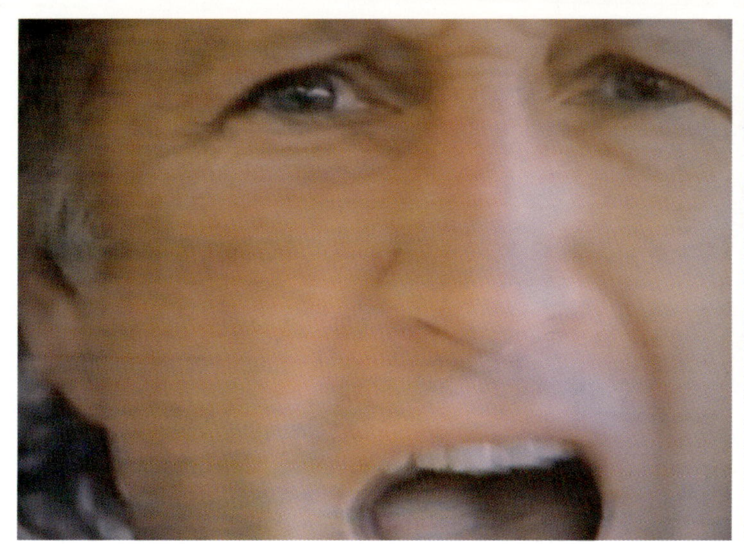

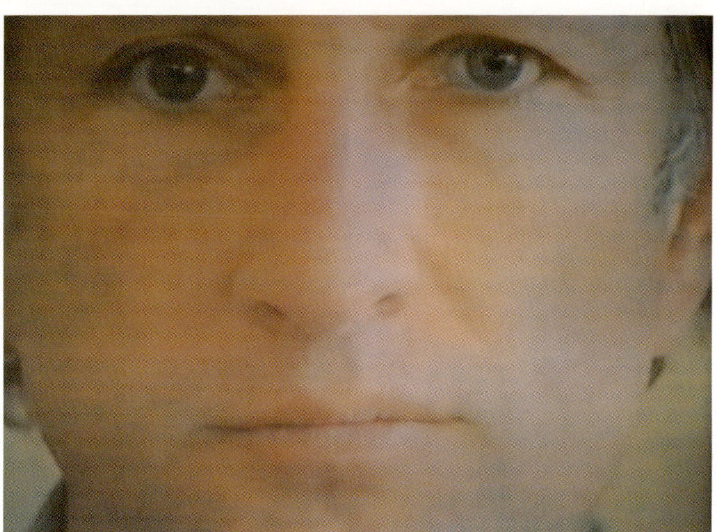

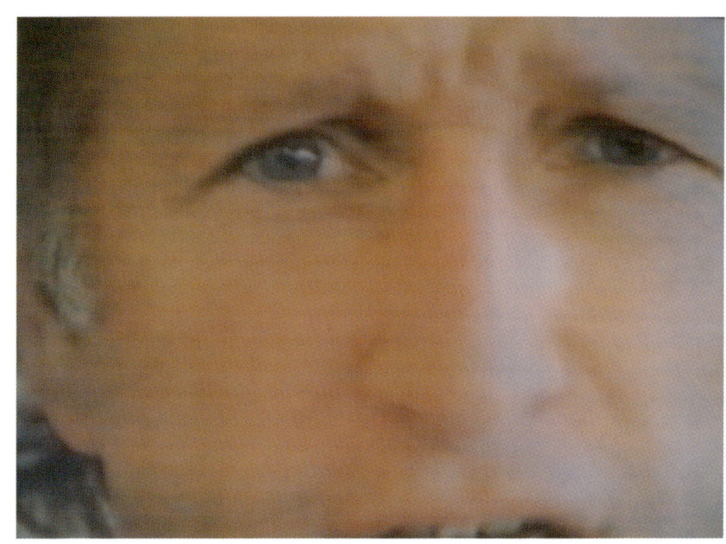

(Figs.14–16)

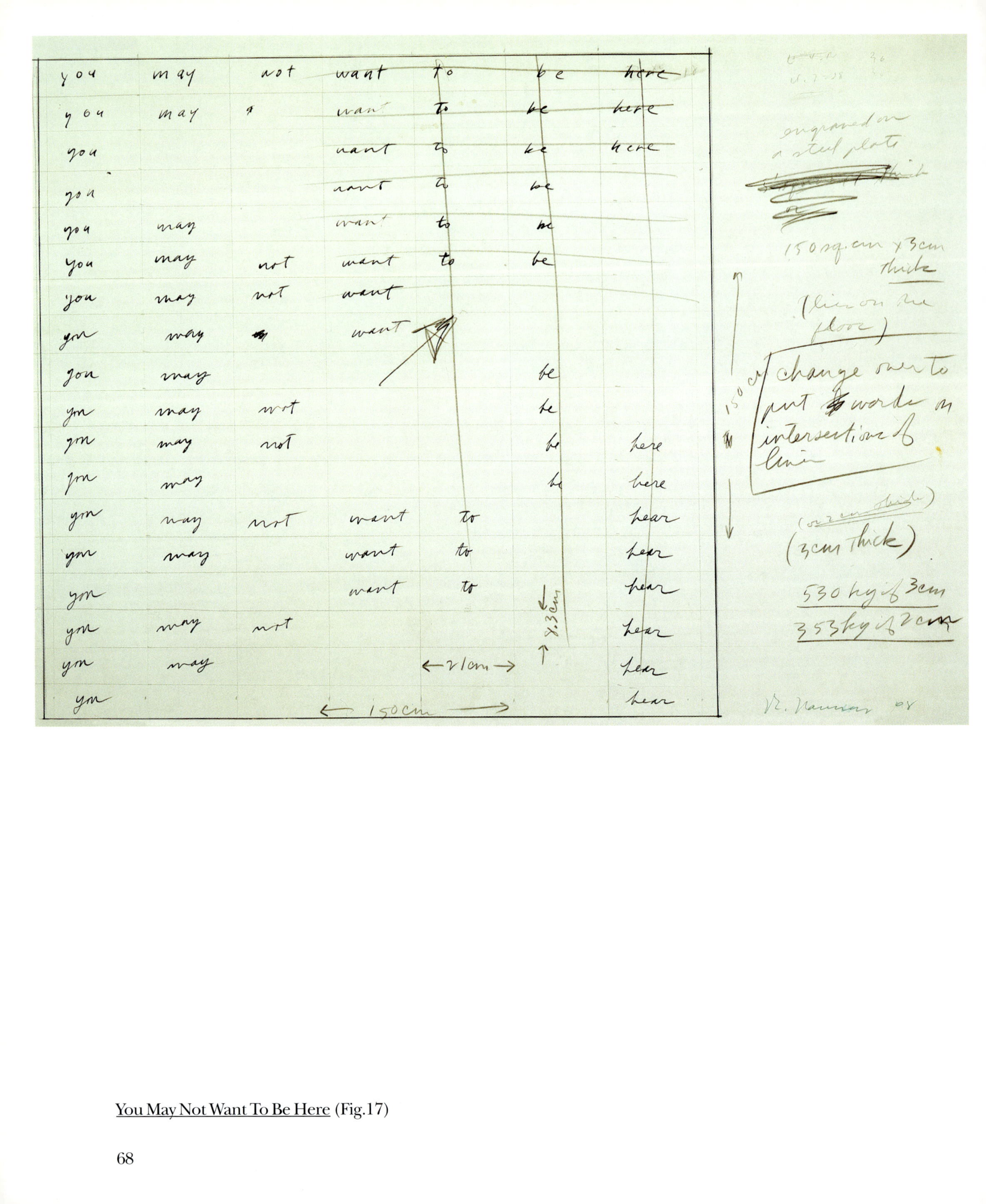

You May Not Want To Be Here (Fig.17)

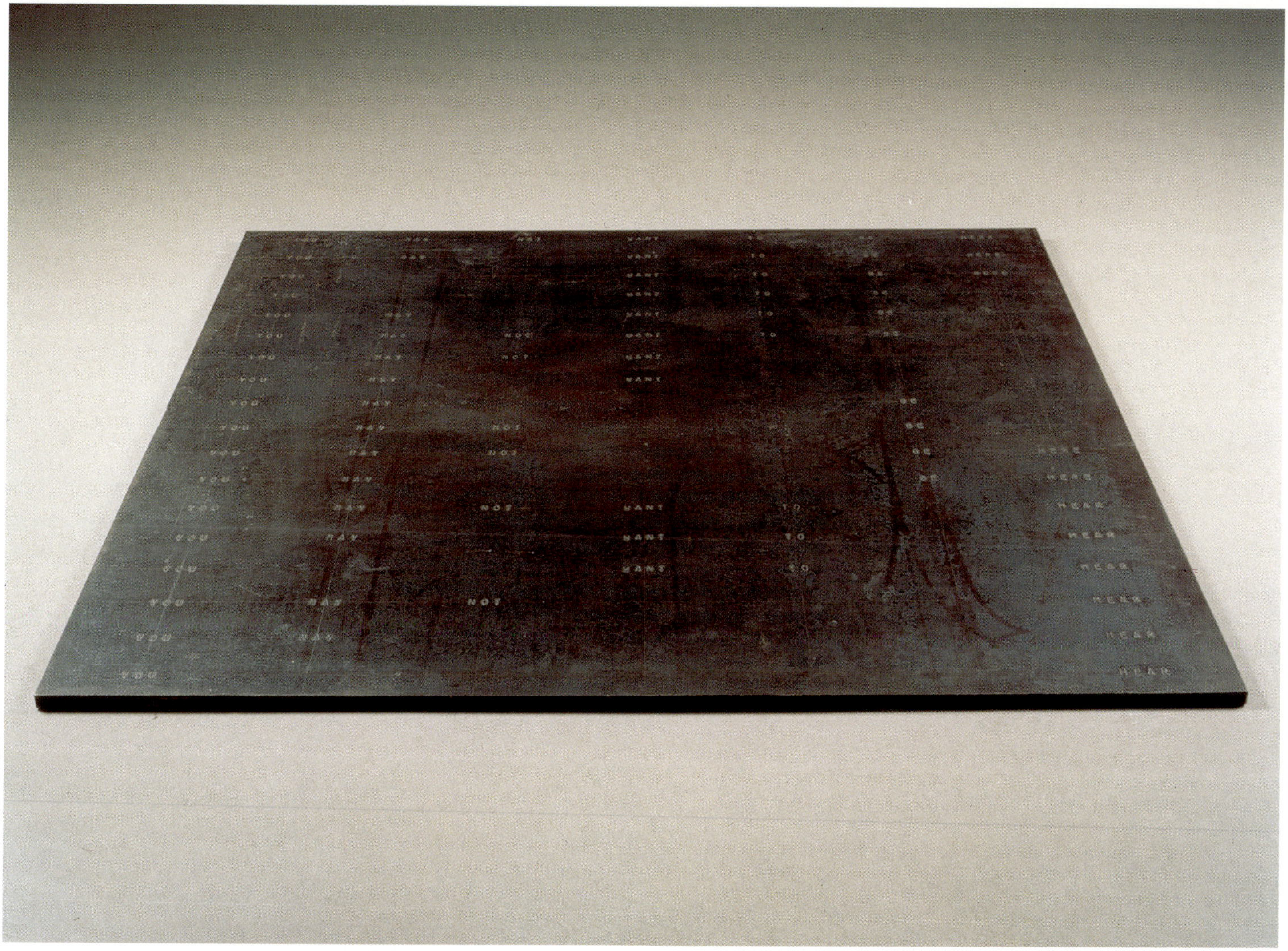

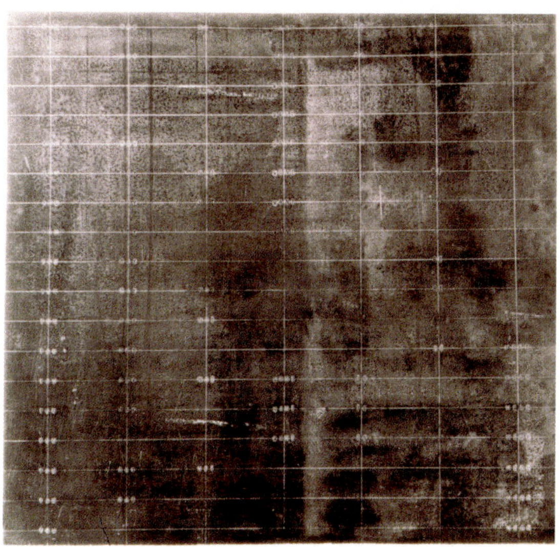

(Figs.18–19)

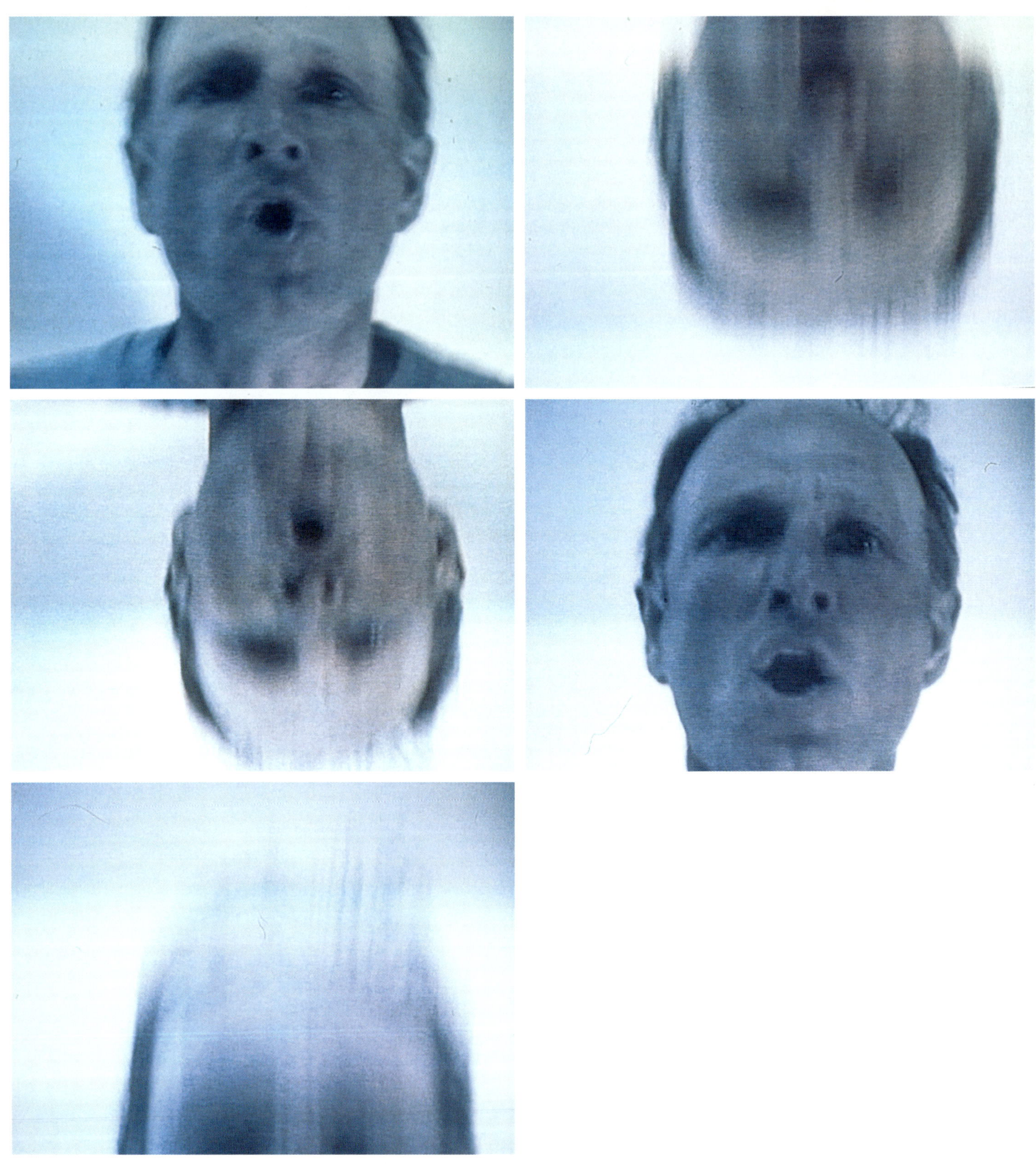

Work Work (Figs.20–4)

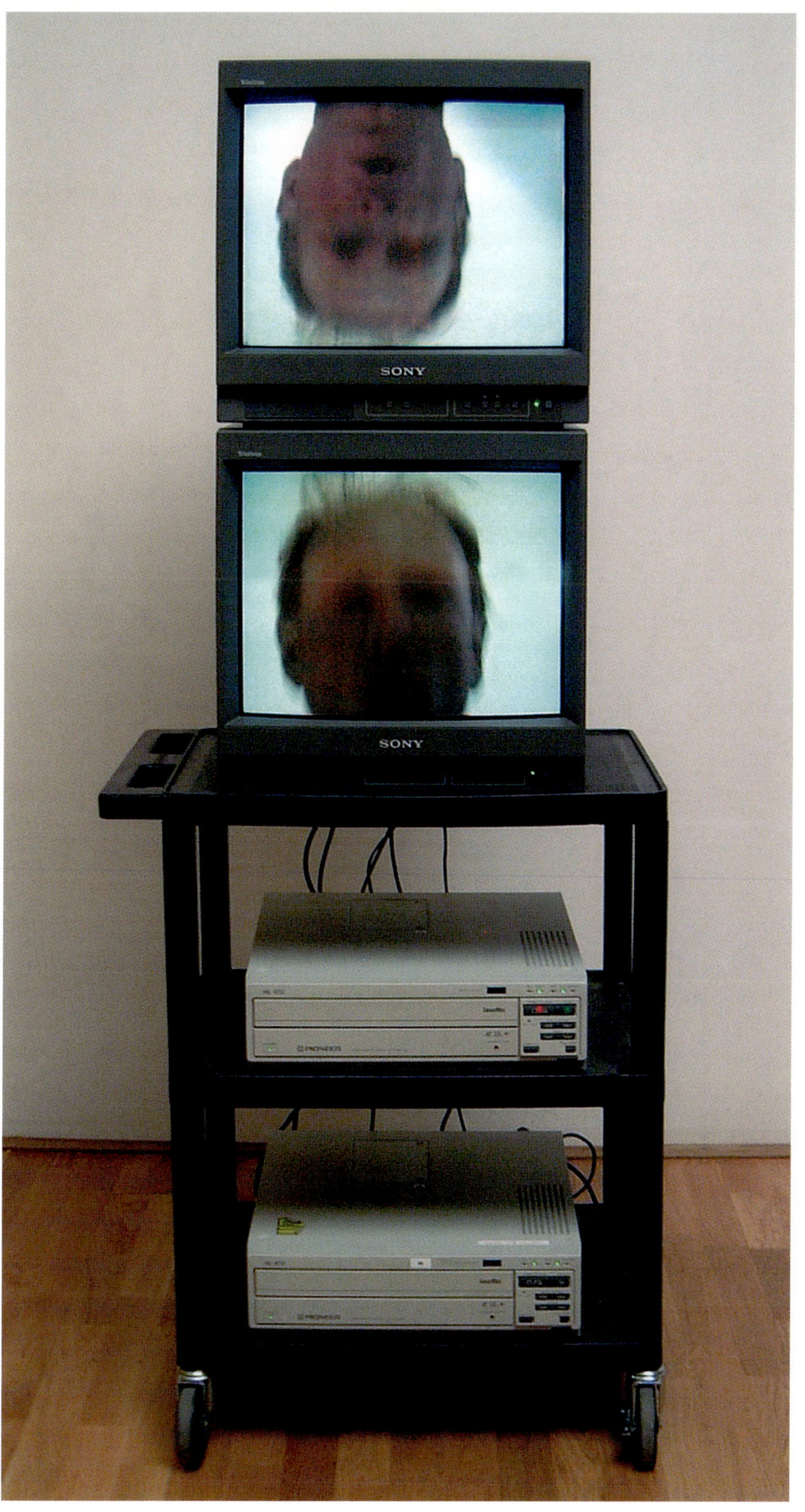

(Fig.25)

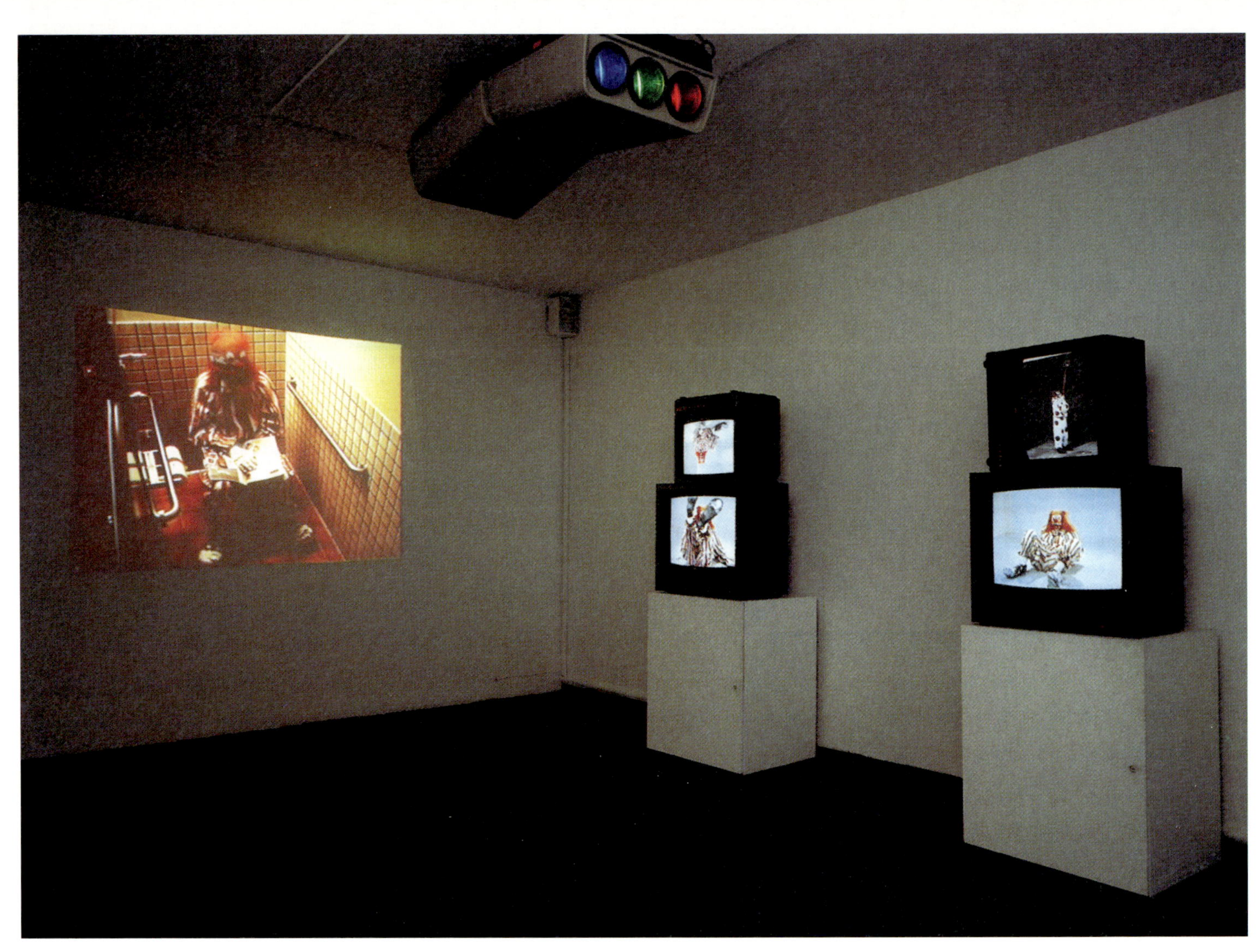

<u>Pete and Repeat/Dark and Stormy Night</u> (Fig.26)

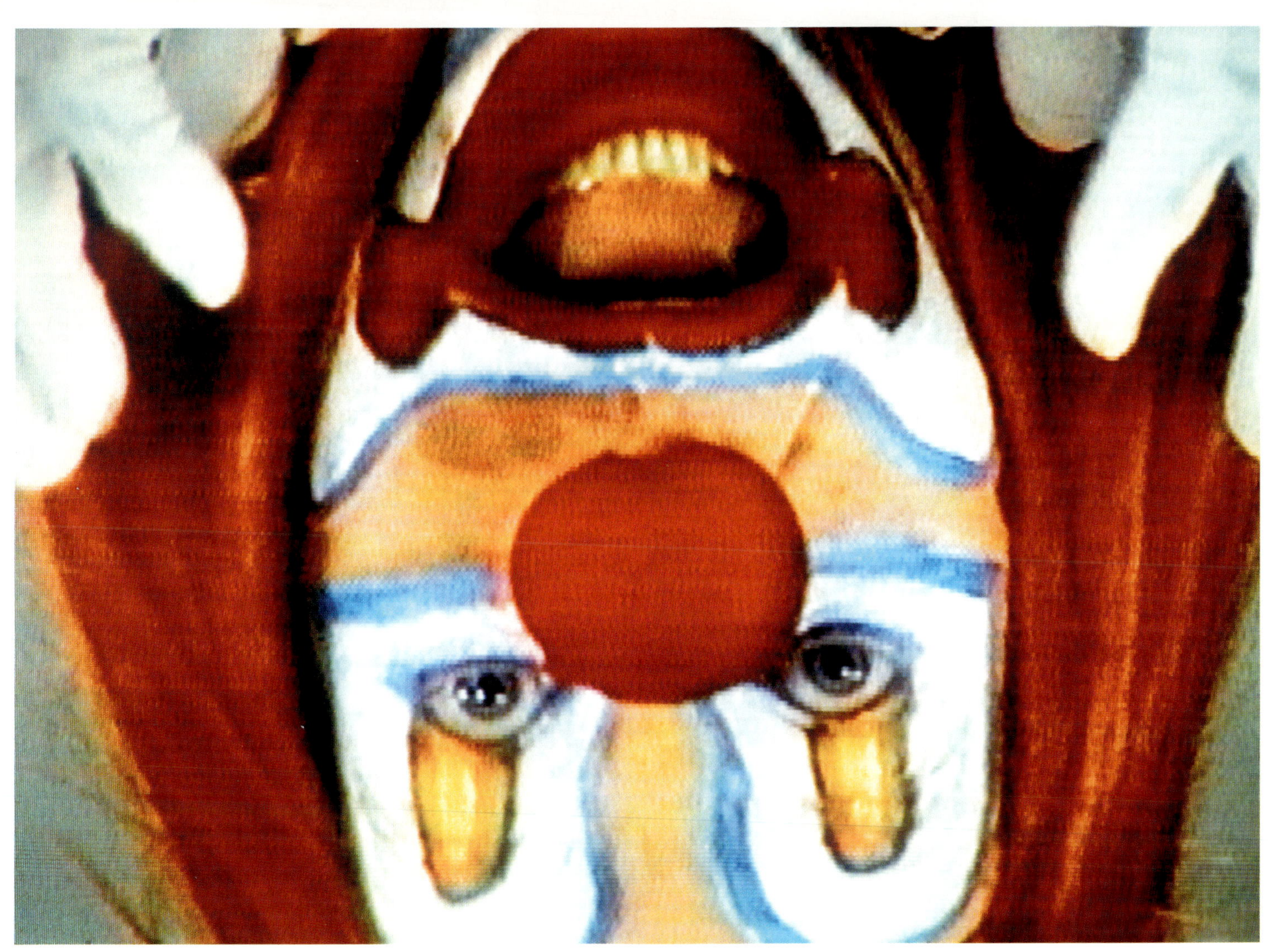

(Fig.27)

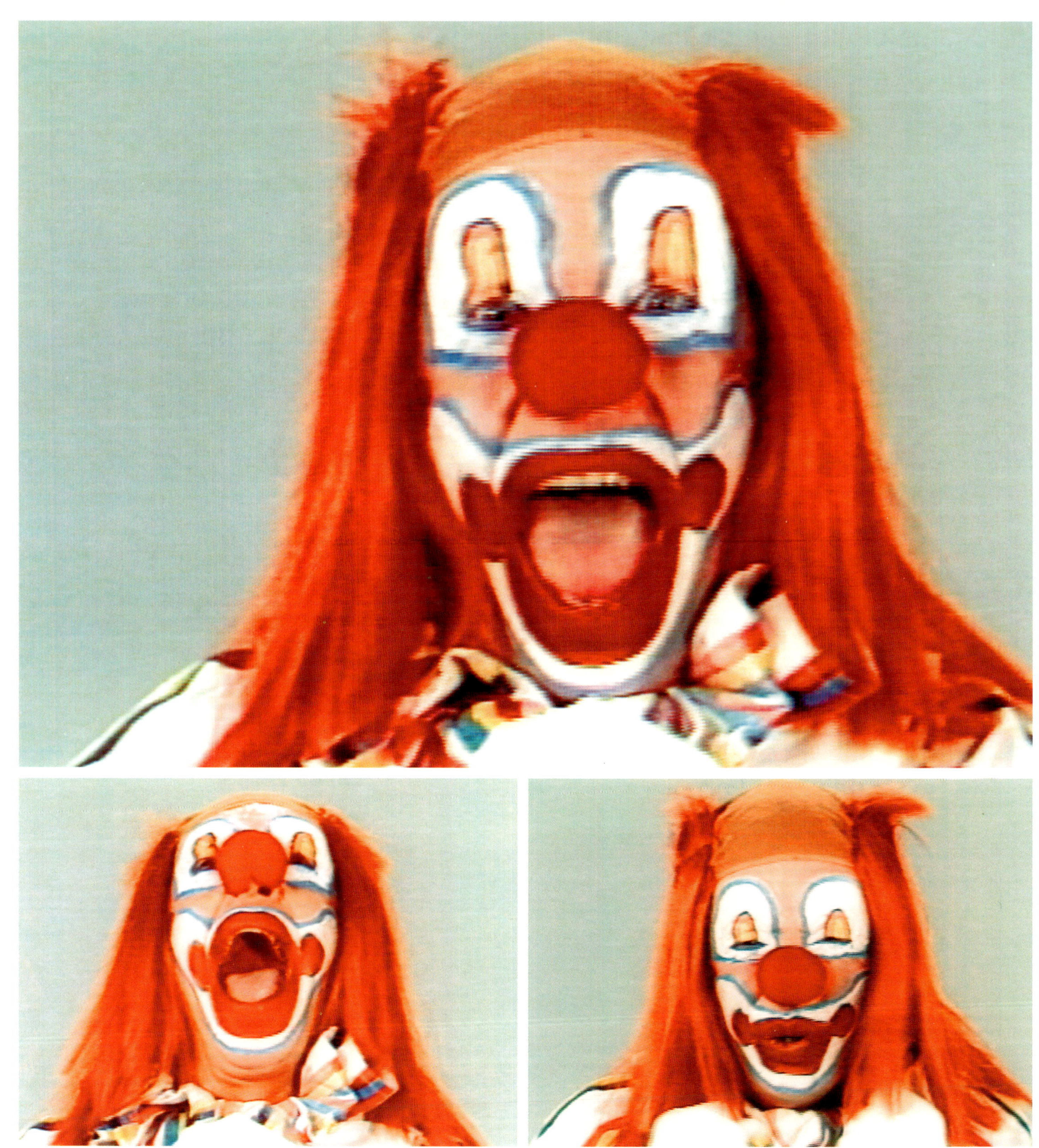

Pete and Repeat/Dark and Stormy Night (Figs.28–30)

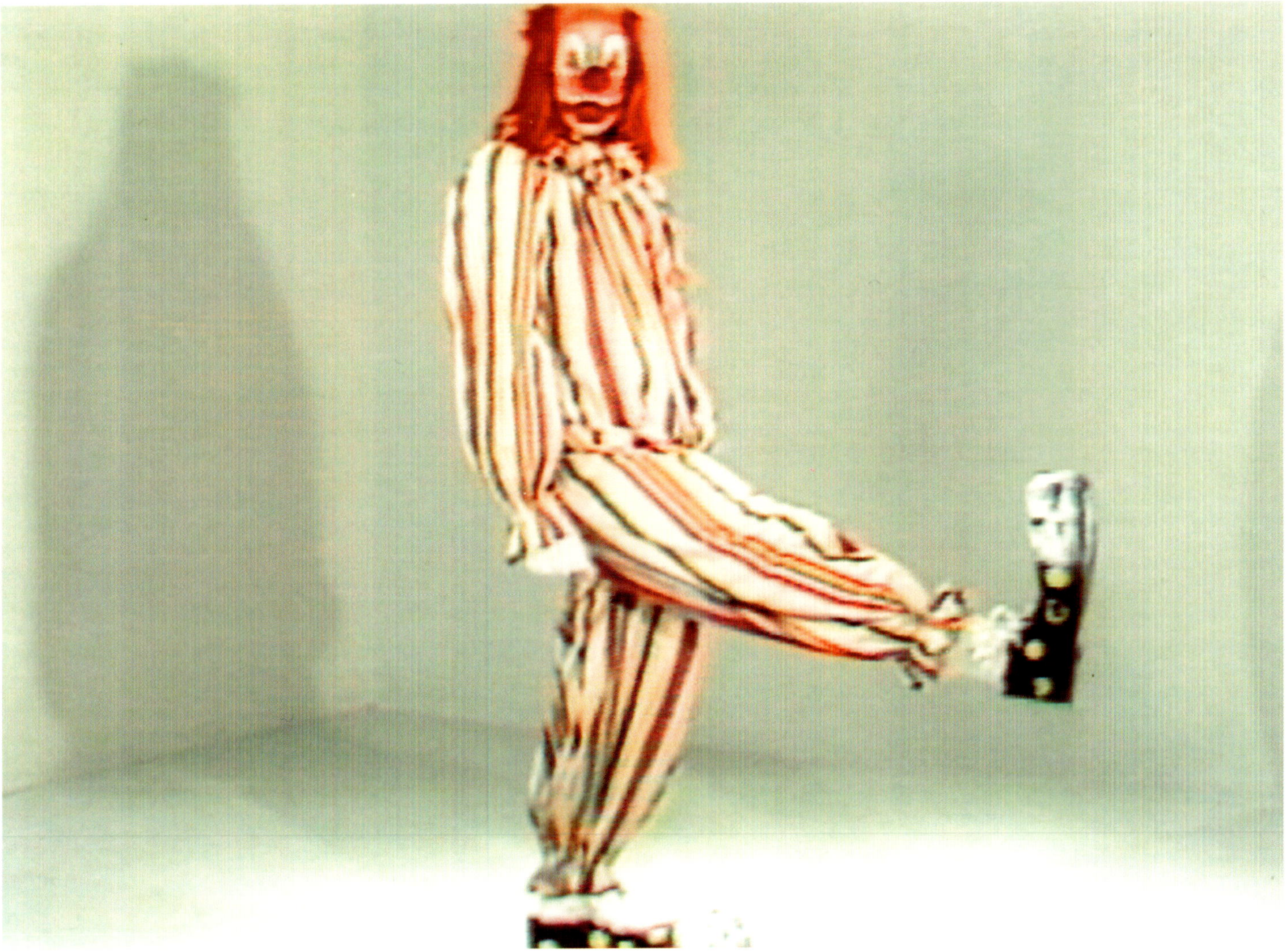

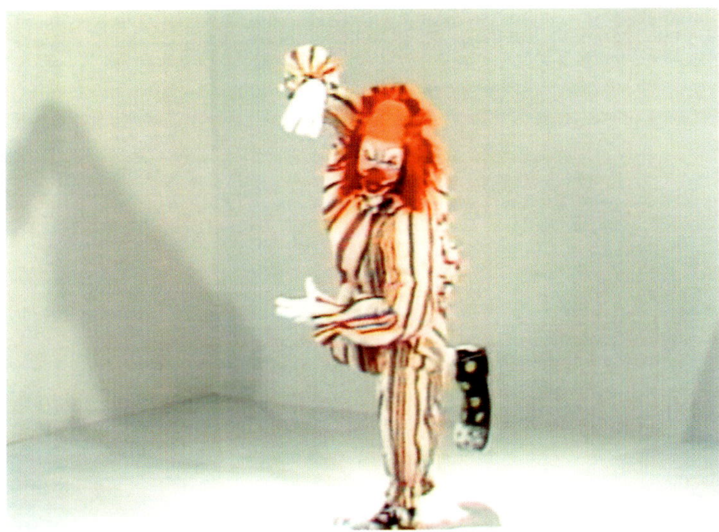

(Figs.31–2)

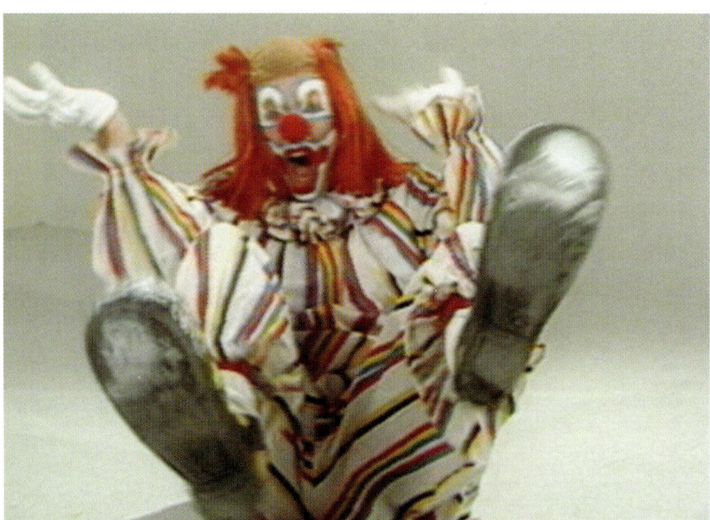

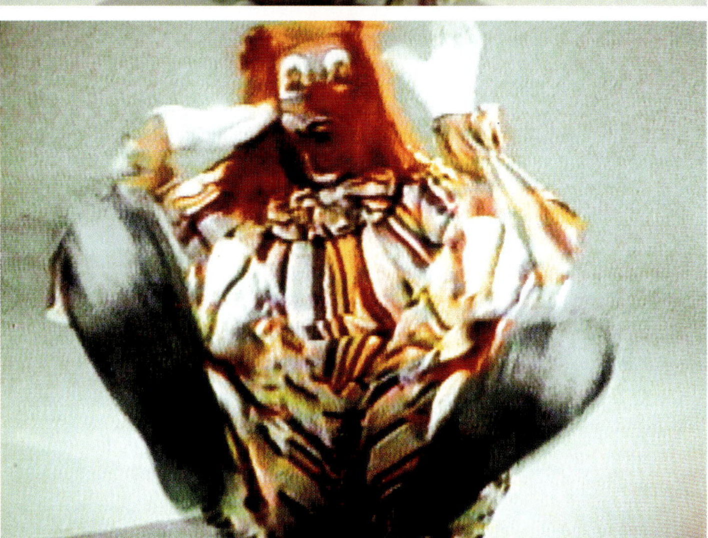

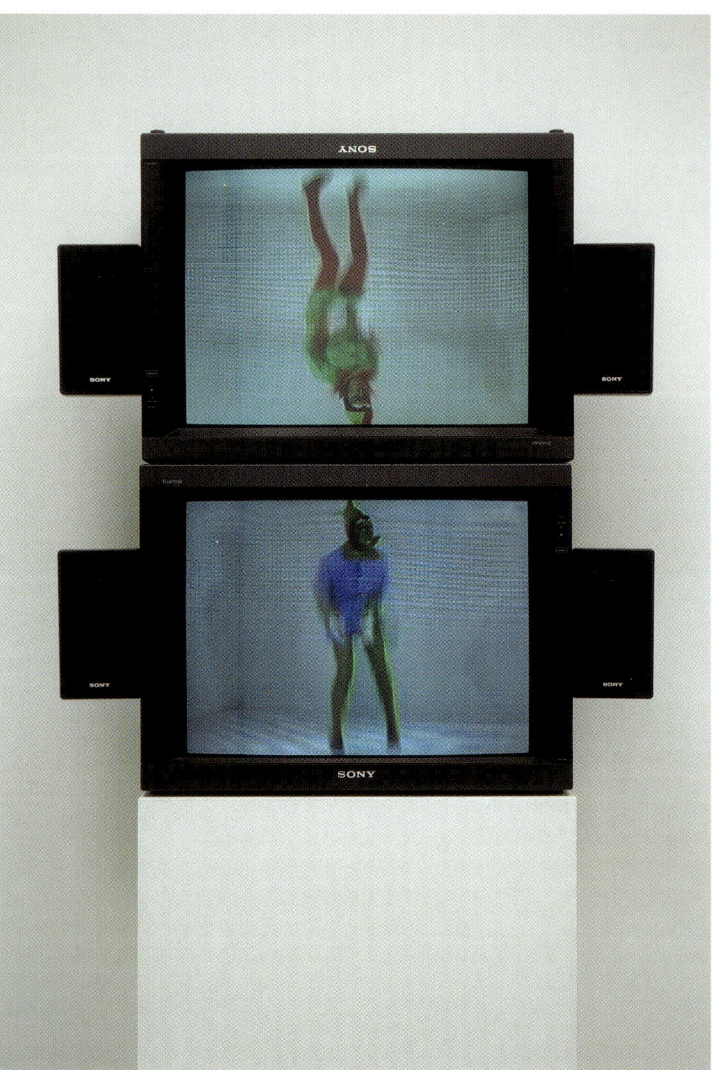

No No No No — New Museum/Walter (Figs.33–5)

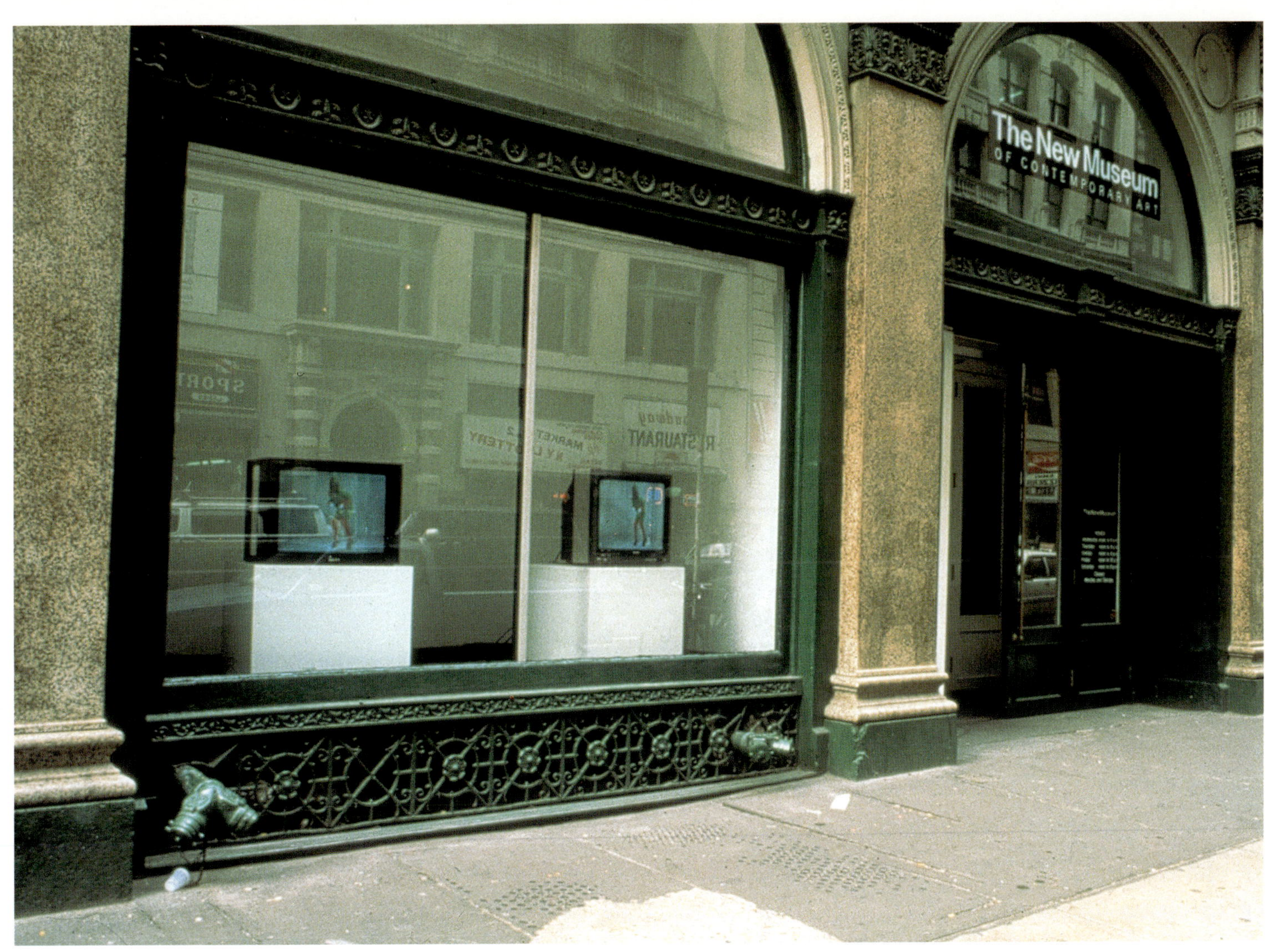

(Fig.36)

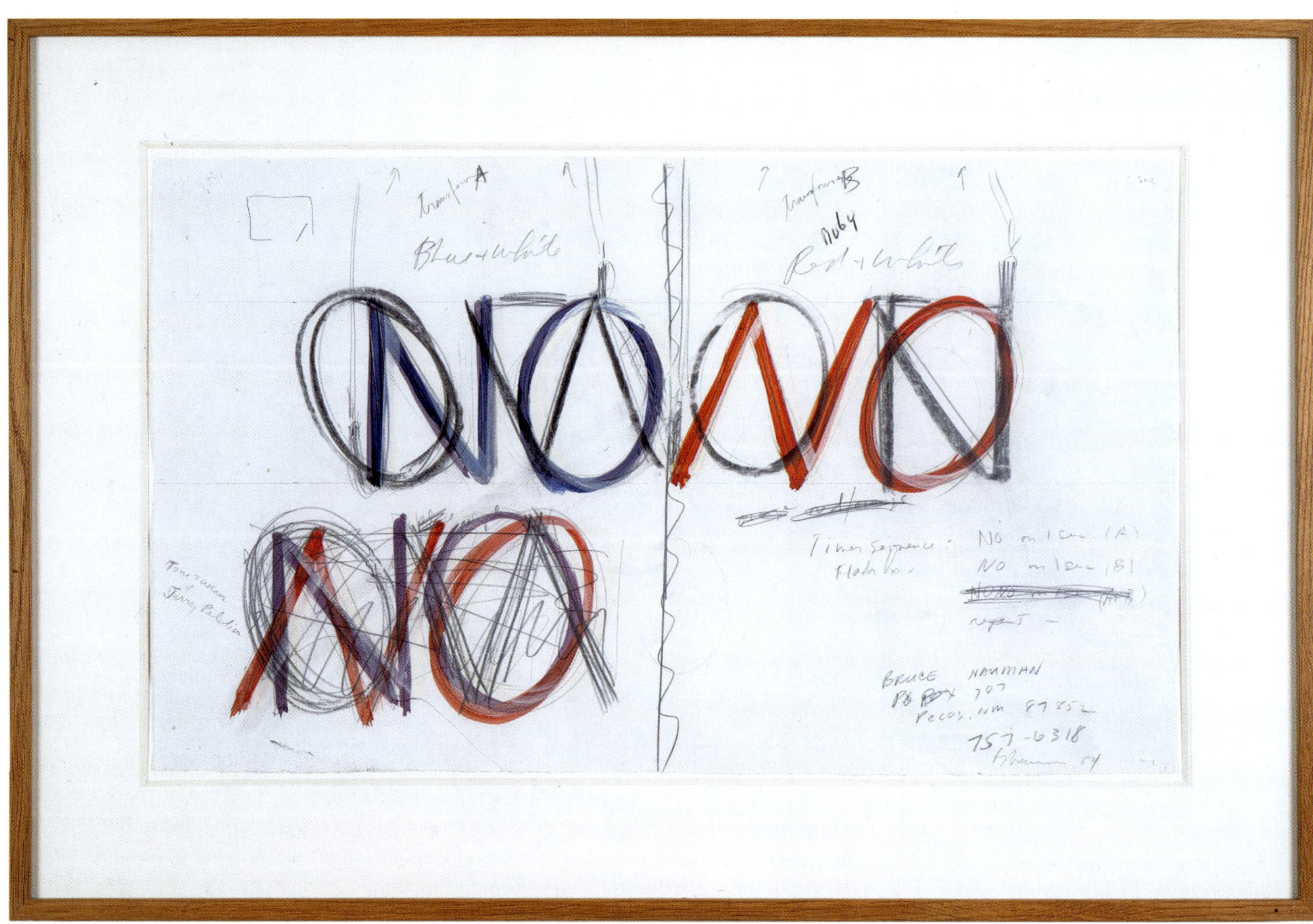

No No No No — New Museum/Walter (Fig.37)

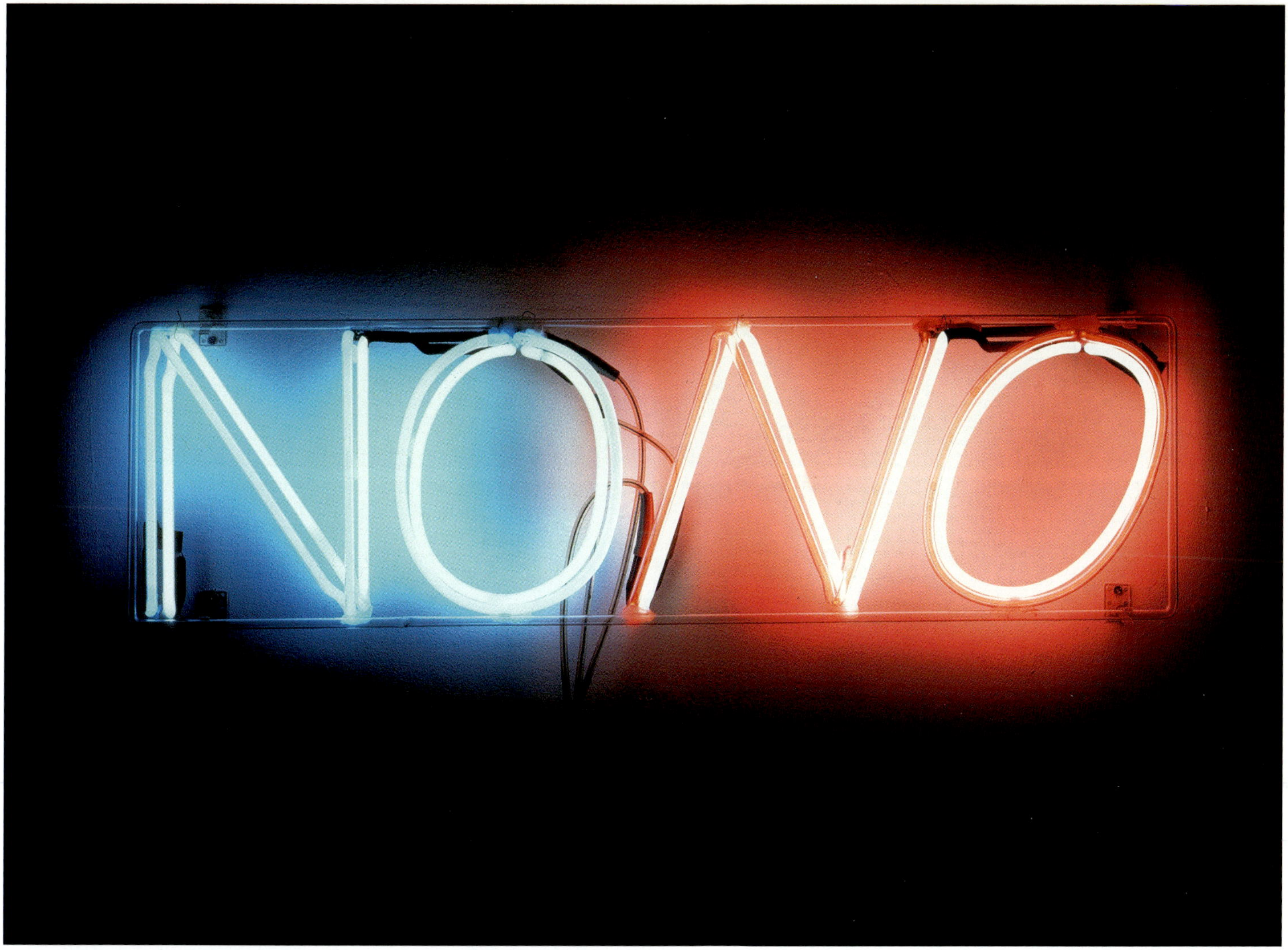

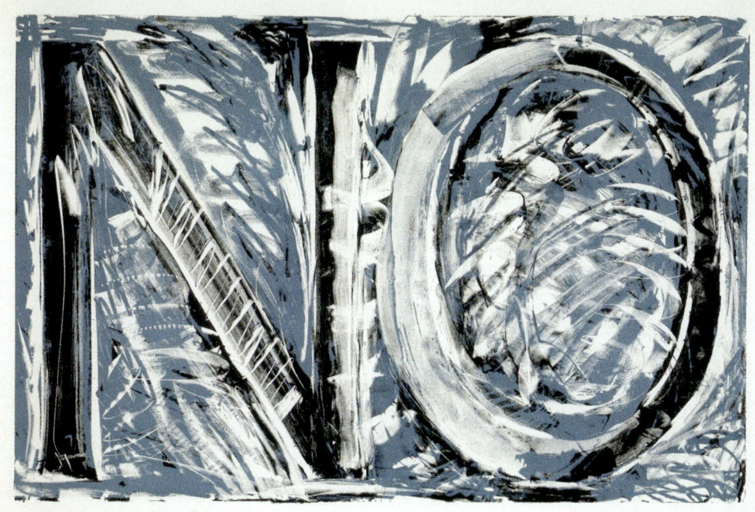

(Figs.38–9)

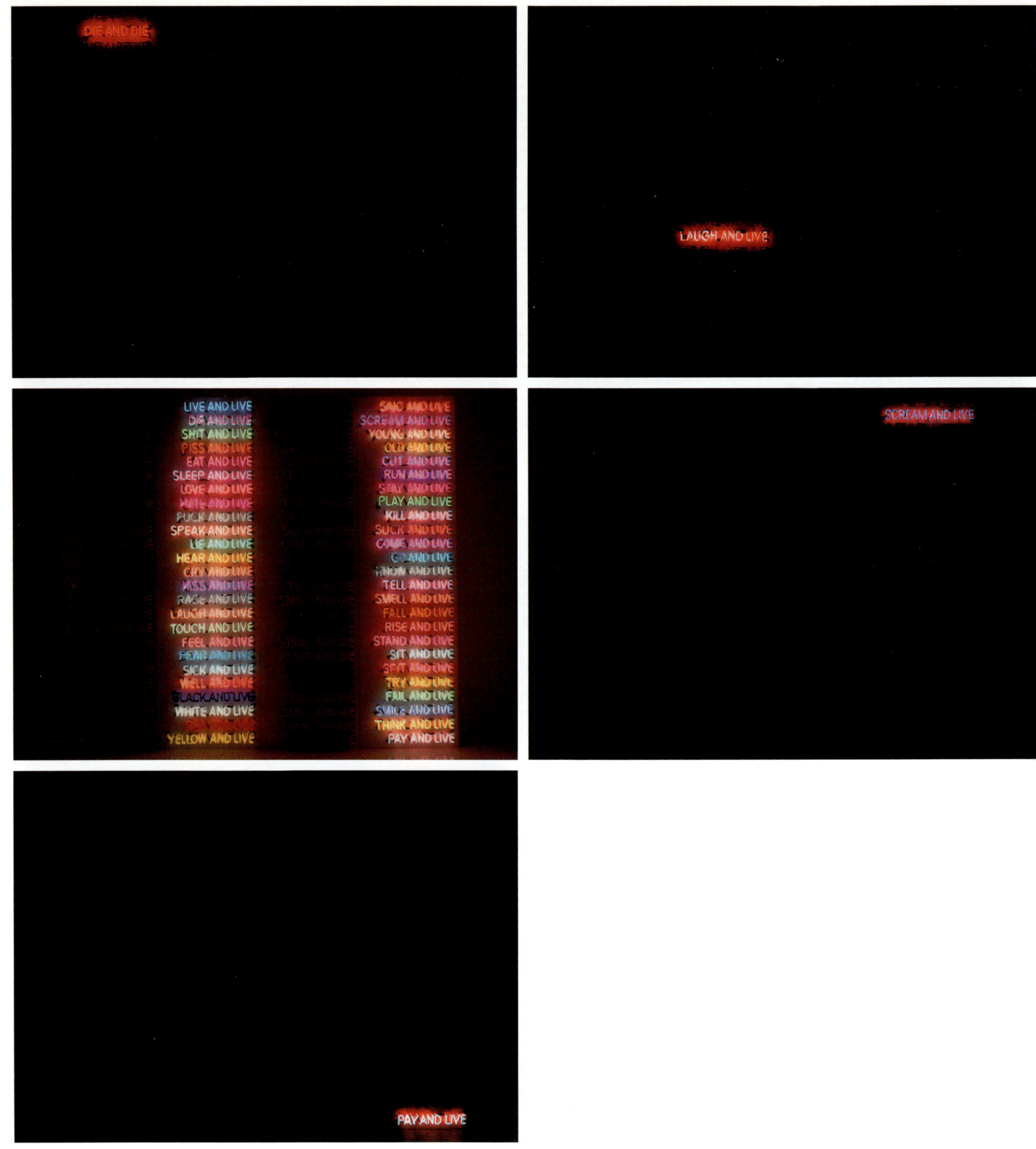

<u>100 Live and Die</u> (Figs.40–4)

(Fig.45)

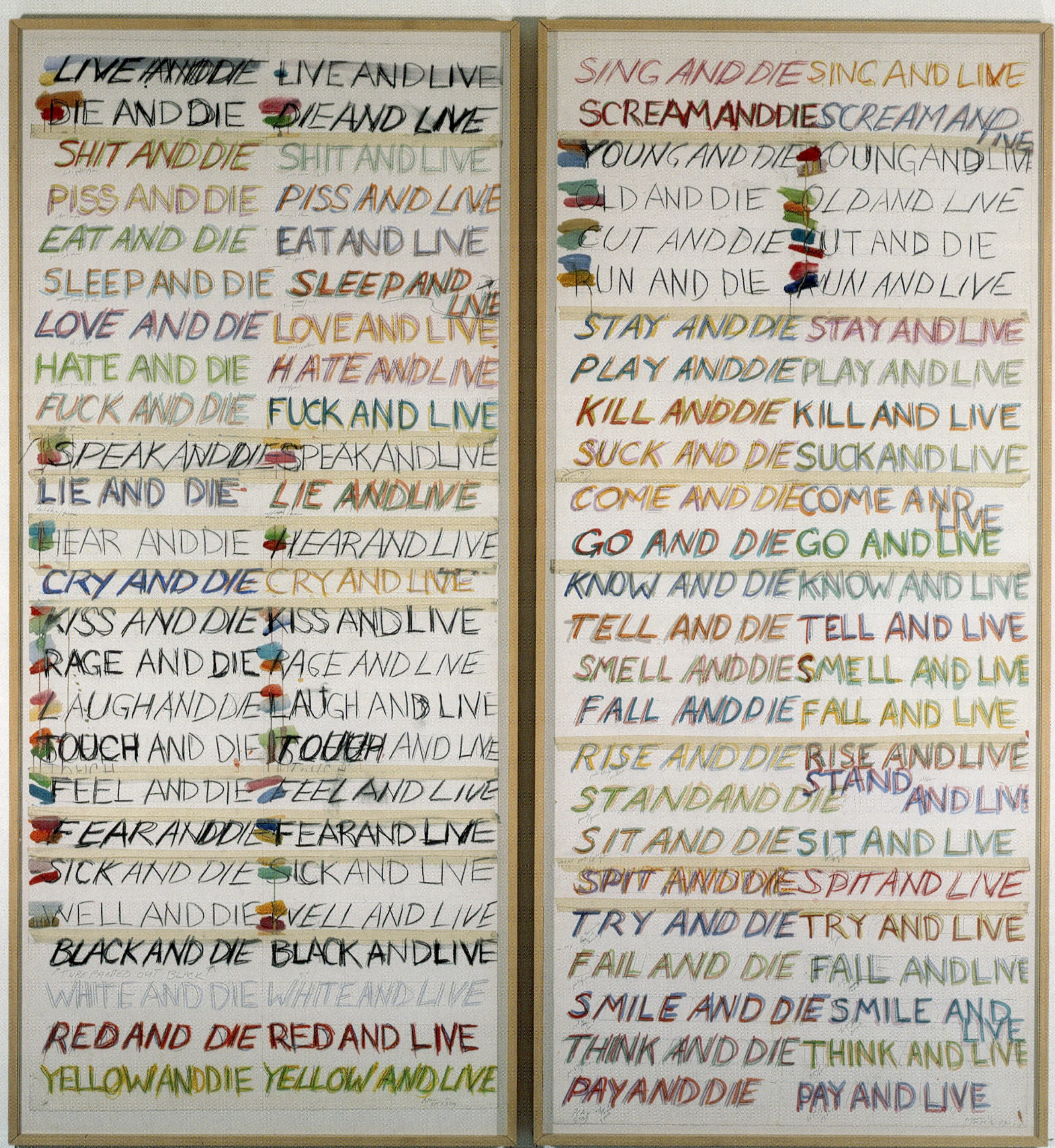

<u>100 Live and Die</u> (Fig.46)

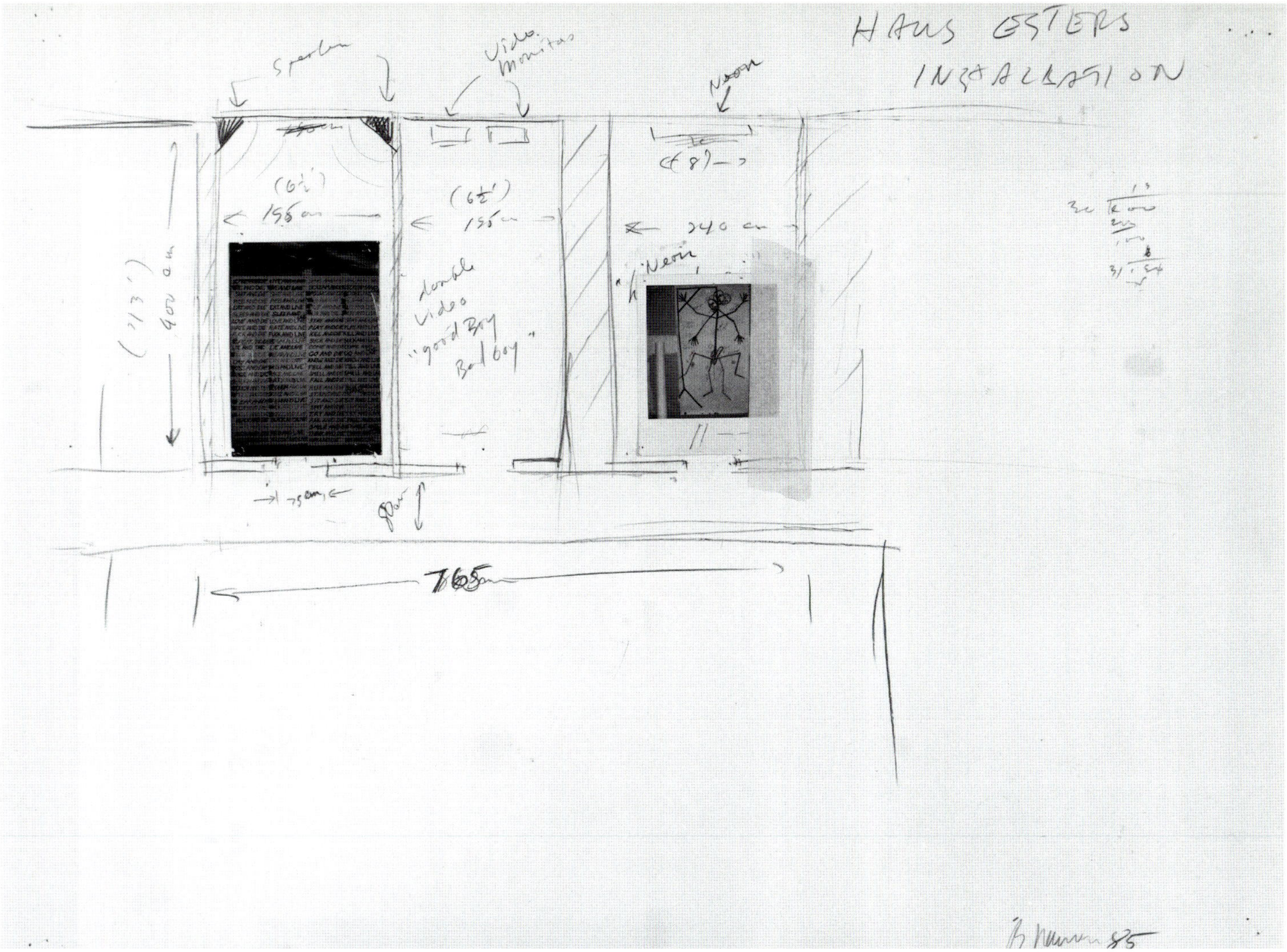

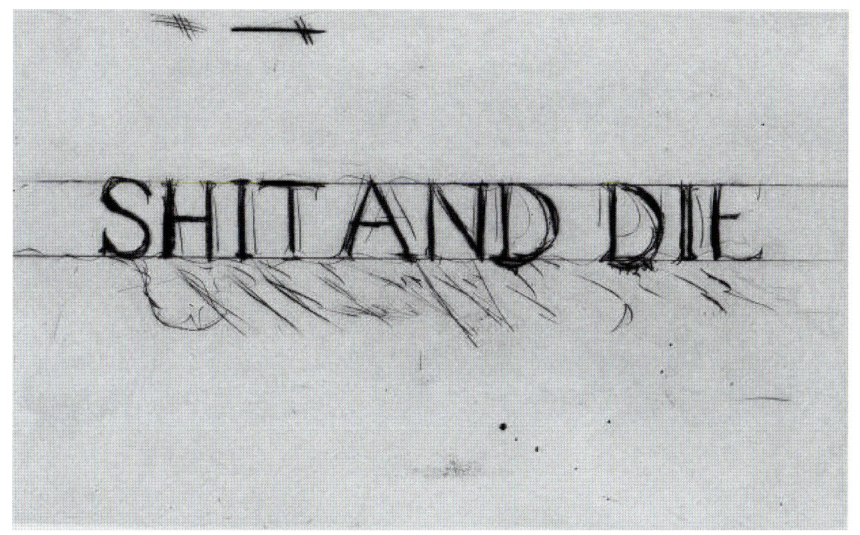

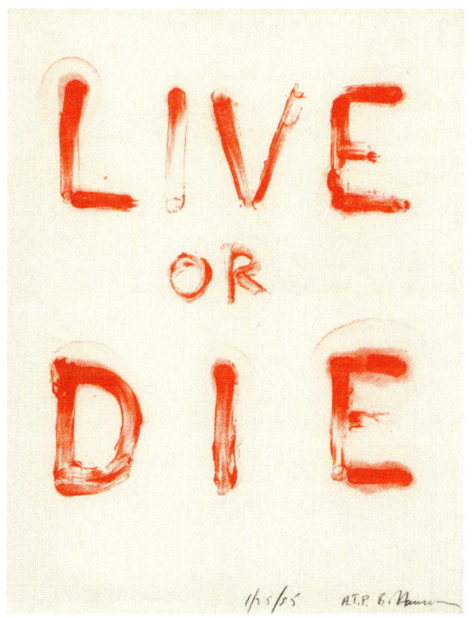

(Figs.47–9)

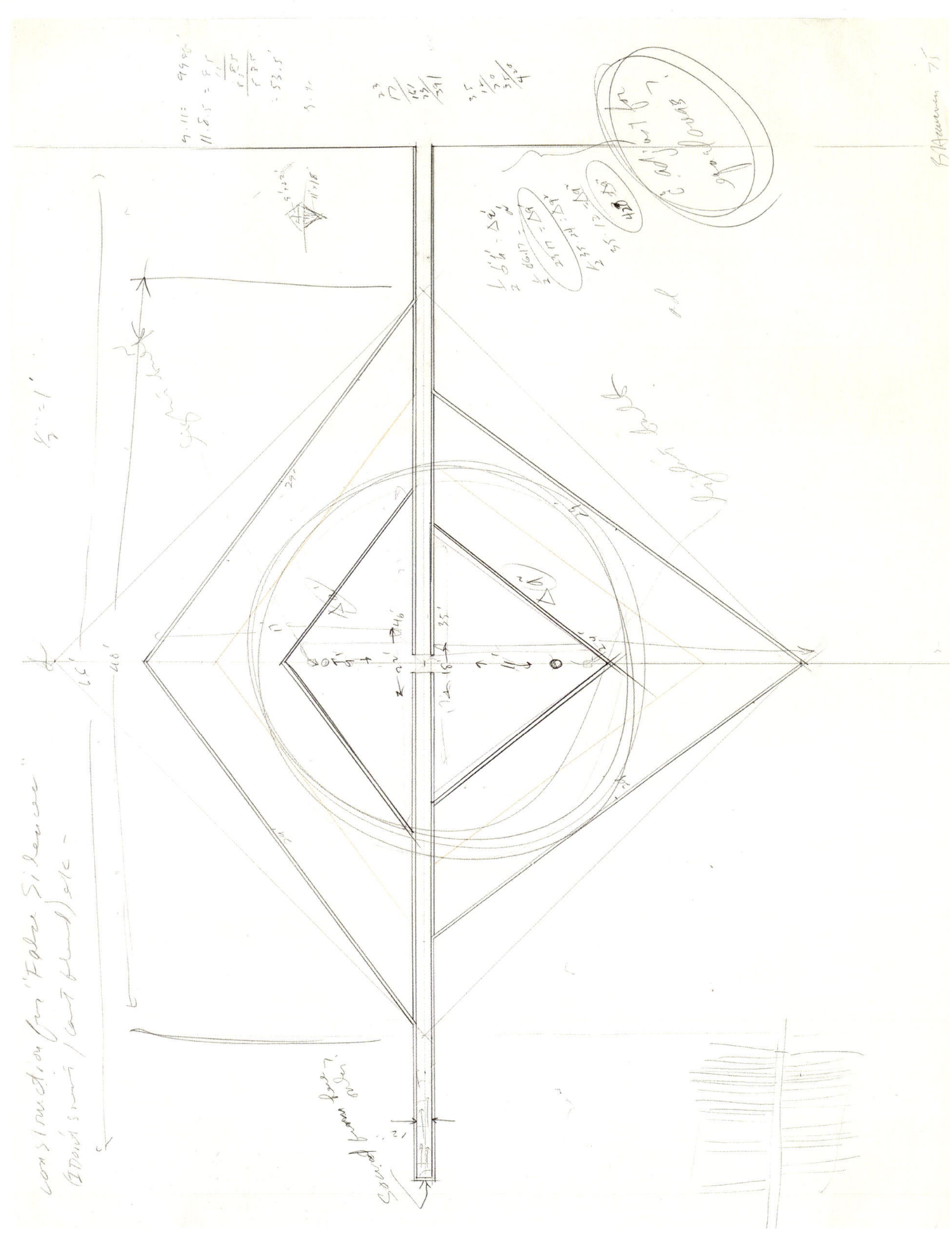

False Silence (Fig.50)

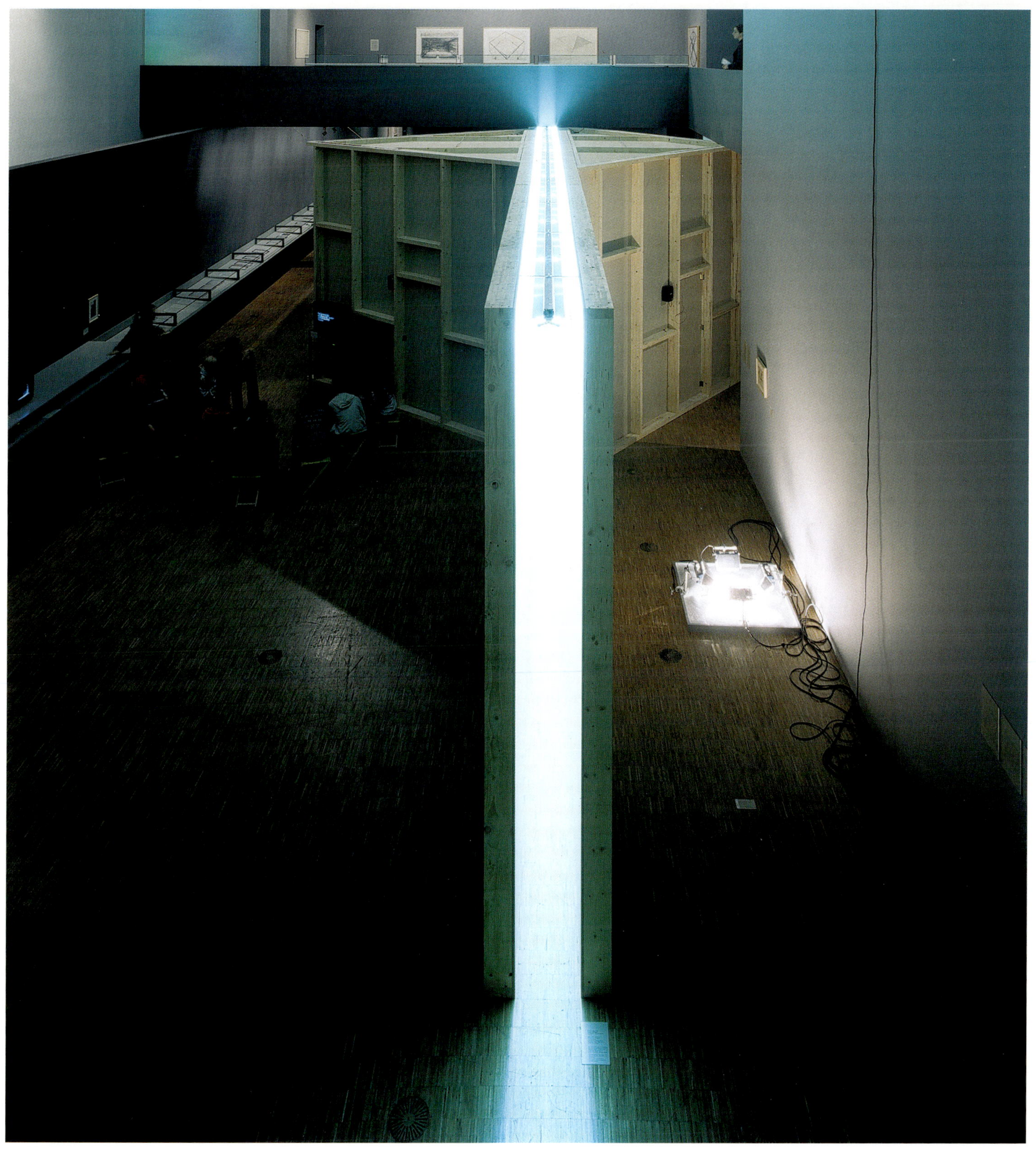

(Fig.51)

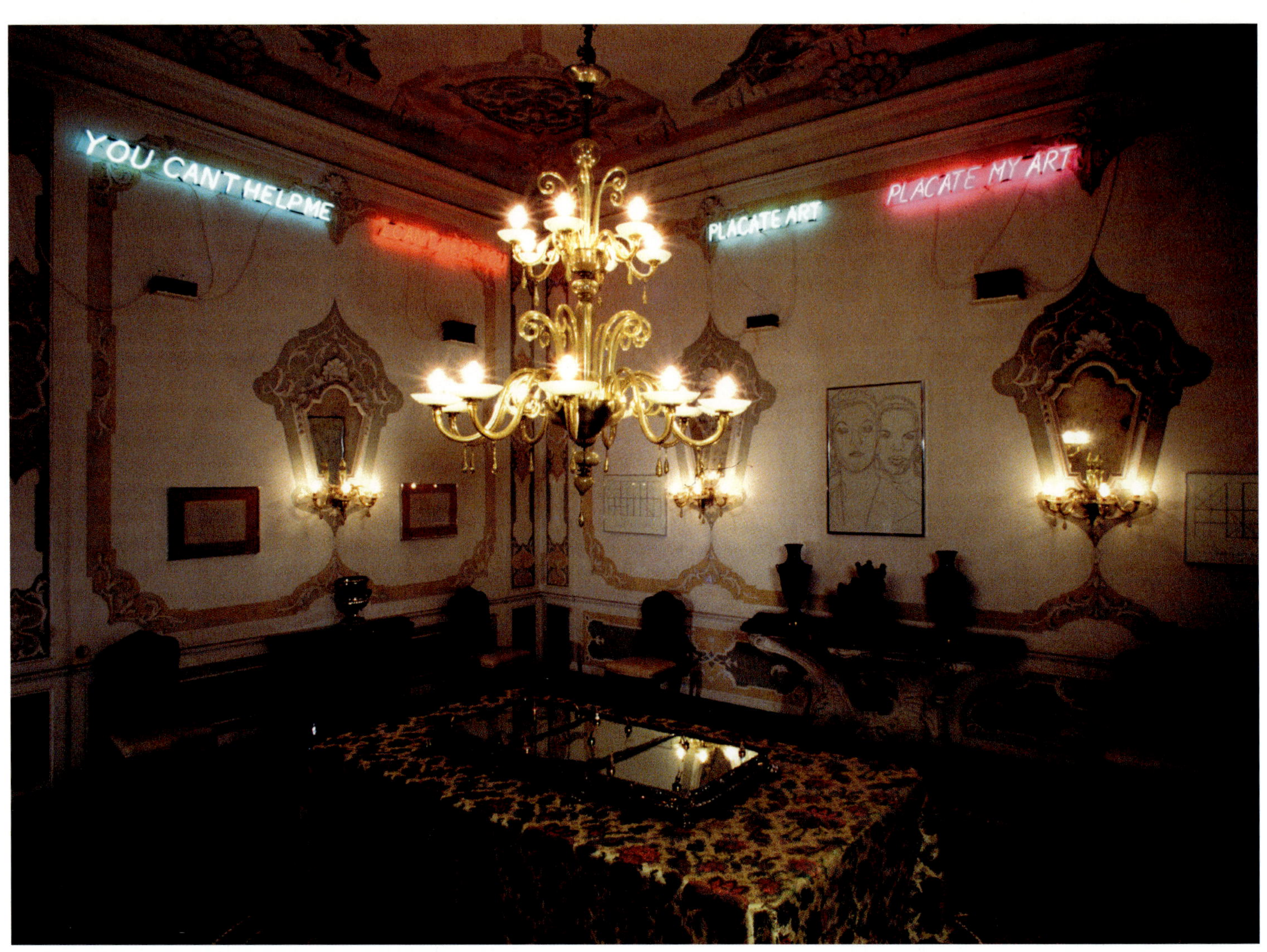

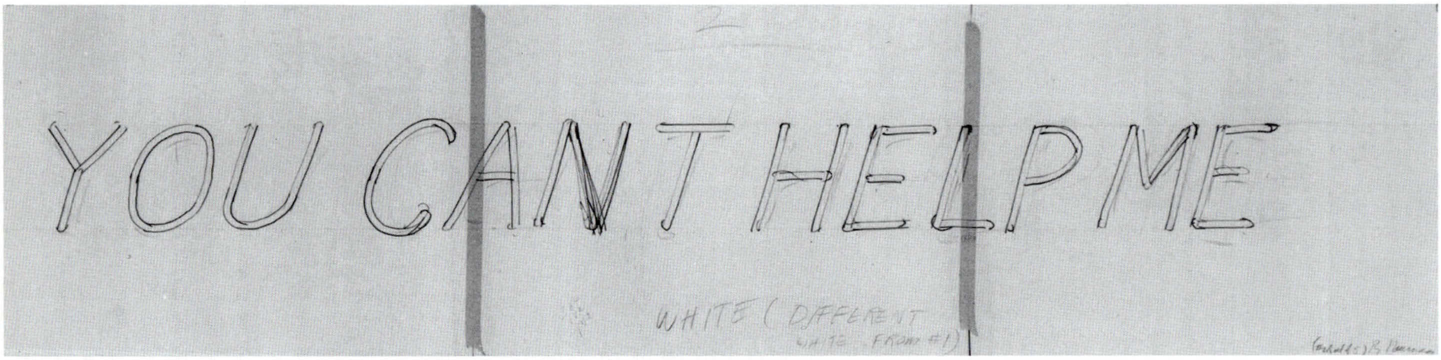

YOU CANT HELPME

WHITE (DIFFERENT WHITE FROM #1)

False Silence (Figs.52–3)

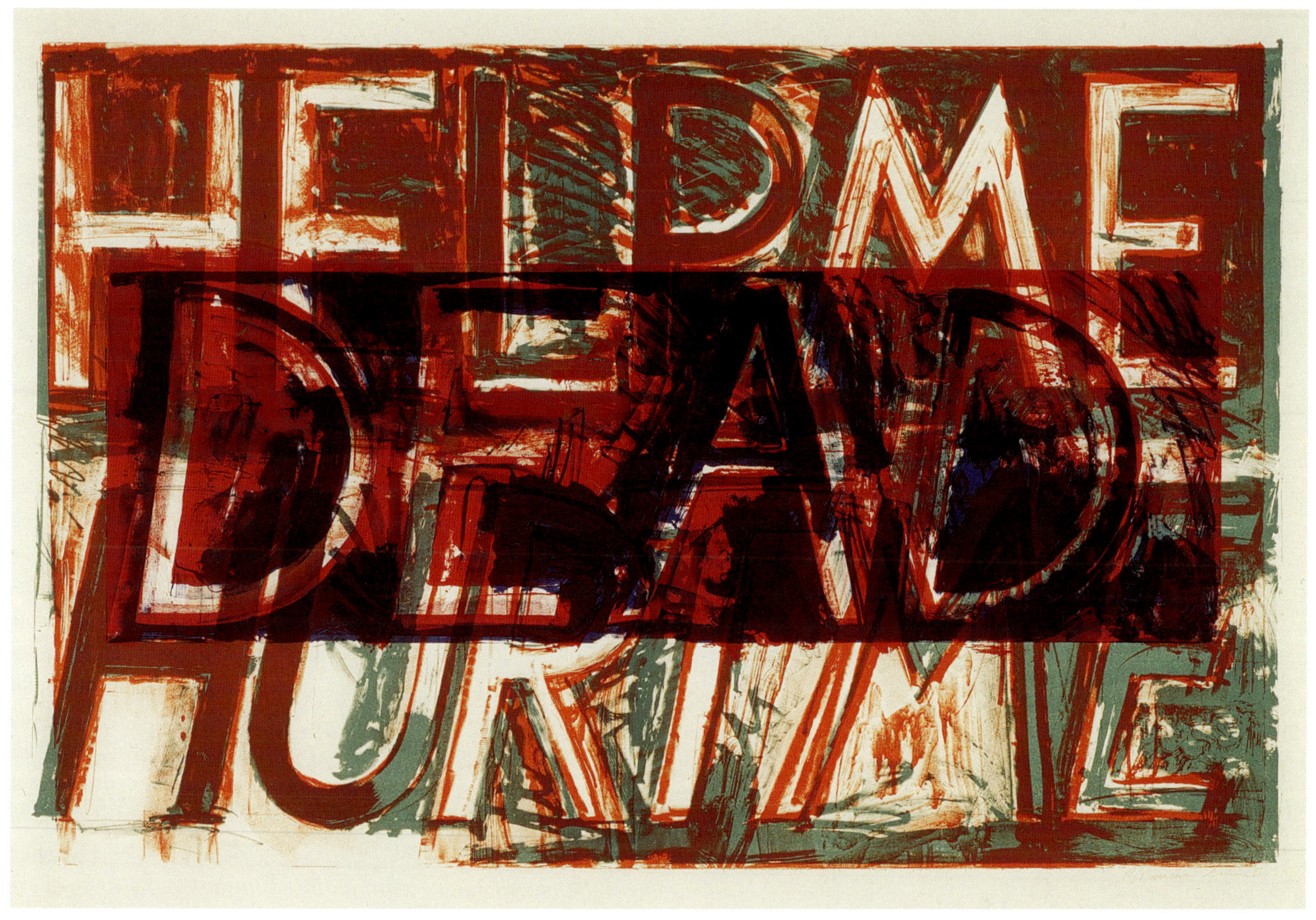

THIS IS THE SILVER GROTTO
YOU CANT HEAR ME
THIS IS THE YELLOW GROTTO
YOU CANT HURT ME
I CAN SUCK YOU DRY

(Figs.54–5)

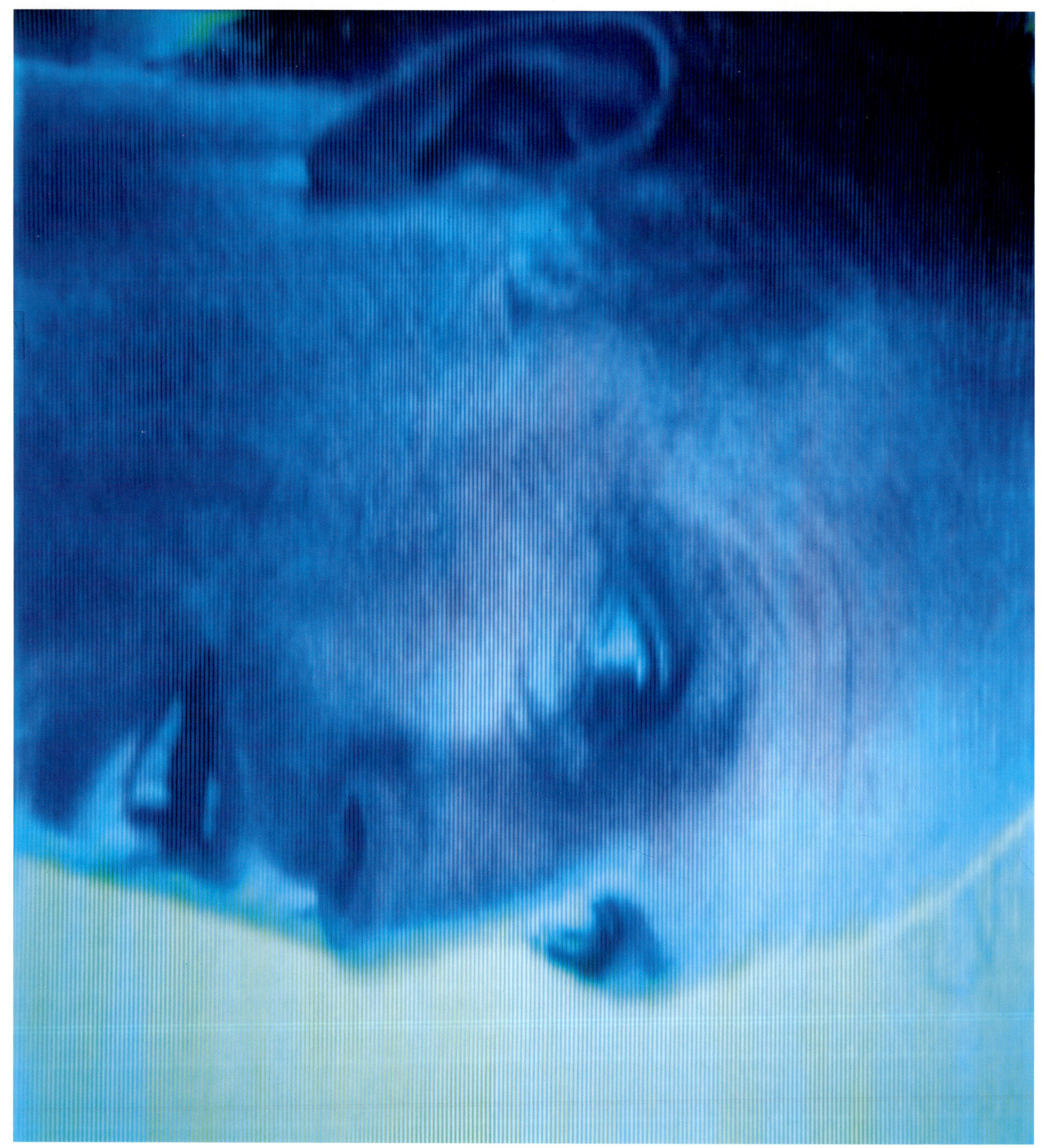

OK OK OK (Fig.56)

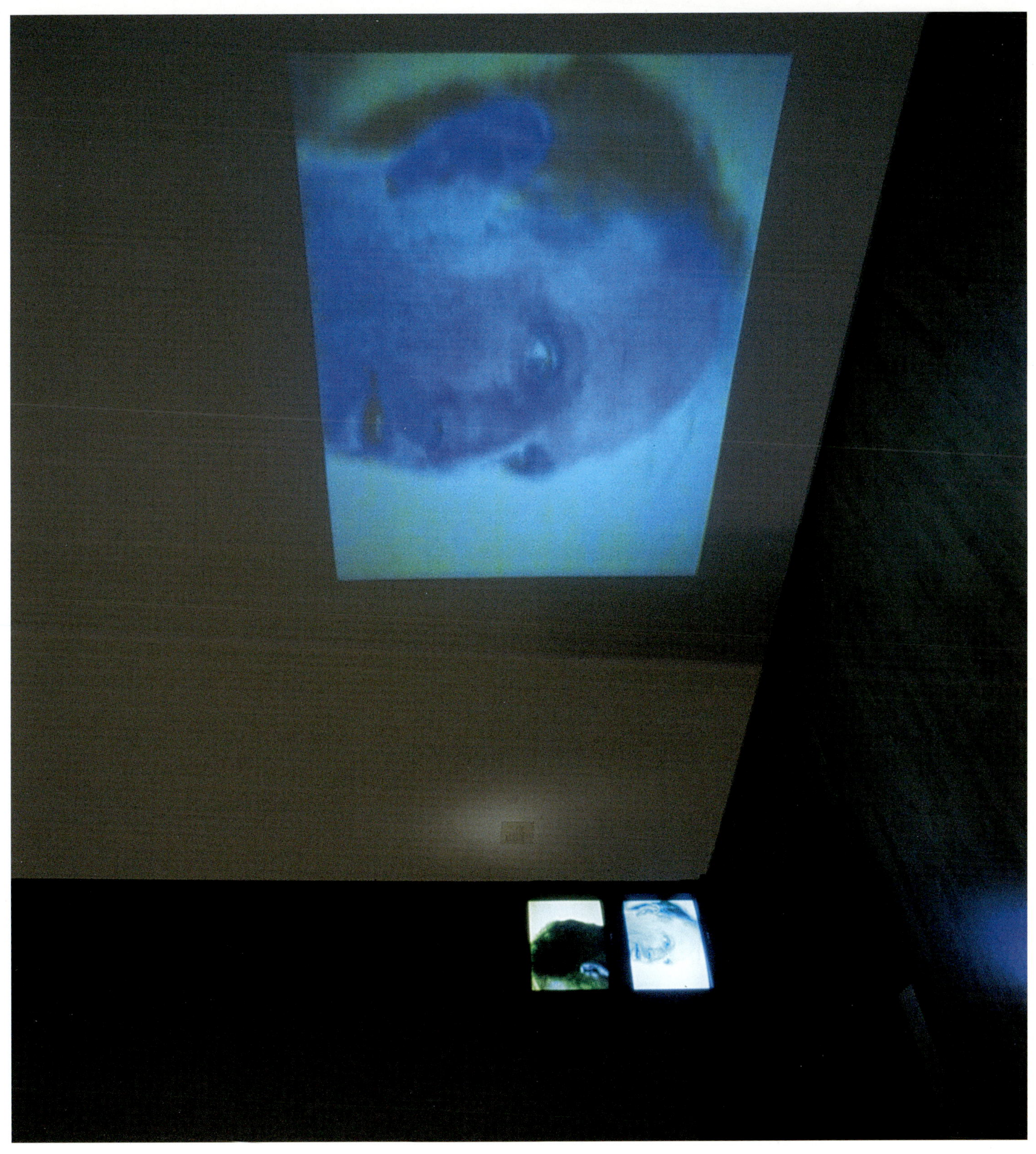

(Fig.57)

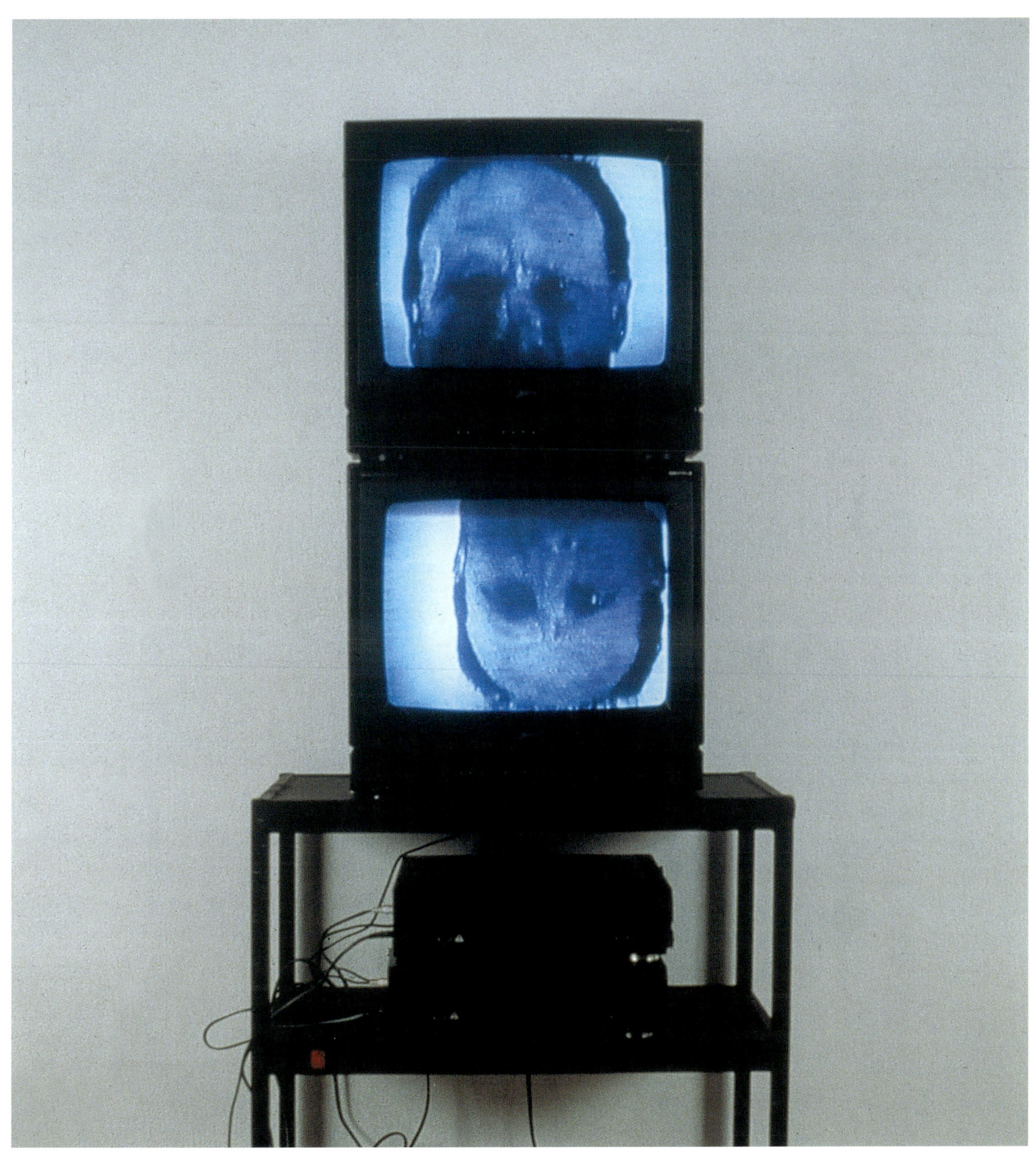

Think Think Think (Fig.58)

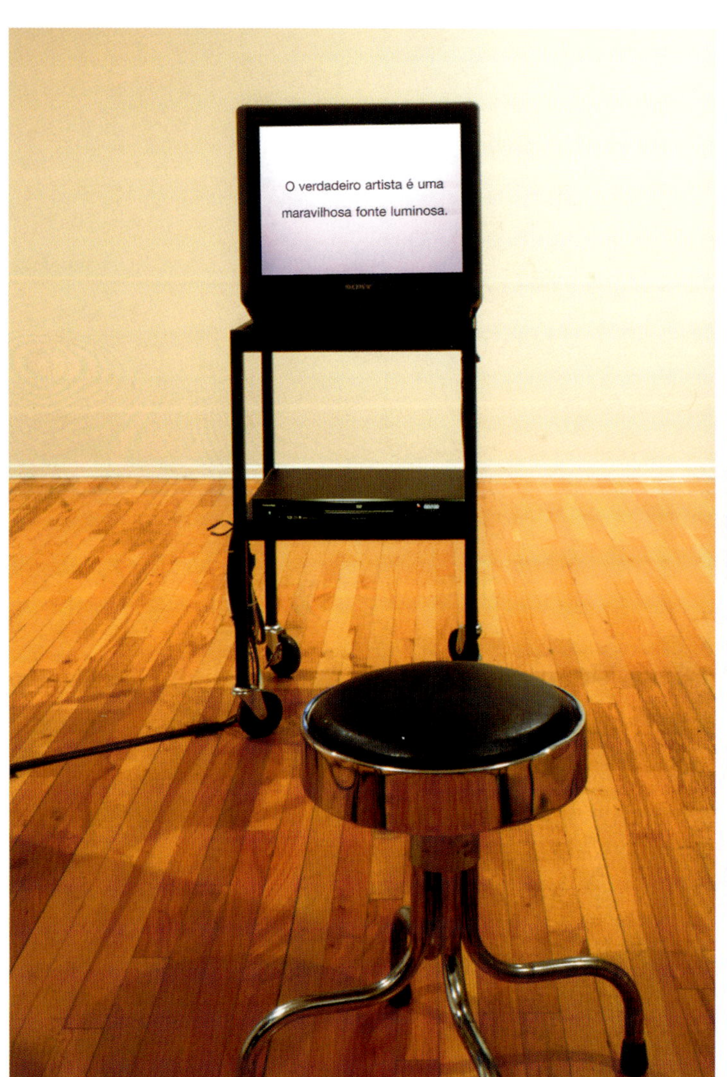

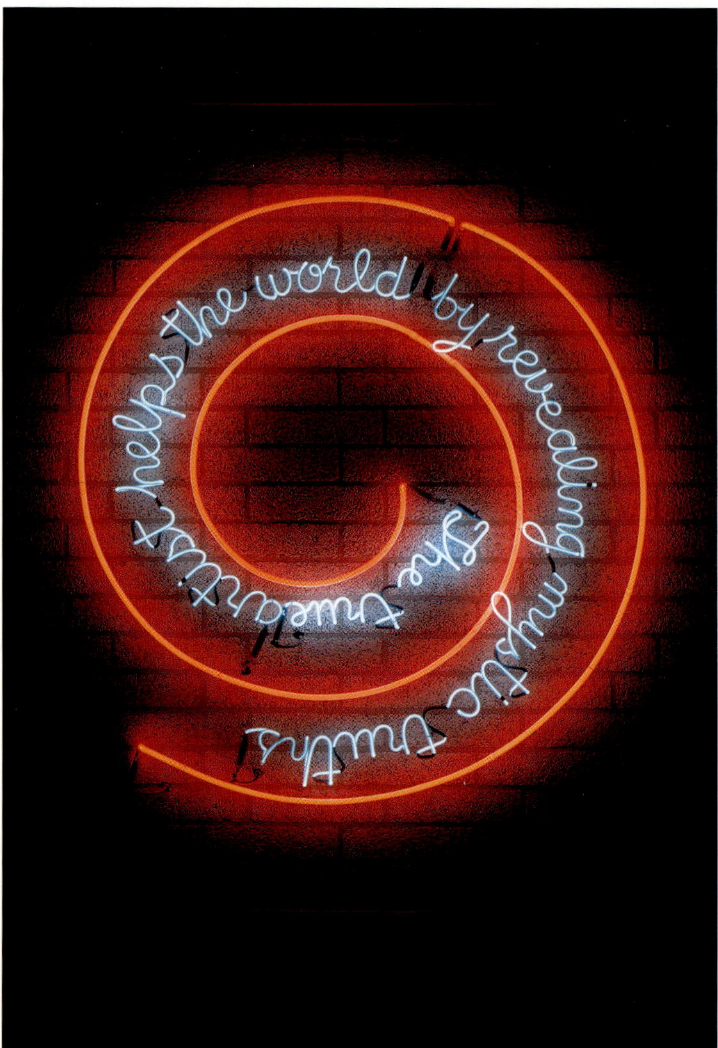

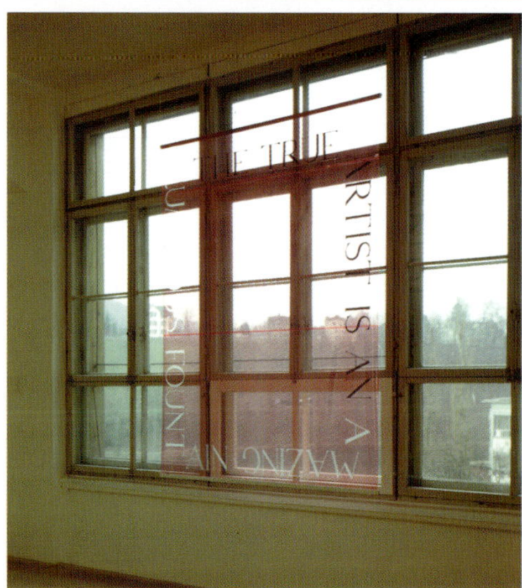

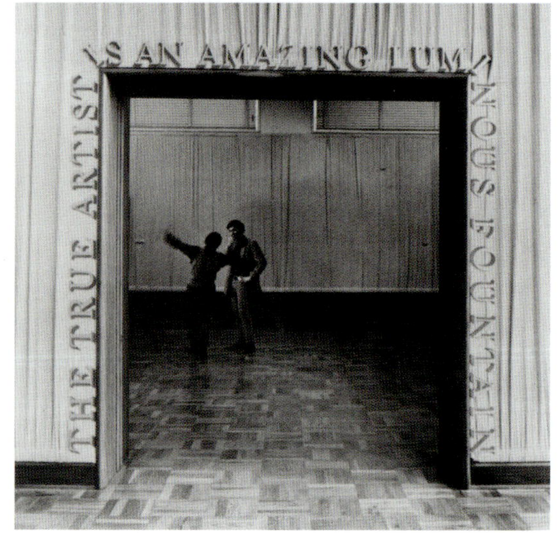

<u>The True Artist Is An Amazing Luminous Fountain</u> (Figs.59–62)

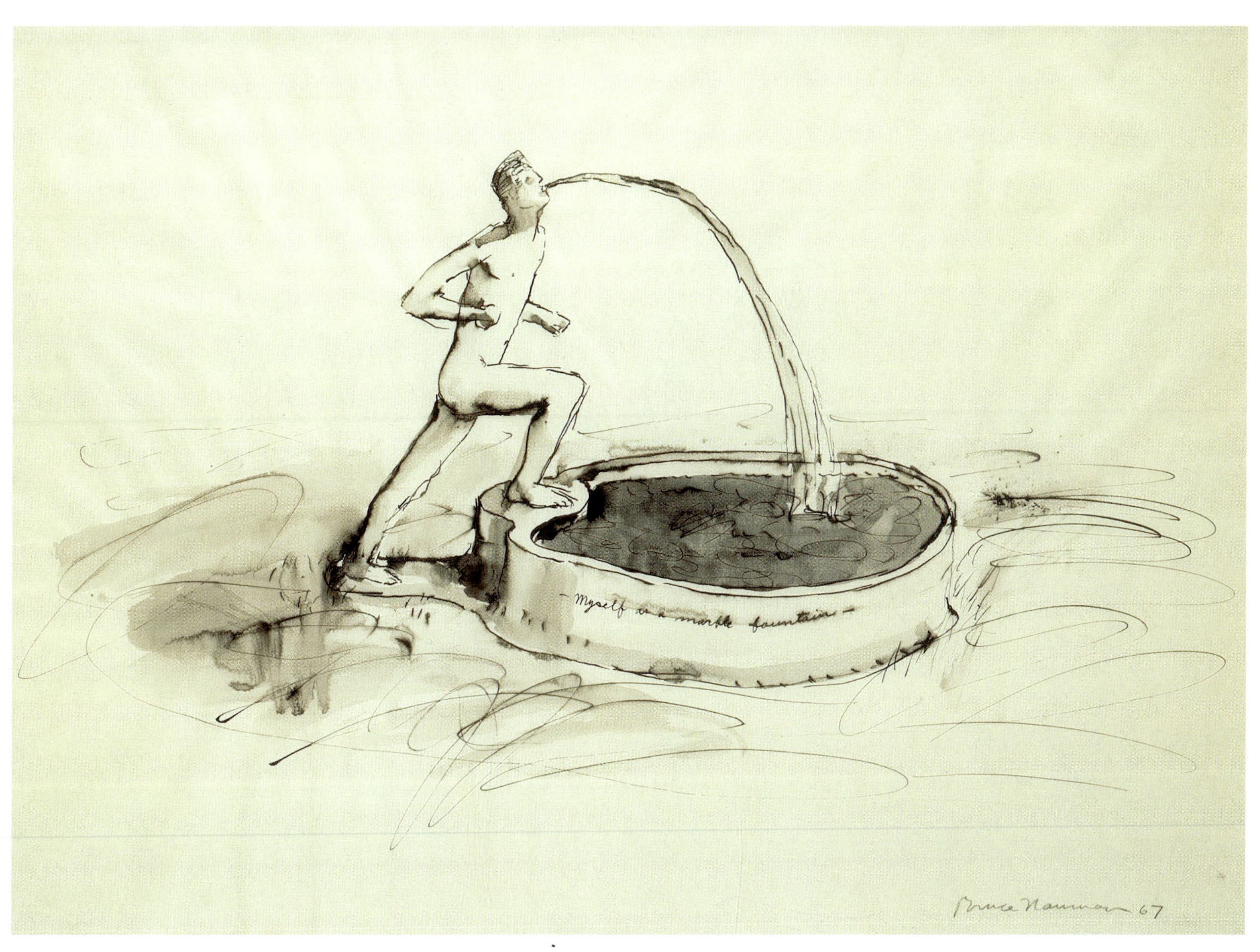

(Fig.63)

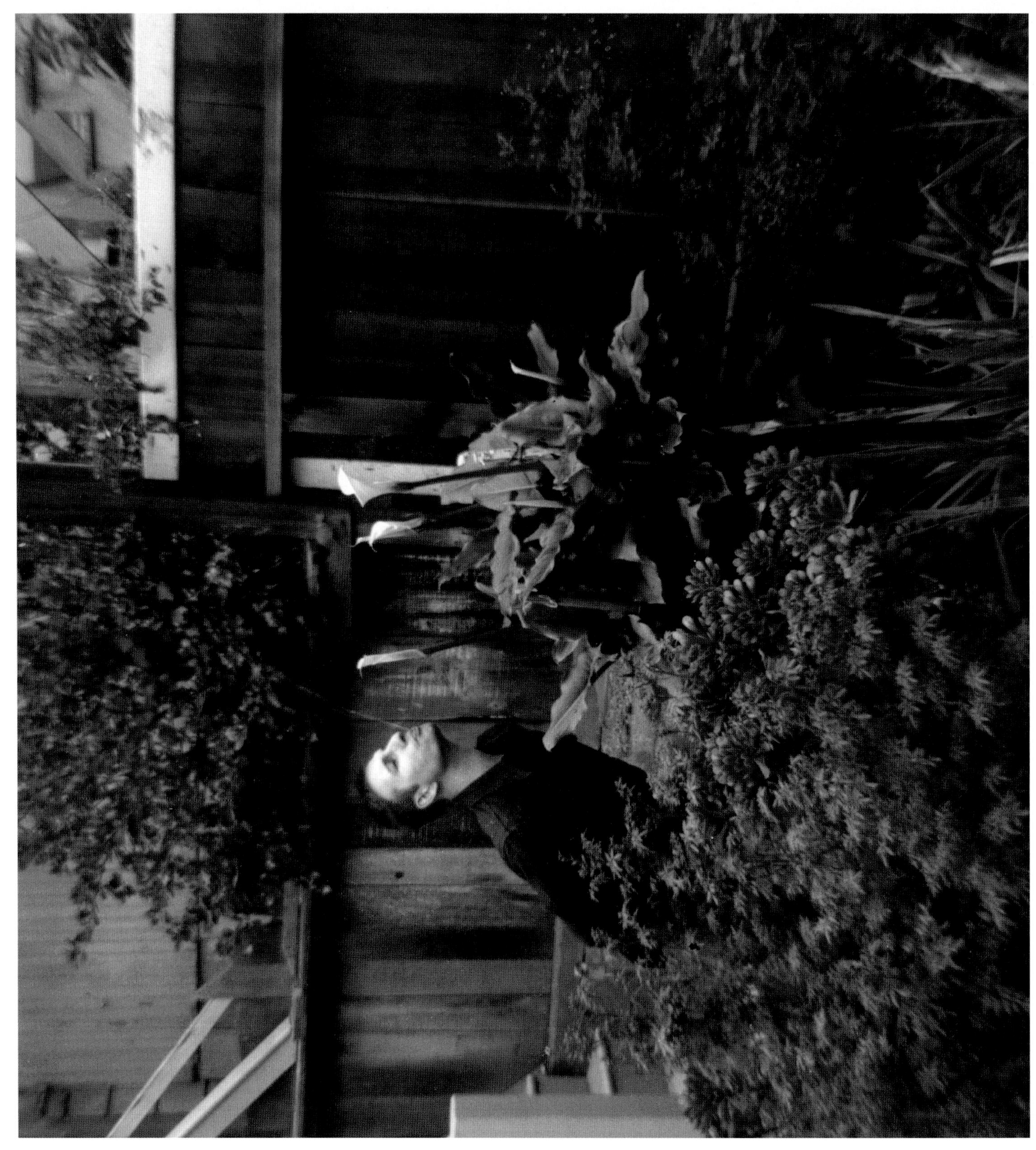

The True Artist Is An Amazing Luminous Fountain (Fig.64)

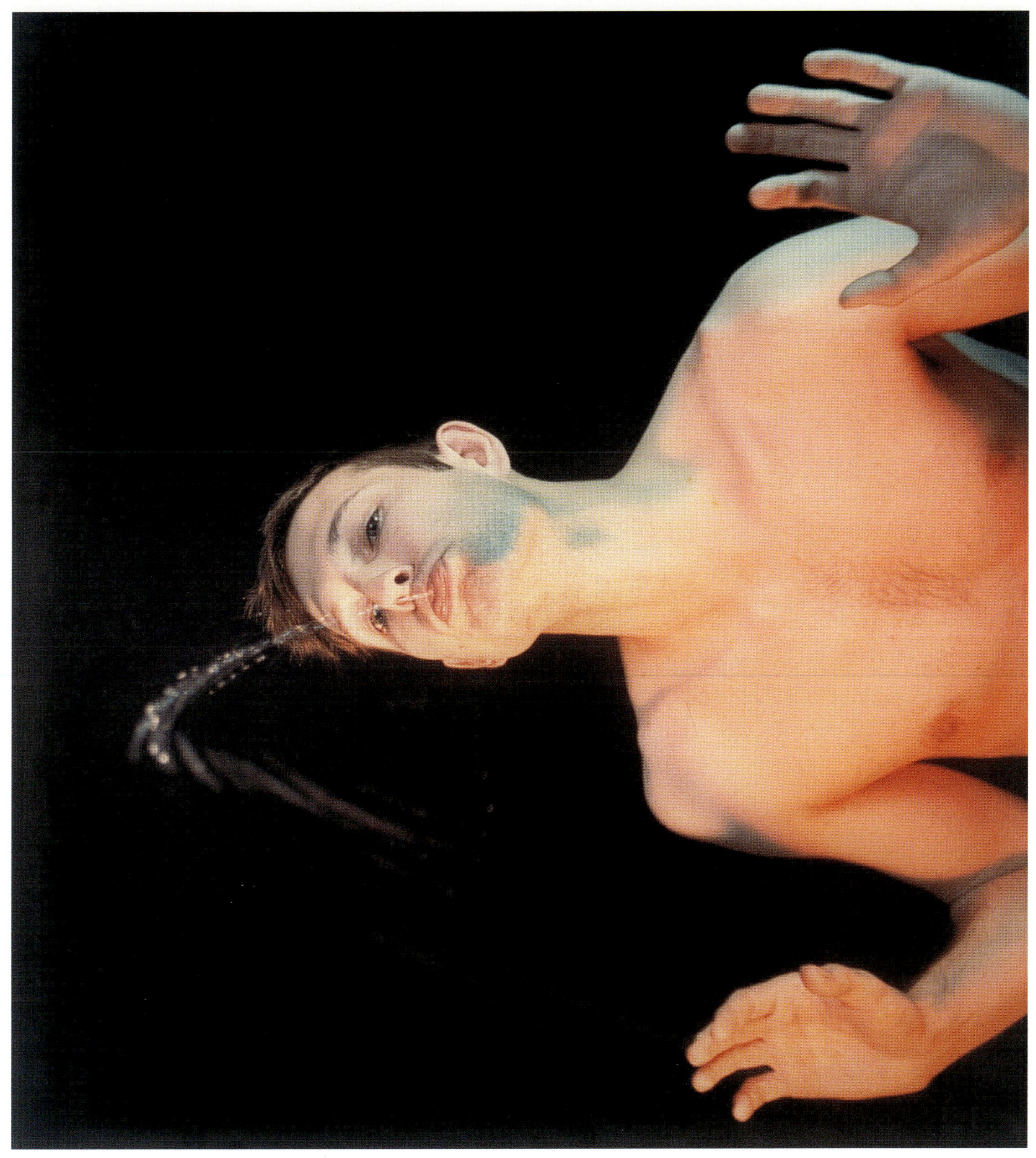

(Fig.65)

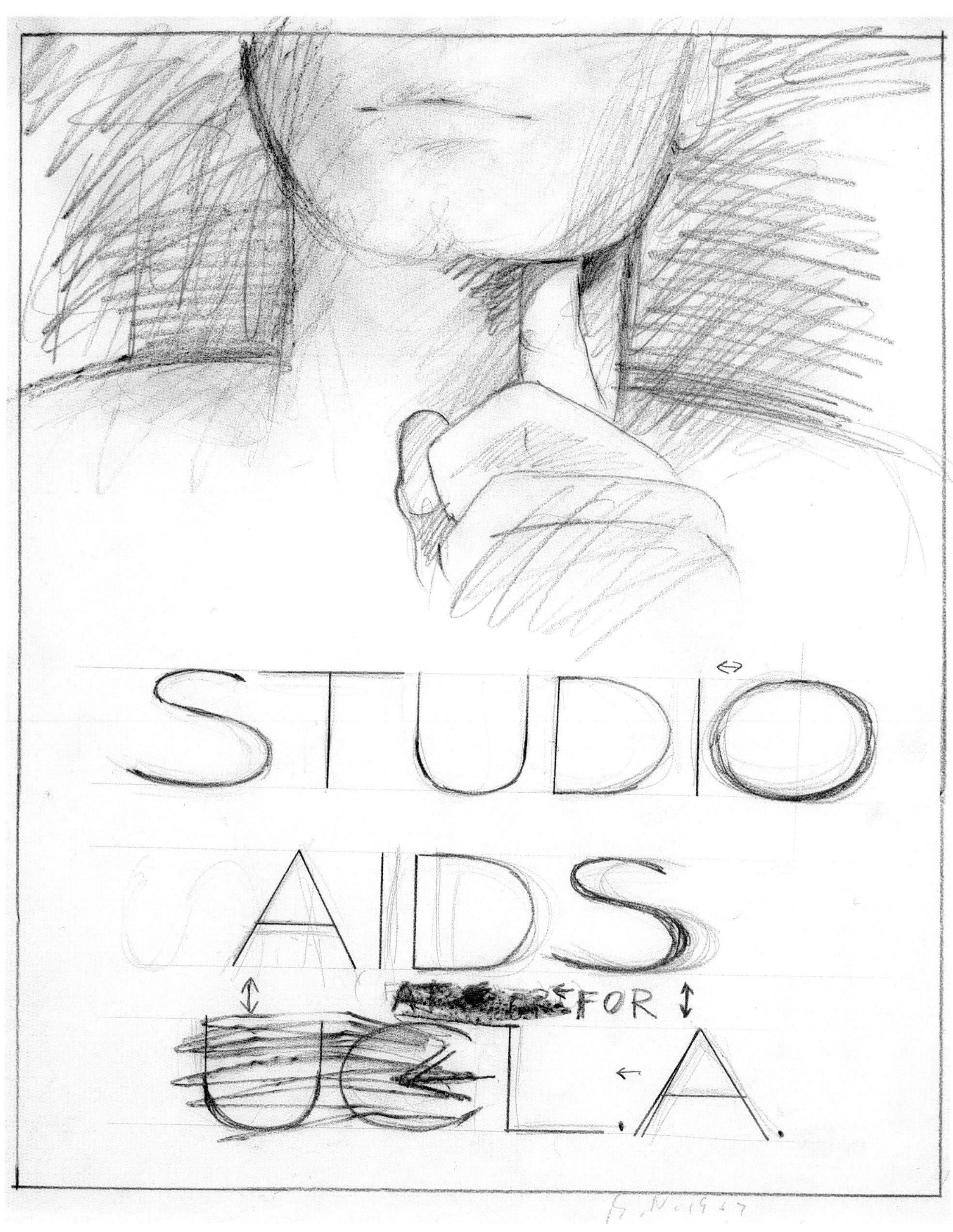

<u>Get Out of My Mind, Get Out of This Room</u> (Fig.66)

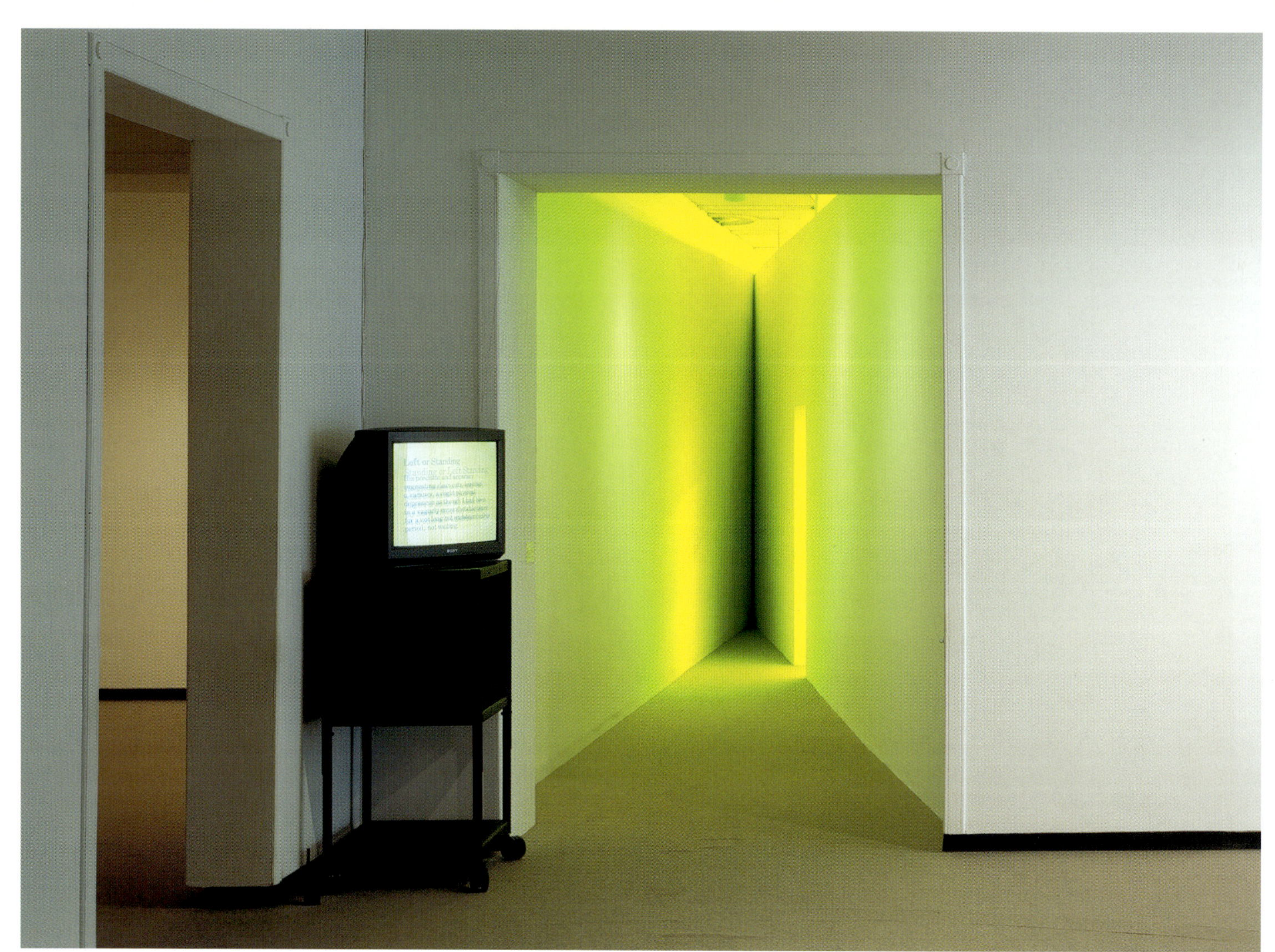

Left or Standing/Standing or Left Standing (Fig.67)

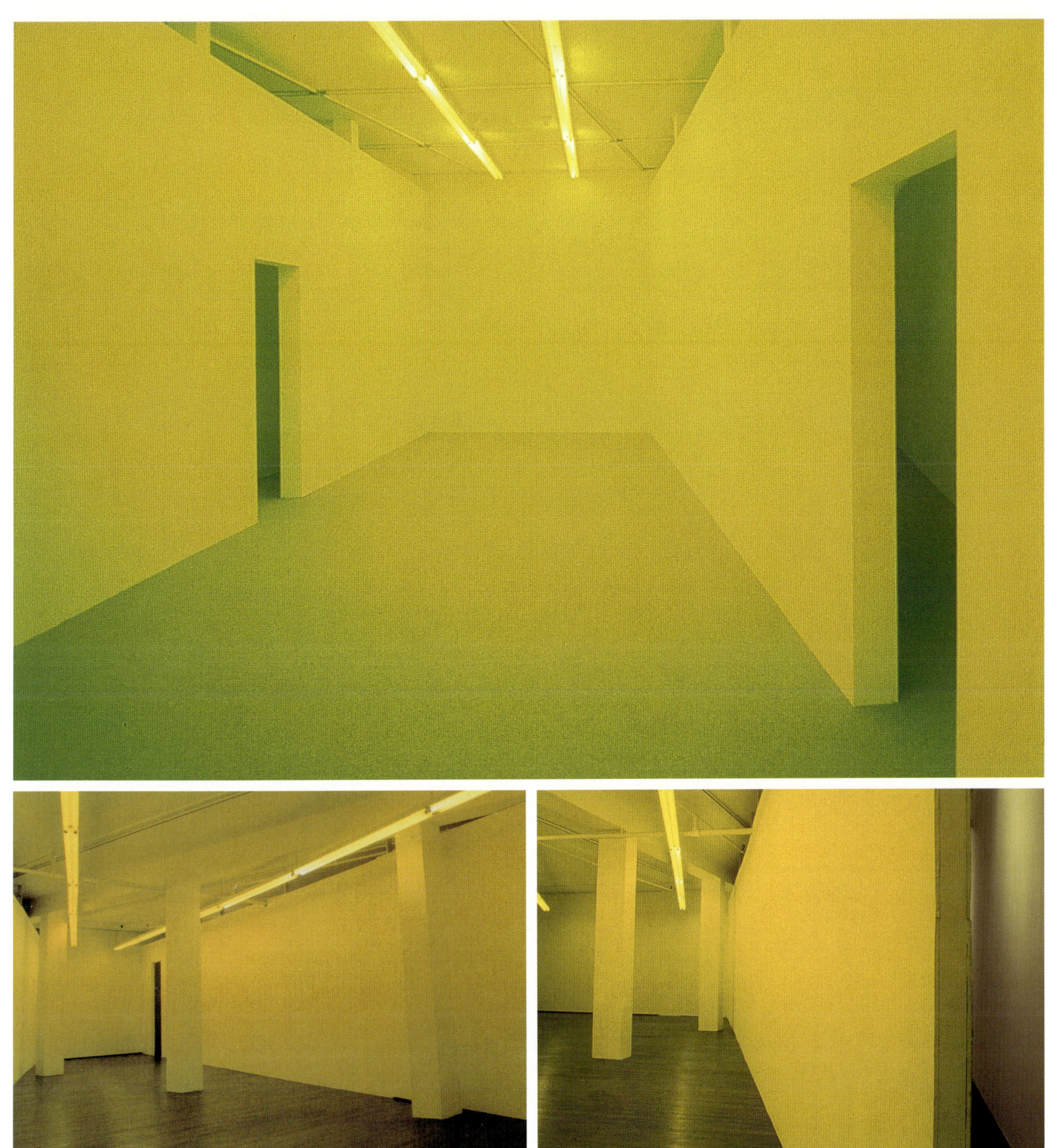

(Figs.68–70)

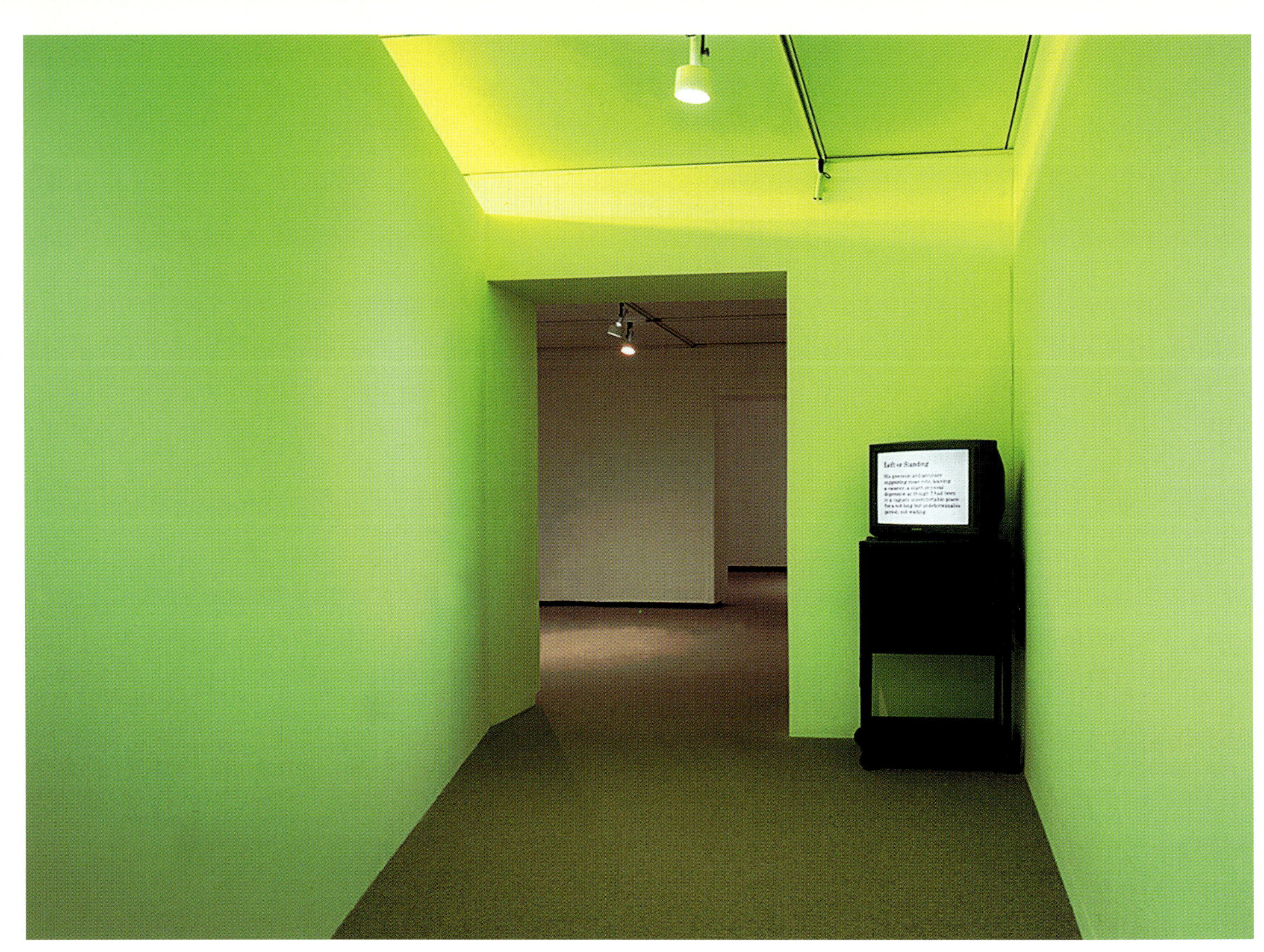

Left or Standing/Standing or Left Standing (Fig.71)

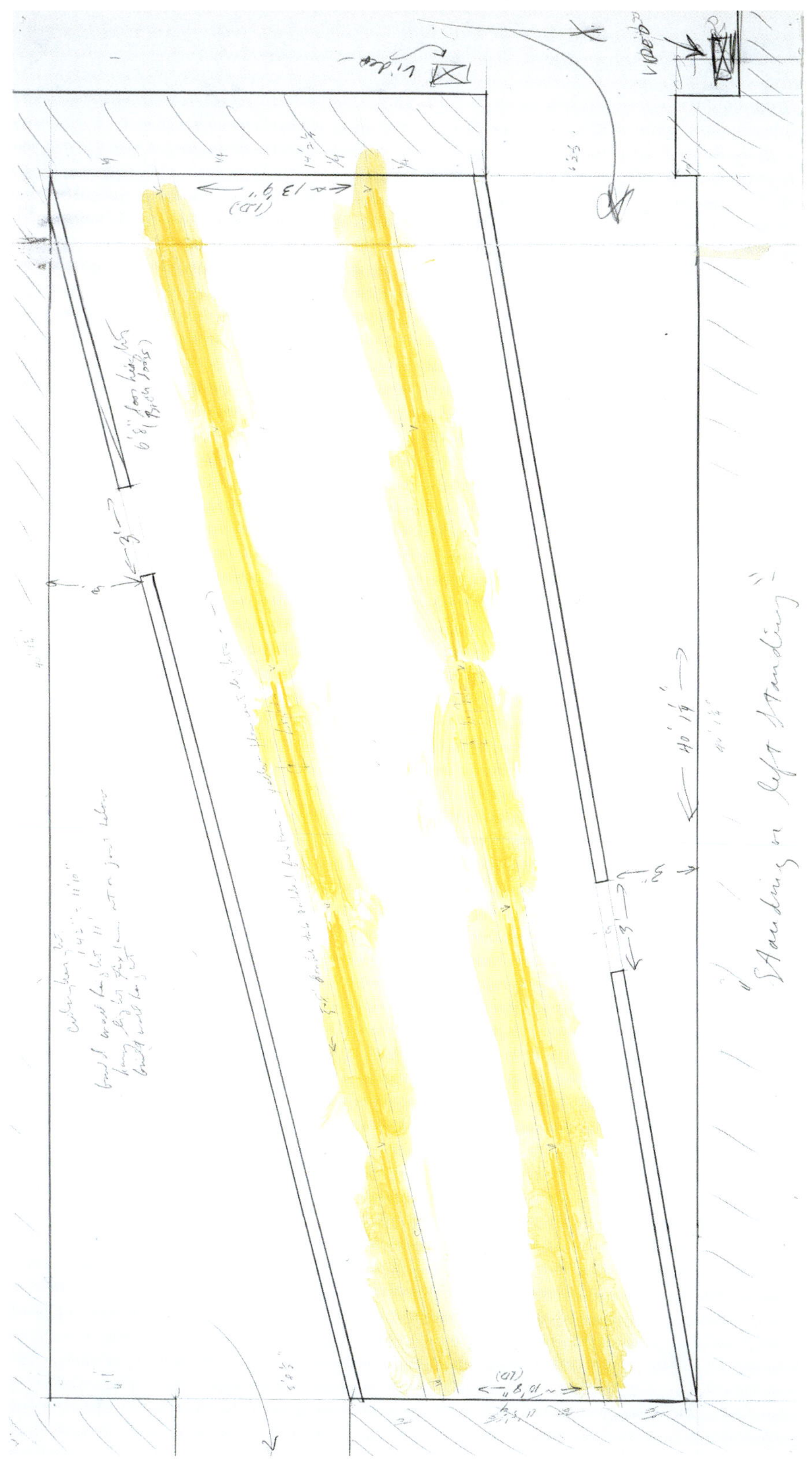

(Fig.72)

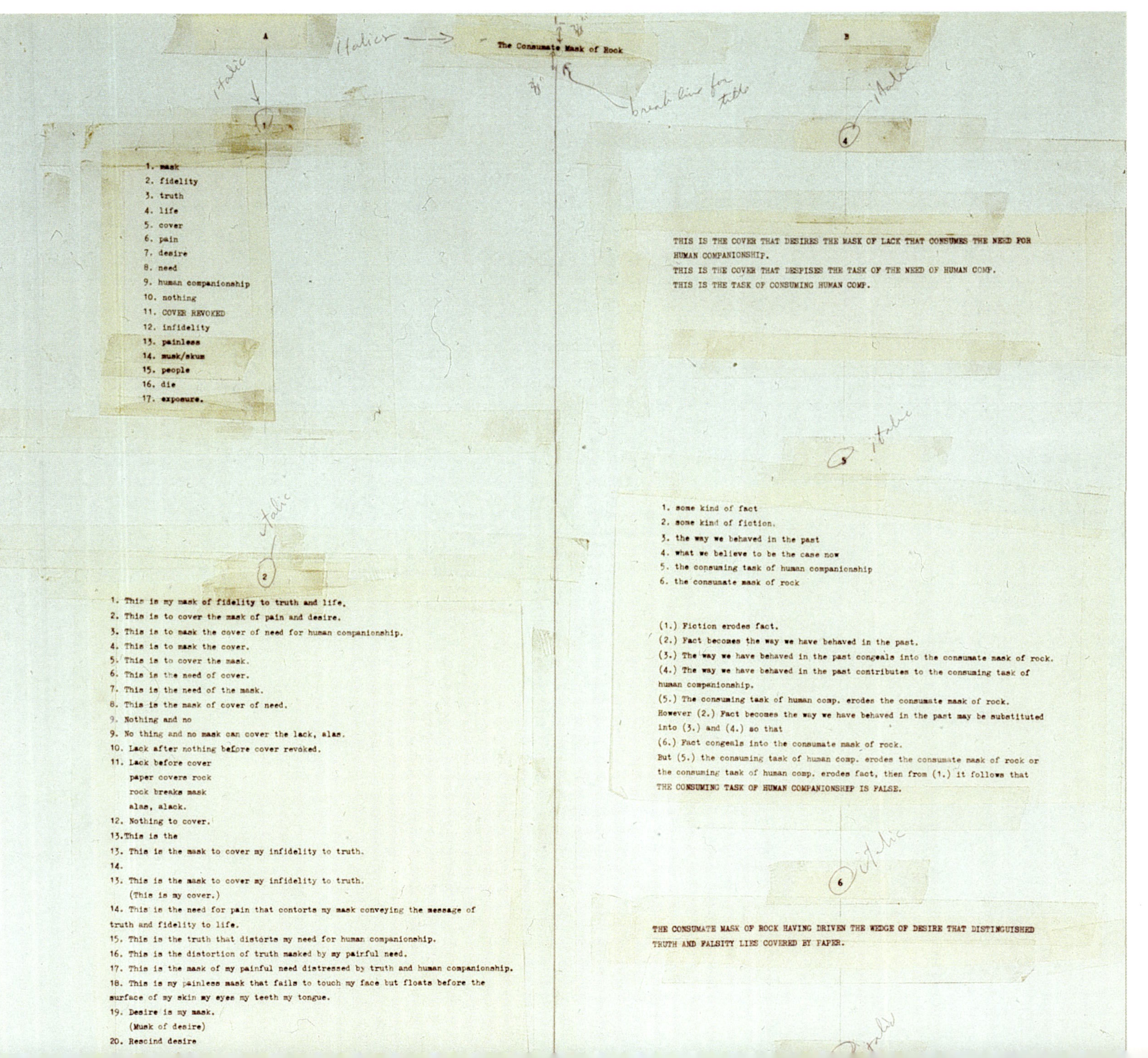

The Consumate Mask of Rock

A

1

1. mask
2. fidelity
3. truth
4. life
5. cover
6. pain
7. desire
8. need
9. human companionship
10. nothing
11. COVER REVOKED
12. infidelity
13. painless
14. musk/skum
15. people
16. die
17. exposure.

2

1. This is my mask of fidelity to truth and life.
2. This is to cover the mask of pain and desire.
3. This is to mask the cover of need for human companionship.
4. This is to mask the cover.
5. This is to cover the mask.
6. This is the need of cover.
7. This is the need of the mask.
8. This is the mask of cover of need.
9. Nothing and no
9. No thing and no mask can cover the lack, alas.
10. Lack after nothing before cover revoked.
11. Lack before cover
paper covers rock
rock breaks mask
alas, alack.
12. Nothing to cover.
13.This is the
13. This is the mask to cover my infidelity to truth.
14.
13. This is the mask to cover my infidelity to truth.
(This is my cover.)
14. This is the need for pain that contorts my mask conveying the message of truth and fidelity to life.
15. This is the truth that distorts my need for human companionship.
16. This is the distortion of truth masked by my pairful need.
17. This is the mask of my painful need distressed by truth and human companionship.
18. This is my painless mask that fails to touch my face but floats before the surface of my skin my eyes my teeth my tongue.
19. Desire is my mask.
(Musk of desire)
20. Rescind desire

B

4

THIS IS THE COVER THAT DESIRES THE MASK OF LACK THAT CONSUMES THE NEED FOR HUMAN COMPANIONSHIP.
THIS IS THE COVER THAT DESPISES THE TASK OF THE NEED OF HUMAN COMP.
THIS IS THE TASK OF CONSUMING HUMAN COMP.

5

1. some kind of fact
2. some kind of fiction.
3. the way we behaved in the past
4. what we believe to be the case now
5. the consuming task of human companionship
6. the consumate mask of rock

(1.) Fiction erodes fact.
(2.) Fact becomes the way we have behaved in the past.
(3.) The way we have behaved in the past congeals into the consumate mask of rock.
(4.) The way we have behaved in the past contributes to the consuming task of human companionship.
(5.) The consuming task of human comp. erodes the consumate mask of rock.
However (2.) Fact becomes the way we have behaved in the past may be substituted into (3.) and (4.) so that
(6.) Fact congeals into the consumate mask of rock.
But (5.) the consuming task of human comp. erodes the consumate mask of rock or the consuming task of human comp. erodes fact, then from (1.) it follows that THE CONSUMING TASK OF HUMAN COMPANIONSHIP IS FALSE.

6

THE CONSUMATE MASK OF ROCK HAVING DRIVEN THE WEDGE OF DESIRE THAT DISTINGUISHED TRUTH AND FALSITY LIES COVERED BY PAPER.

Consummate Mask of Rock (Fig.73)

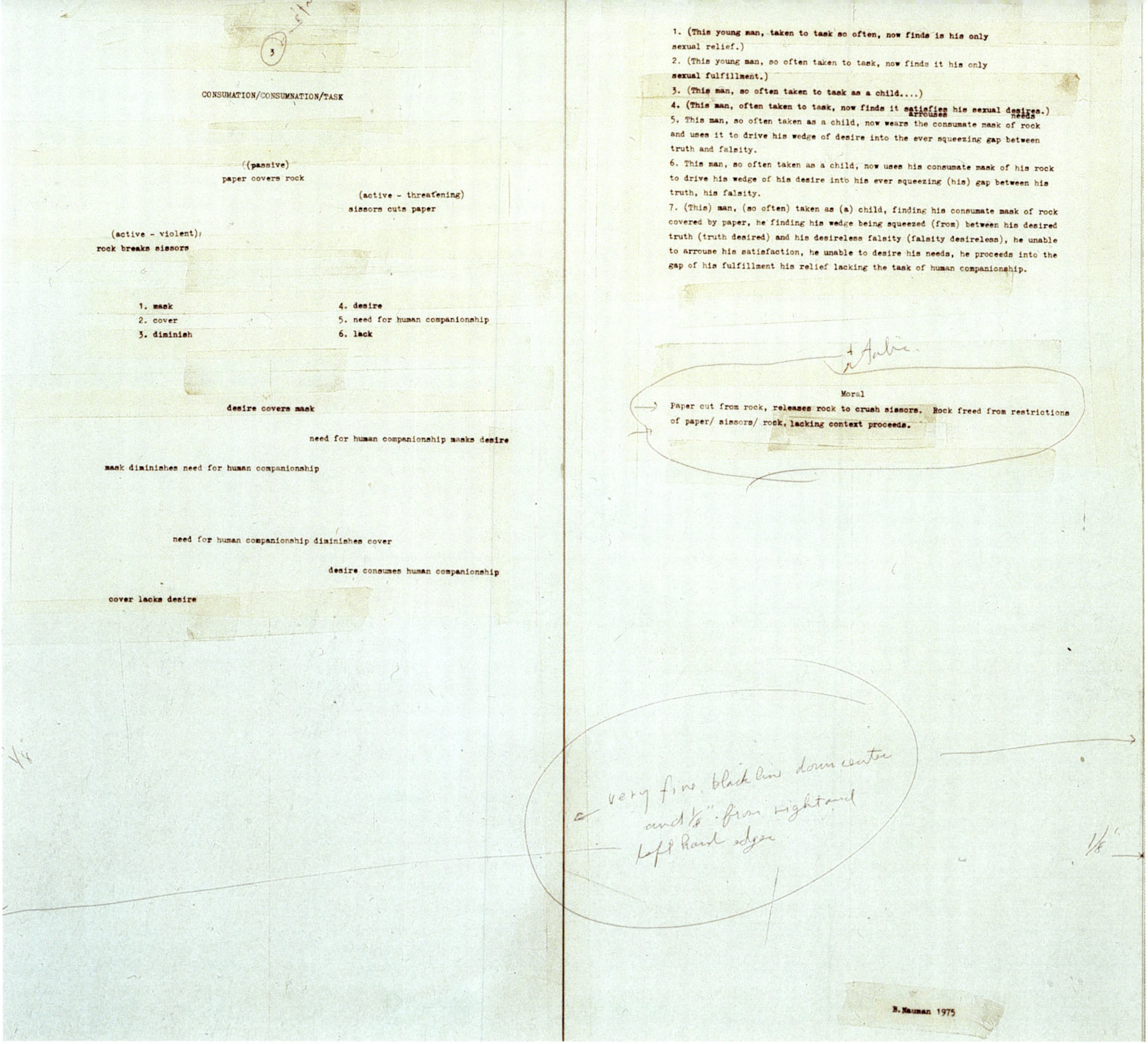

CONSUMATION/CONSUMNATION/TASK

((passive)
paper covers rock

(active - threatening)
sissors cuts paper

(active - violent),
rock breaks sissors

1. mask
2. cover
3. diminish

4. desire
5. need for human companionship
6. lack

desire covers mask

need for human companionship masks desire

mask diminishes need for human companionship

need for human companionship diminishes cover

desire consumes human companionship

cover lacks desire

1. (This young man, taken to task so often, now finds is his only sexual relief.)
2. (This young man, so often taken to task, now finds it his only sexual fulfillment.)
3. (This man, so often taken to task as a child....)
4. (This man, often taken to task, now finds it satisfies arrouses his sexual desires needs.)
5. This man, so often taken as a child, now wears the consumate mask of rock and uses it to drive his wedge of desire into the ever squeezing gap between truth and falsity.
6. This man, so often taken as a child, now uses his consumate mask of his rock to drive his wedge of his desire into his ever squeezing (his) gap between his truth, his falsity.
7. (This) man, (so often) taken as (a) child, finding his consumate mask of rock covered by paper, he finding his wedge being squeezed (from) between his desired truth (truth desired) and his desireless falsity (falsity desireless), he unable to arrouse his satisfaction, he unable to desire his needs, he proceeds into the gap of his fulfillment his relief lacking the task of human companionship.

Moral

Paper cut from rock, releases rock to crush sissors. Rock freed from restrictions of paper/ sissors/ rock, lacking context proceeds.

very fine black line down center and 1/8" from right and left hand edges

1/8"

B.Nauman 1975

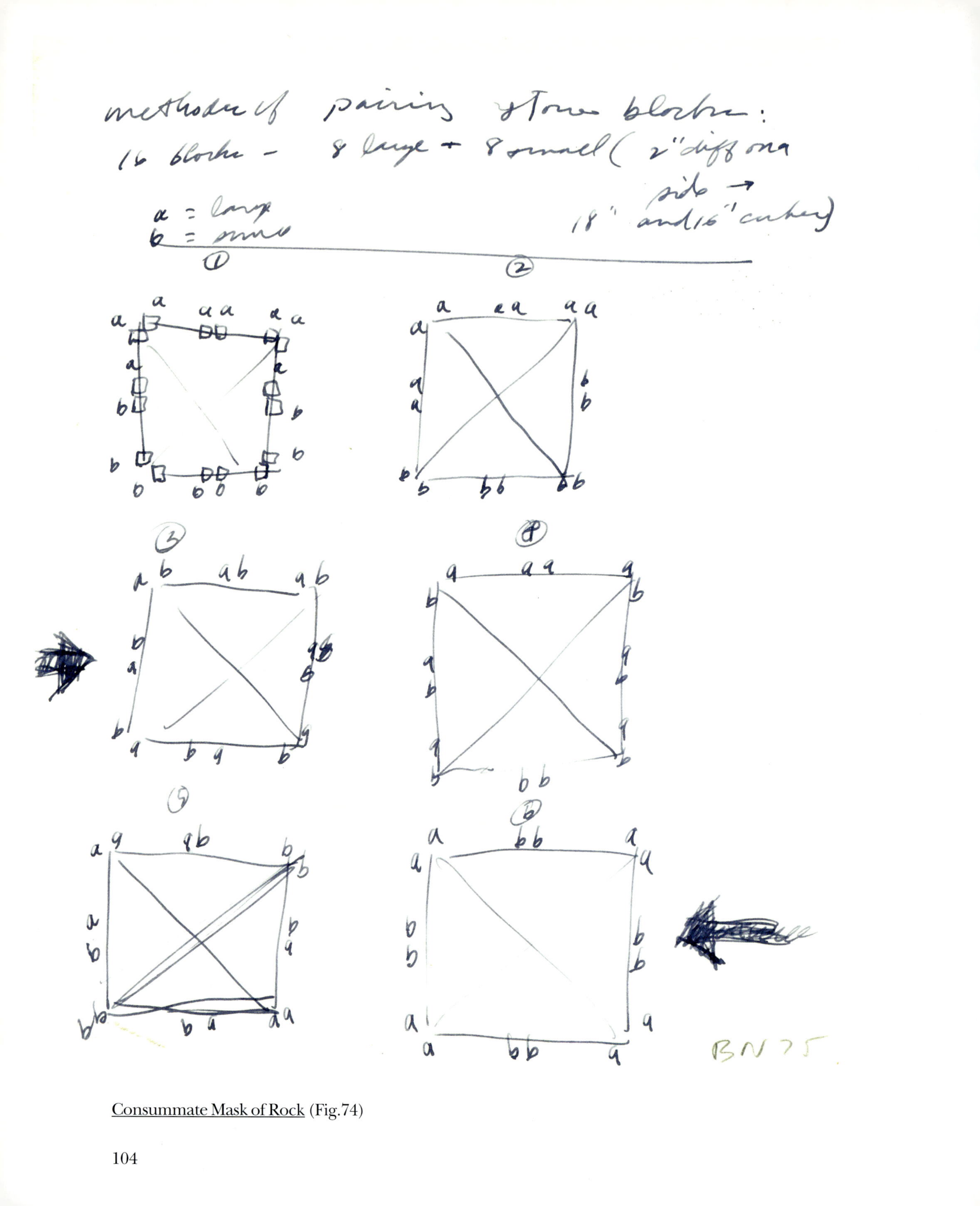

methods of pairing stone blocks:
16 blocks – 8 large + 8 small (2" diff on a side → 18" and 16" cubes)

a = large
b = small

Consummate Mask of Rock (Fig.74)

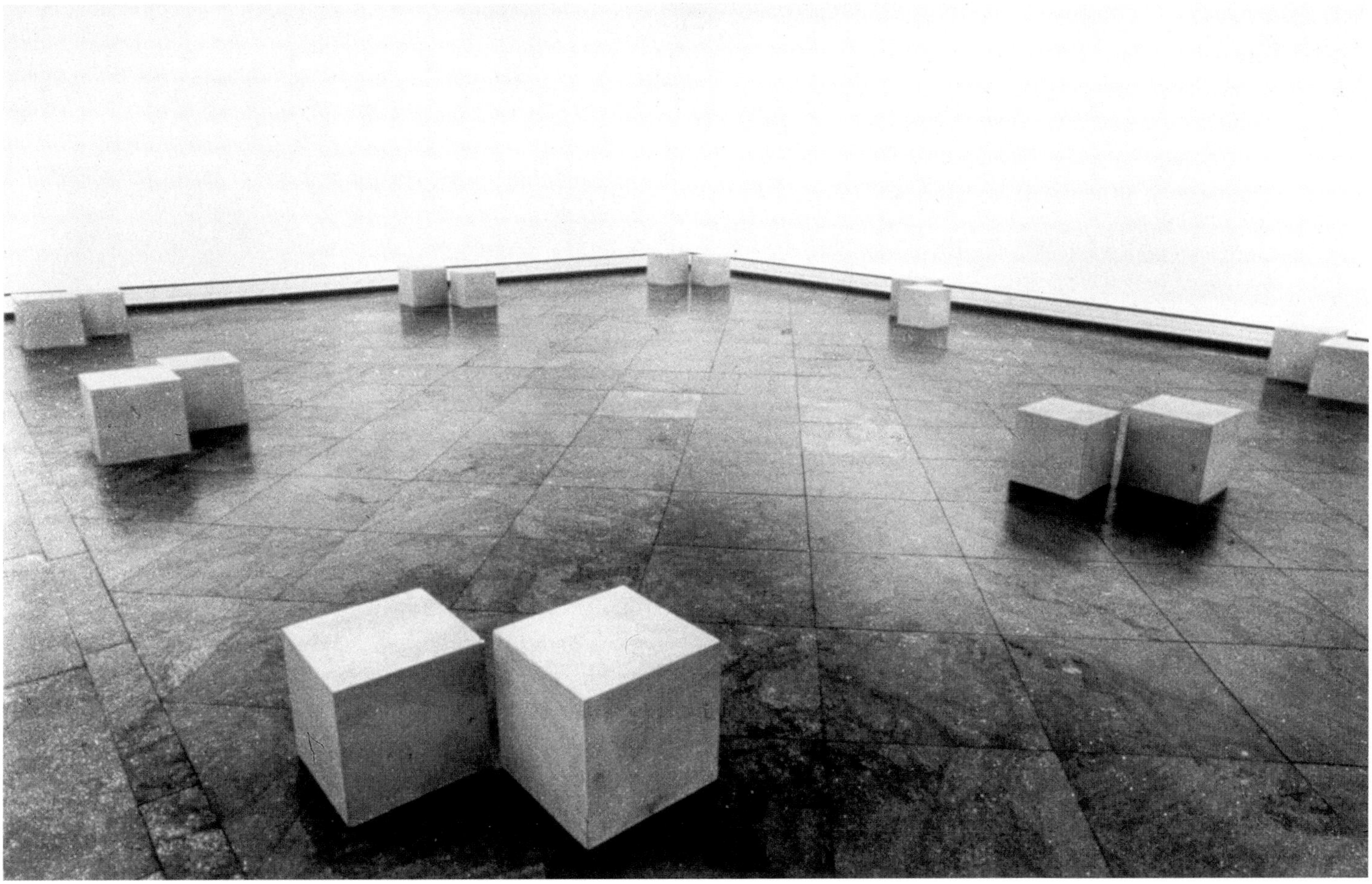

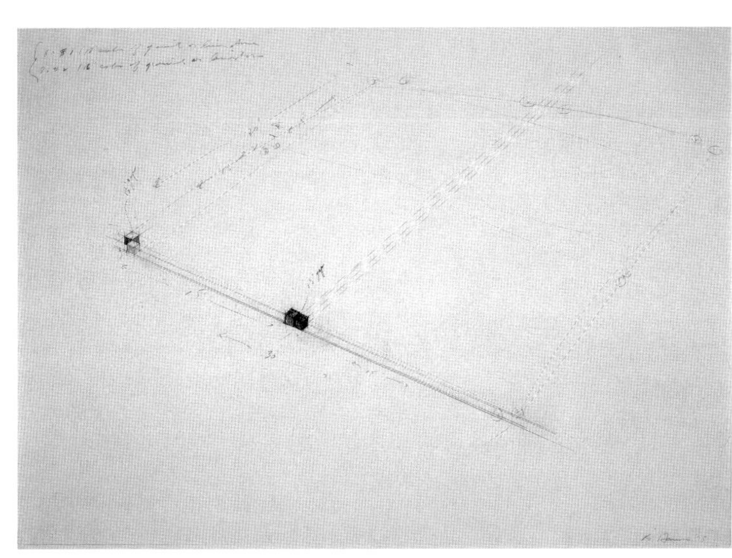

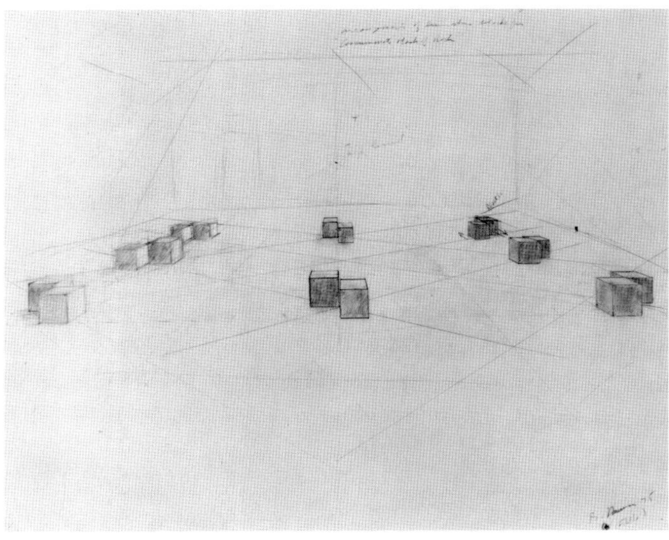

(Figs.75–7)

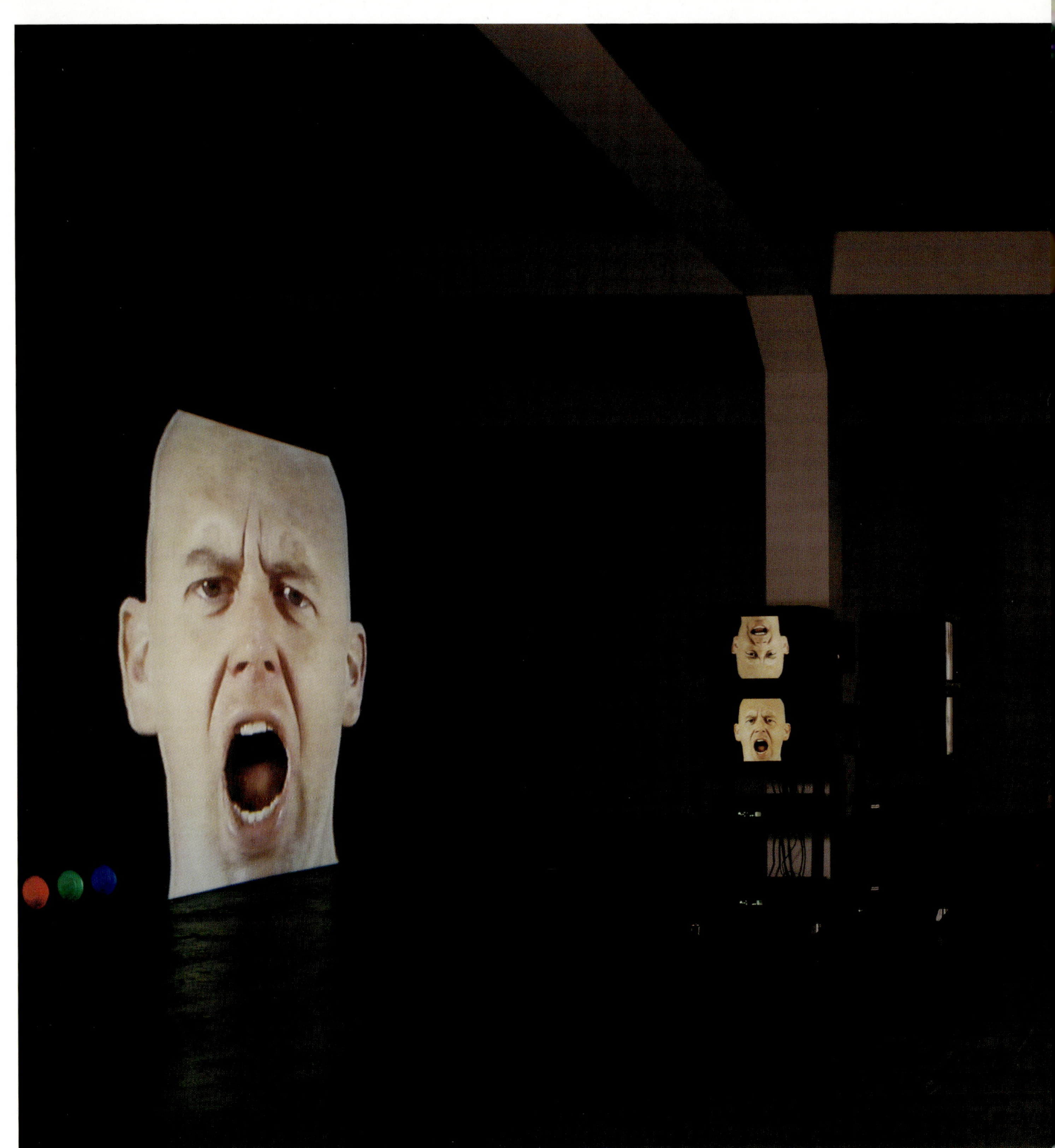

<u>Anthro/Socio</u> (Fig.78)

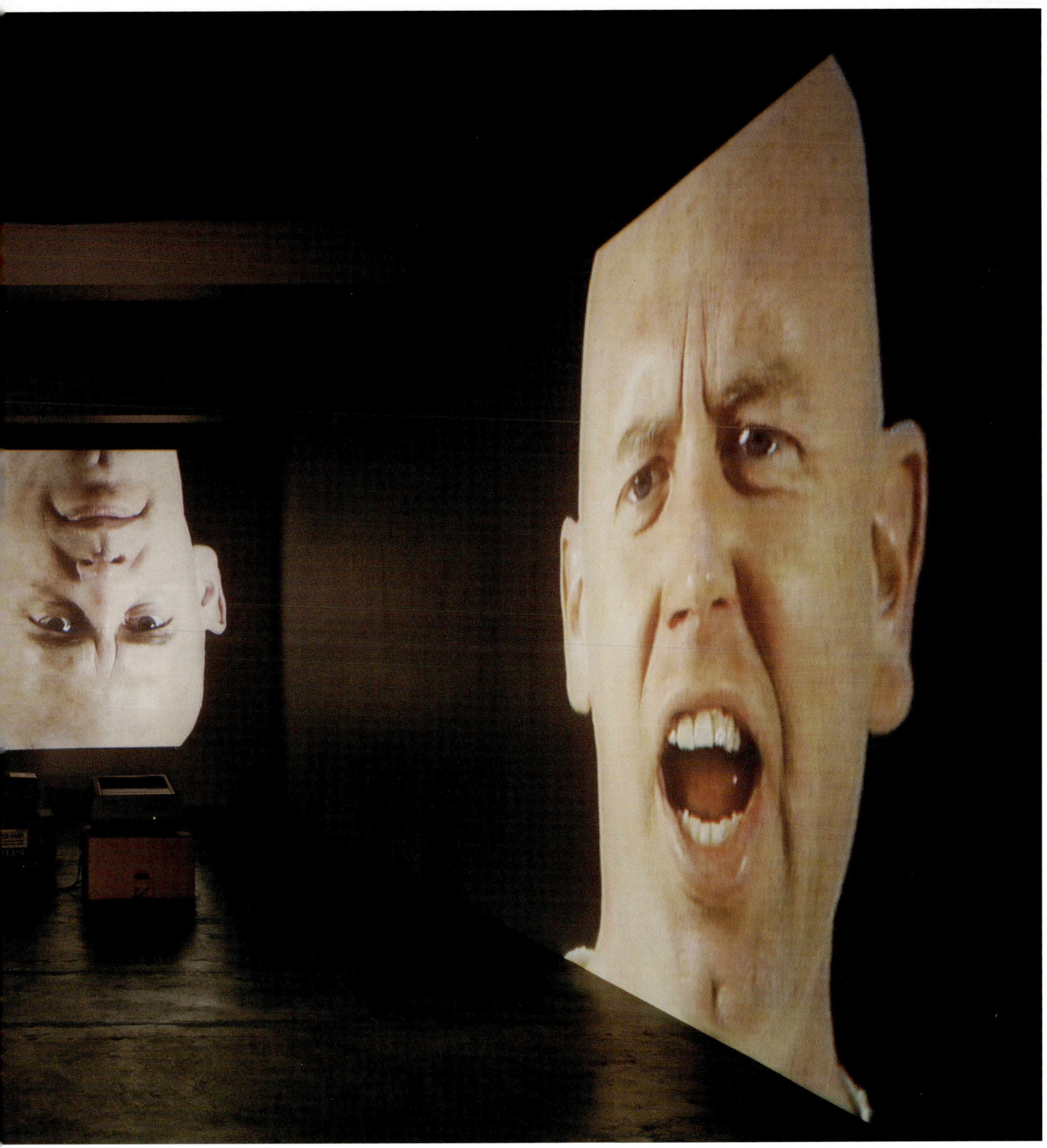

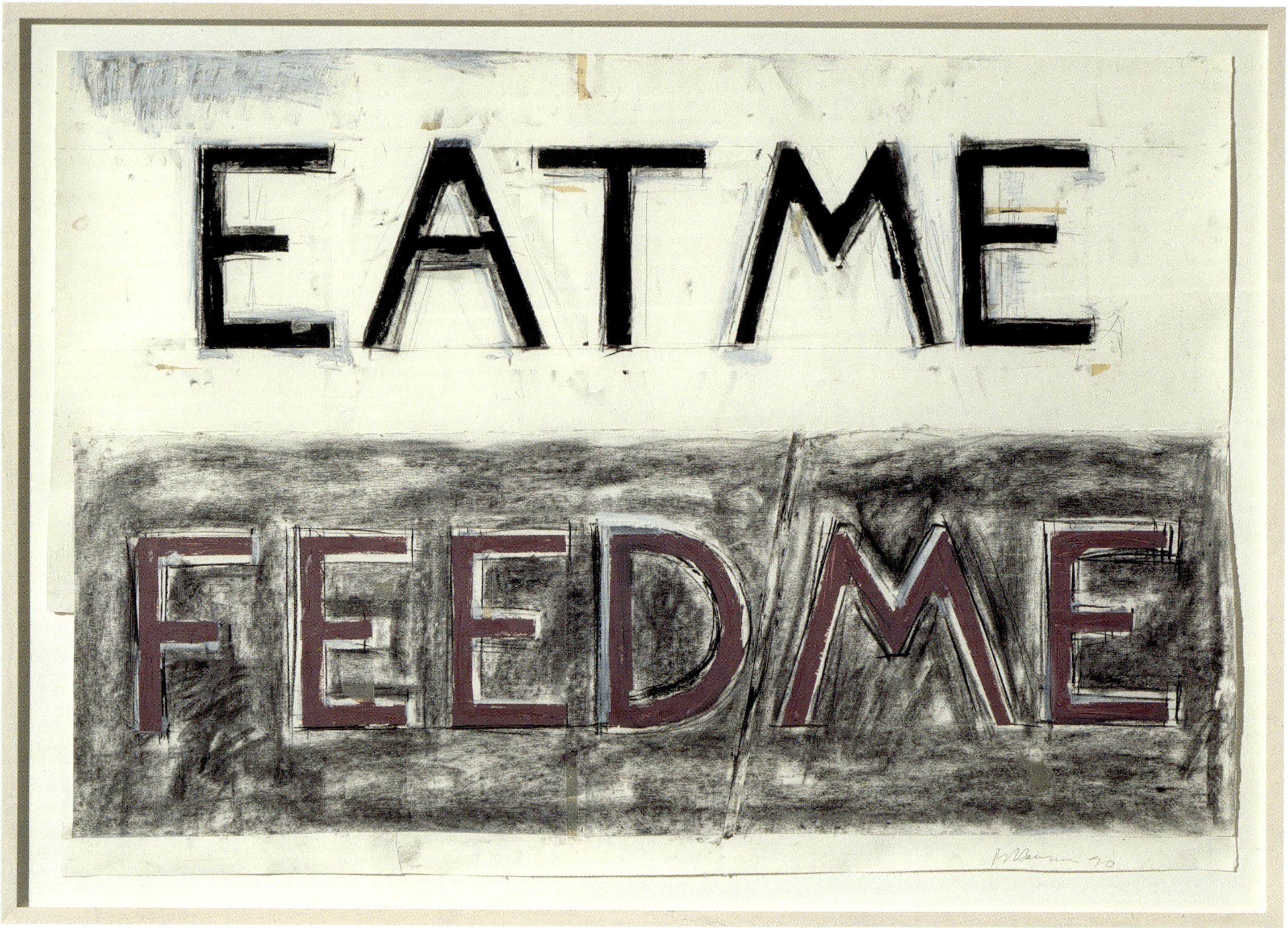

EATME

FEEDME

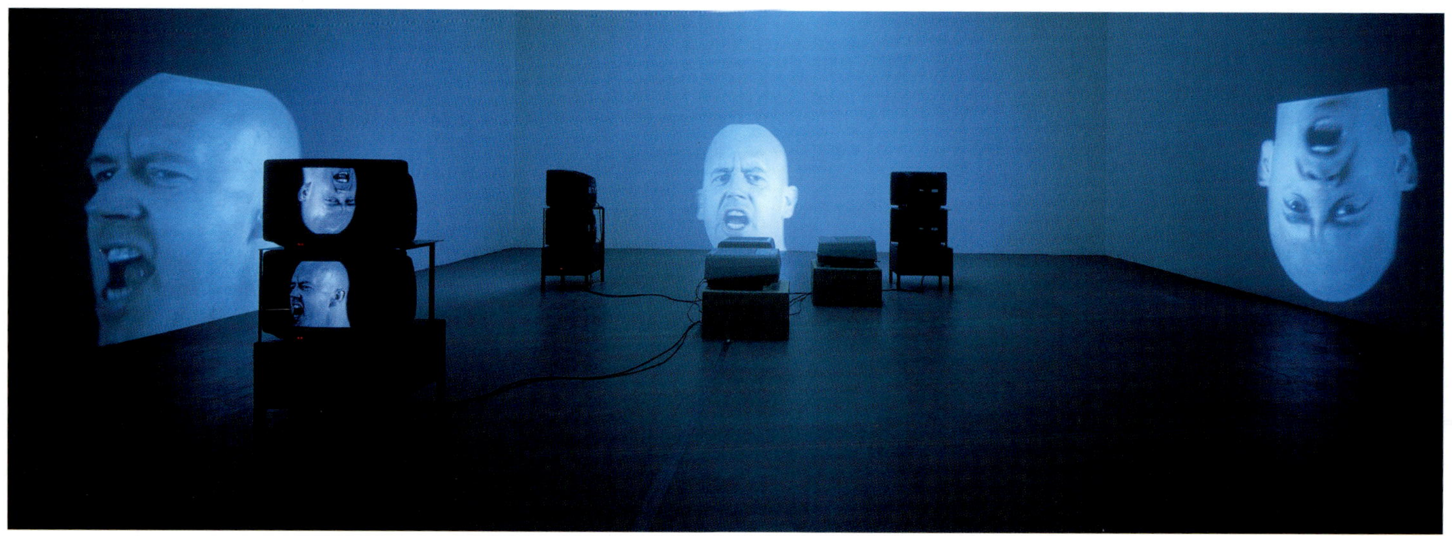

<u>Anthro/Socio</u> (Figs.79–80)

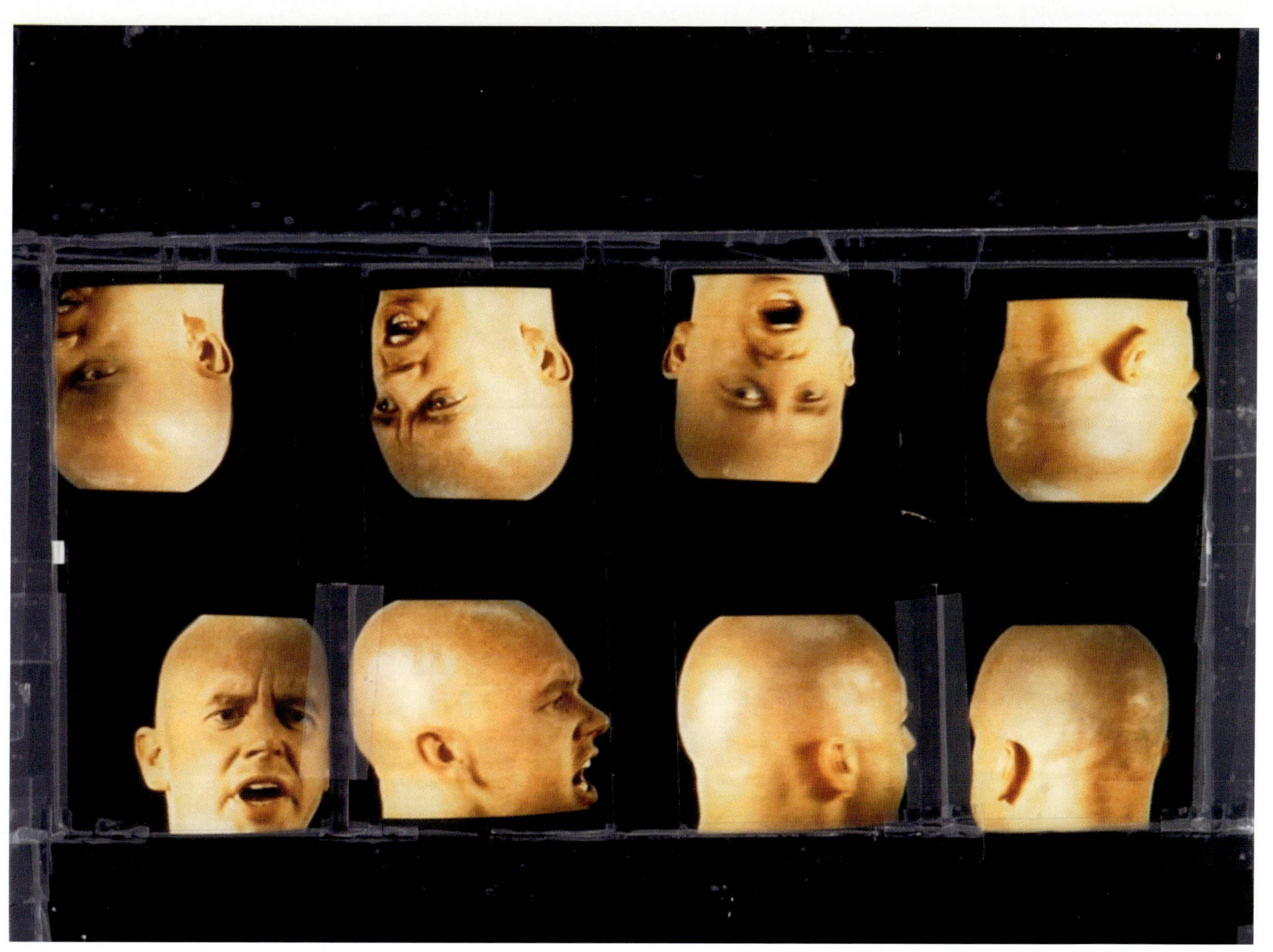

(Fig.81)

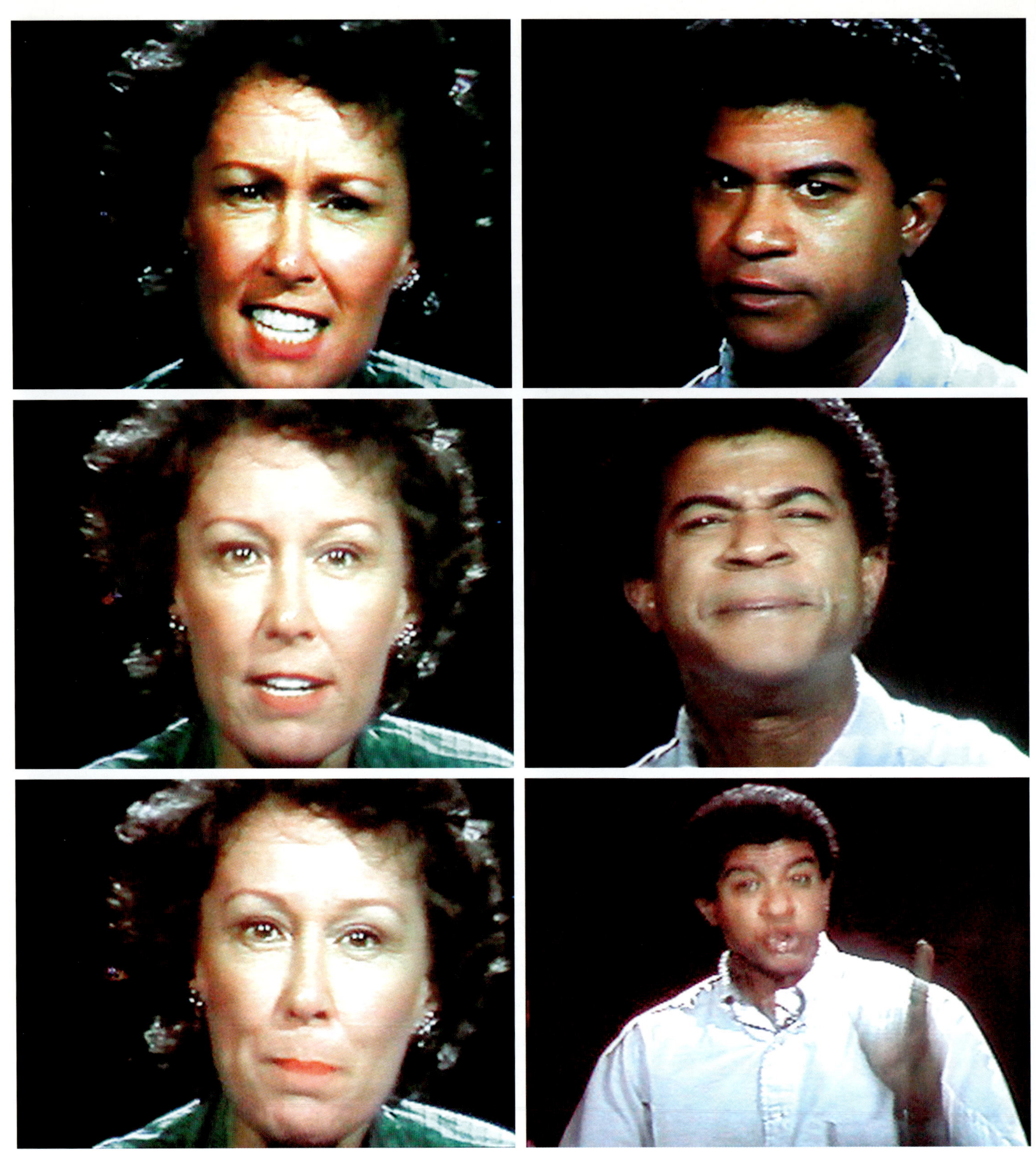

Good Boy Bad Boy — Tucker/Joan (Figs.82–93)

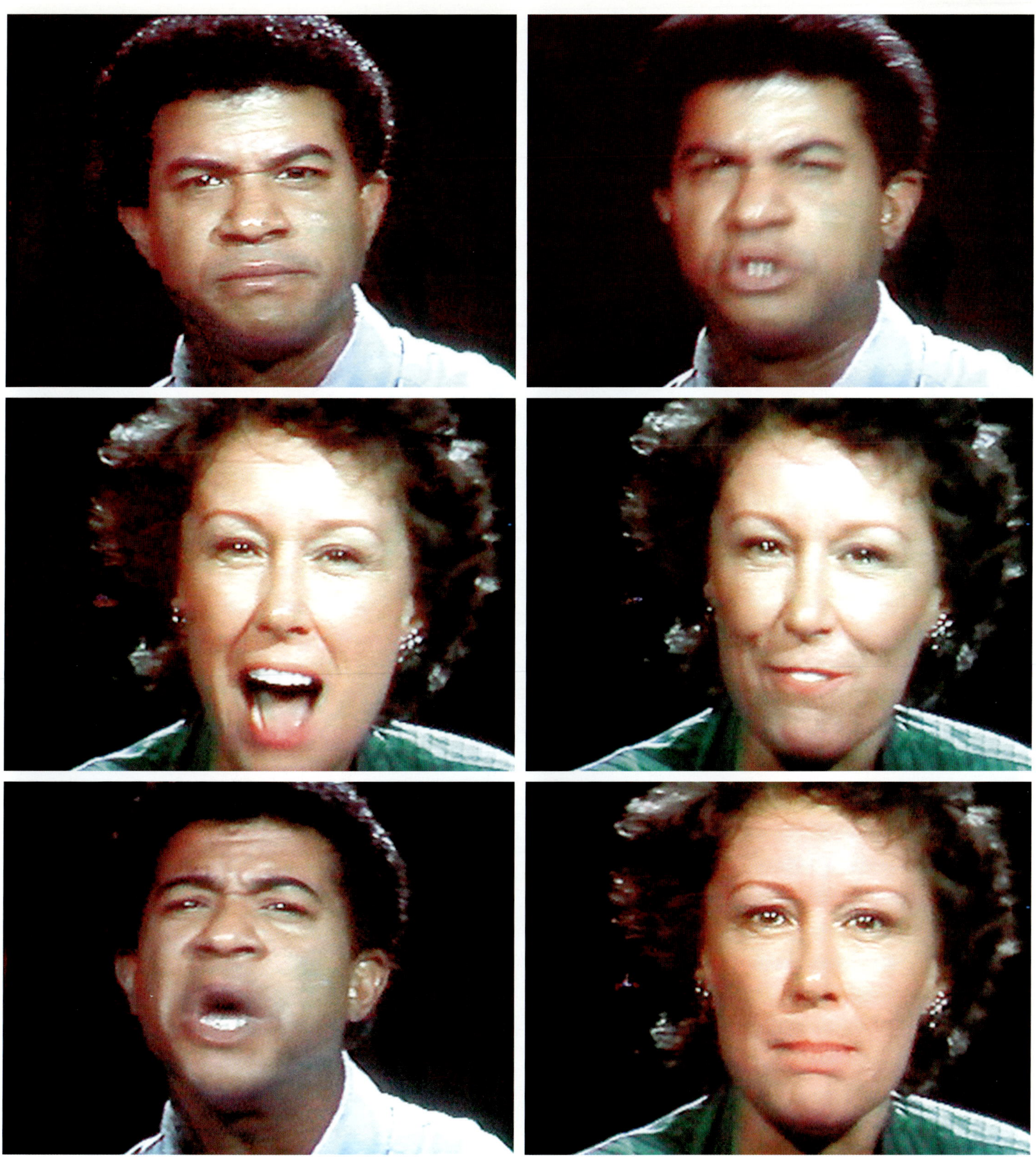

Good Boy Bad Boy — Tucker/Joan (Fig.94)

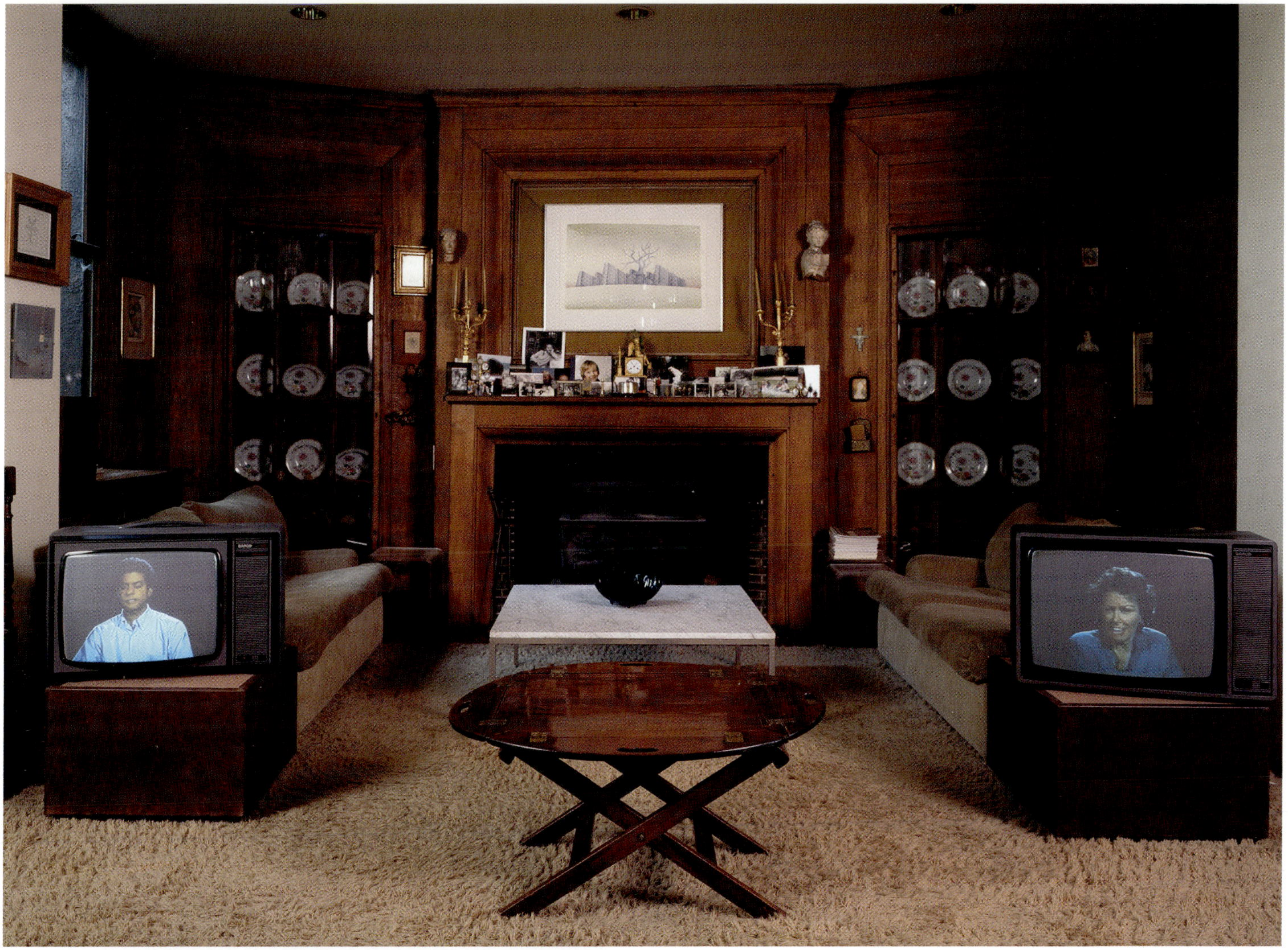

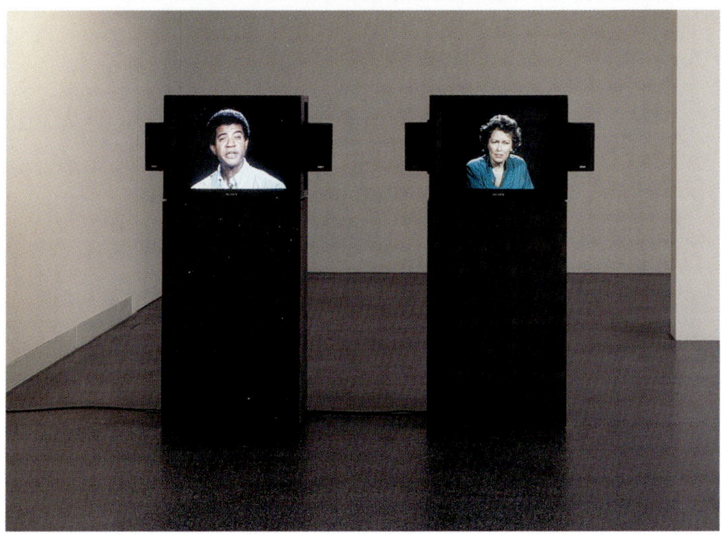

(Figs.95–6)

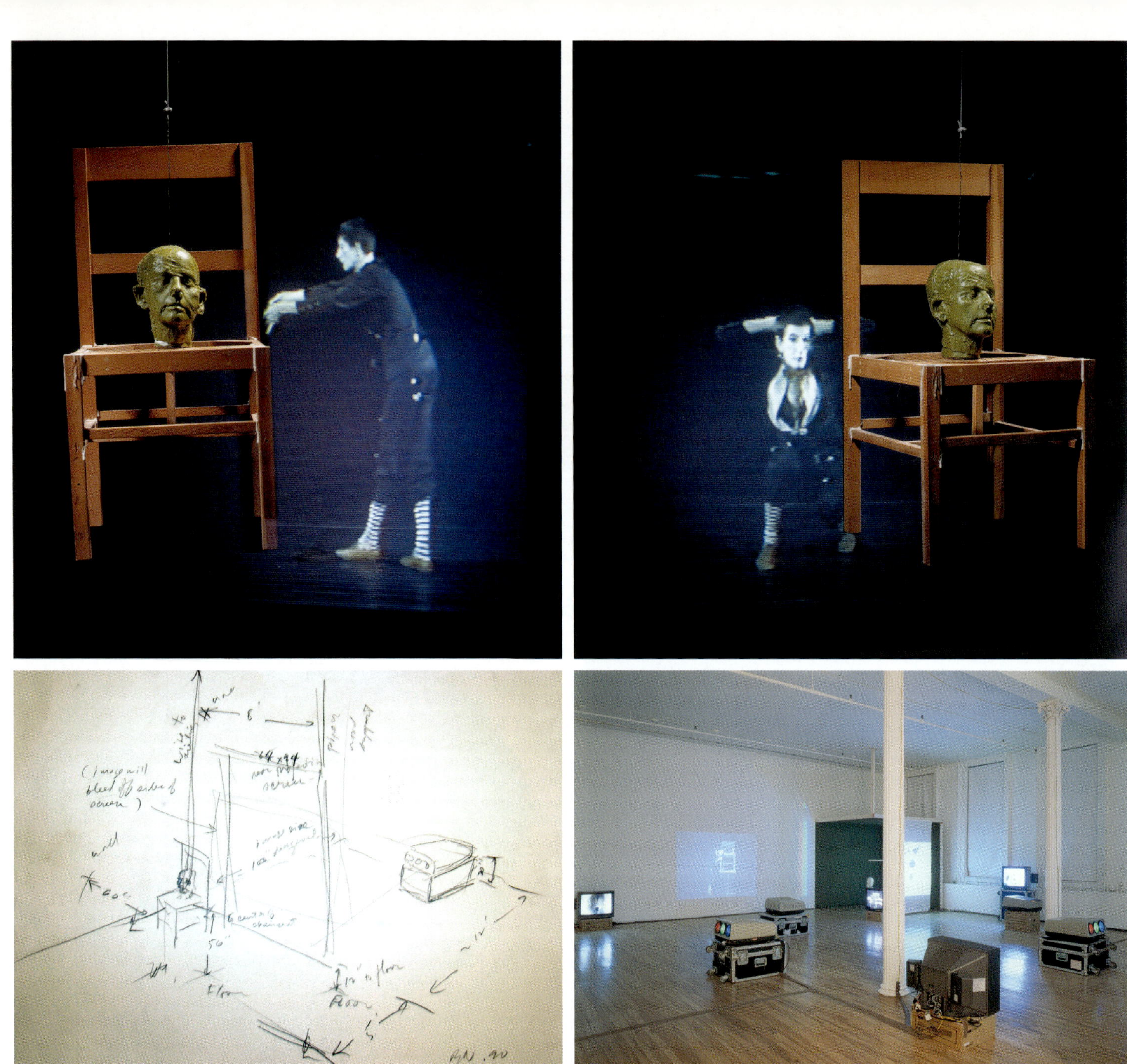

Shit In Your Hat — Head On A Chair (Figs.97–100)

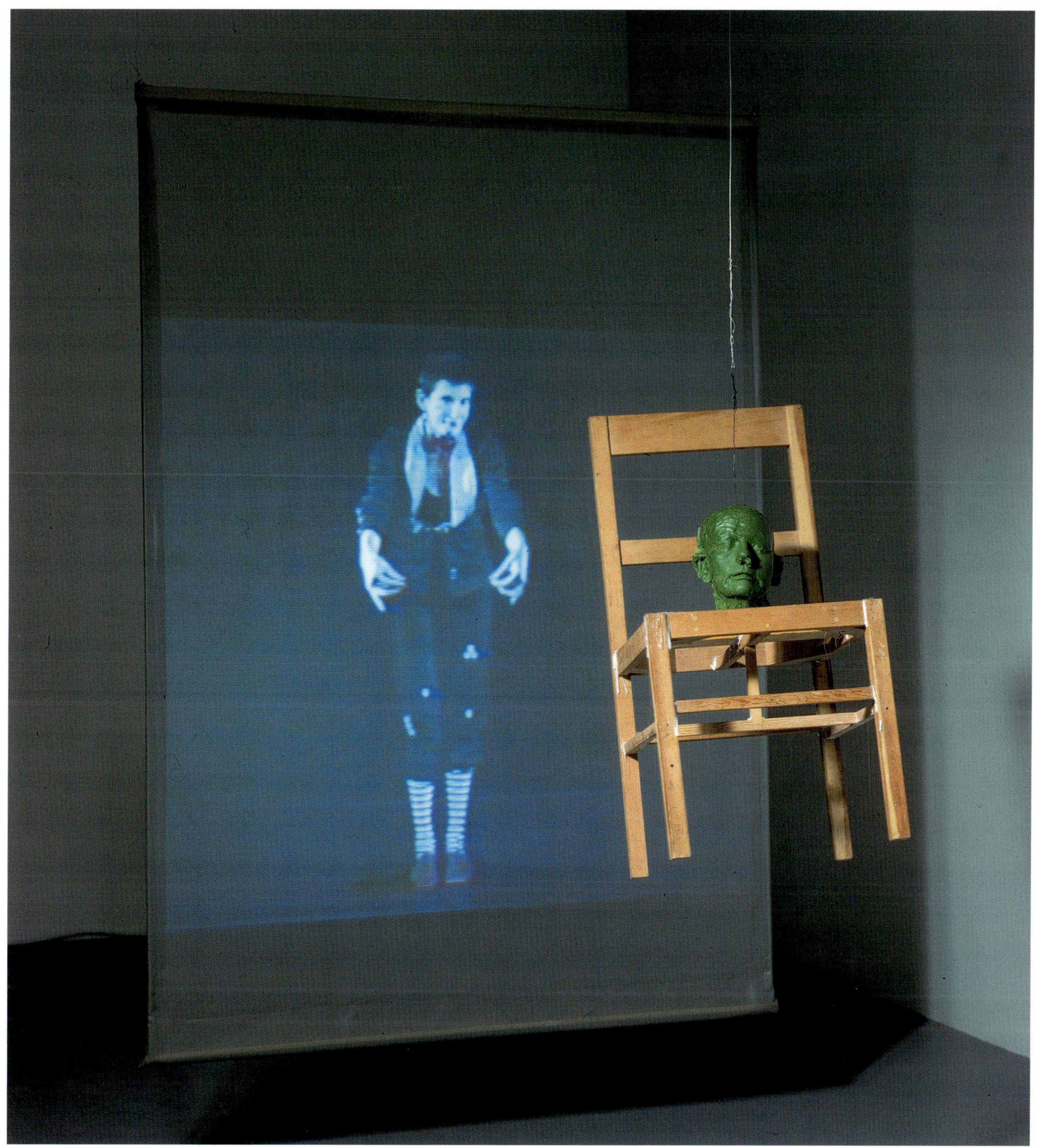

(Fig.101)

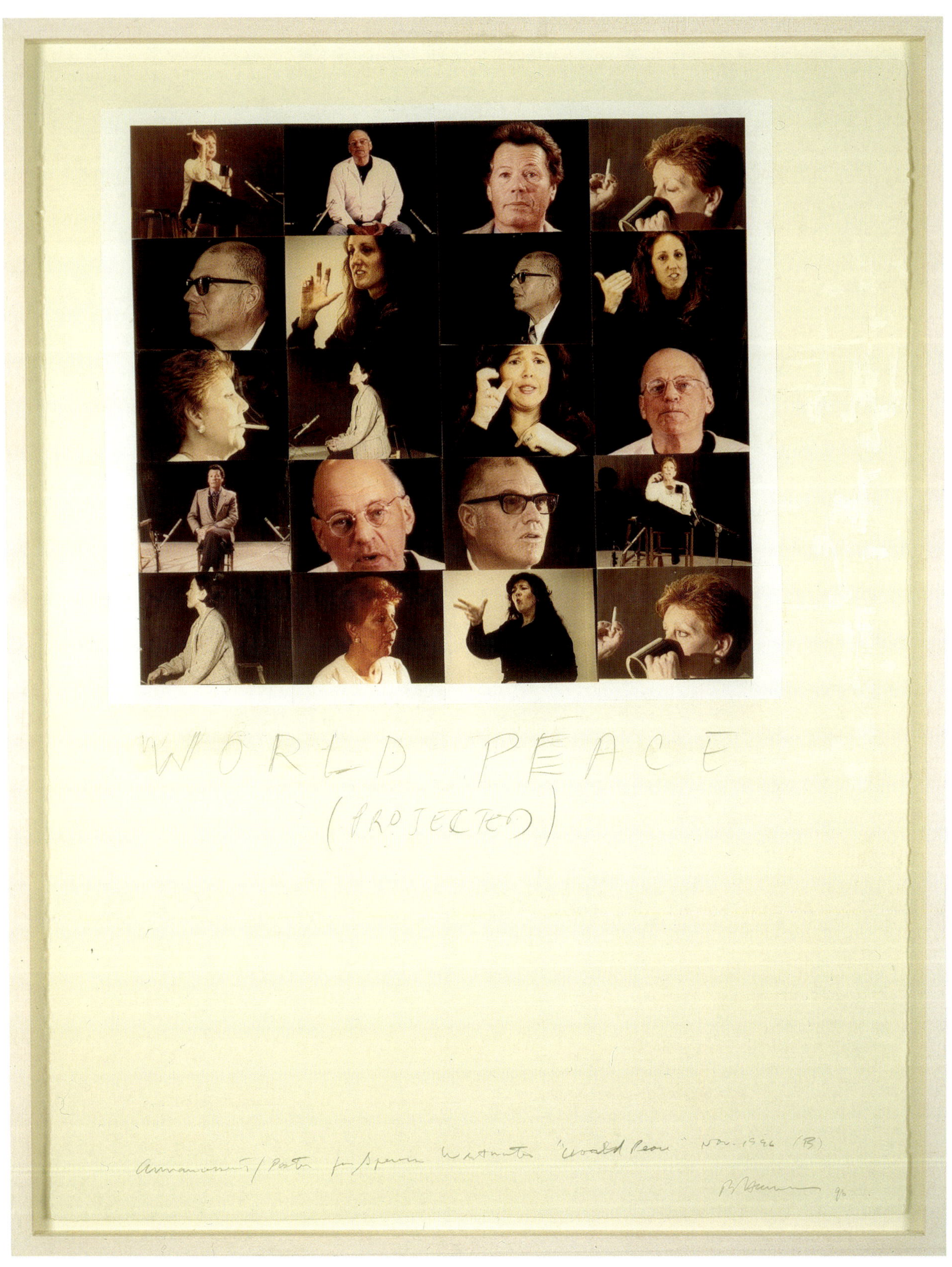

World Peace — Bernard/mei mei (Fig.102)

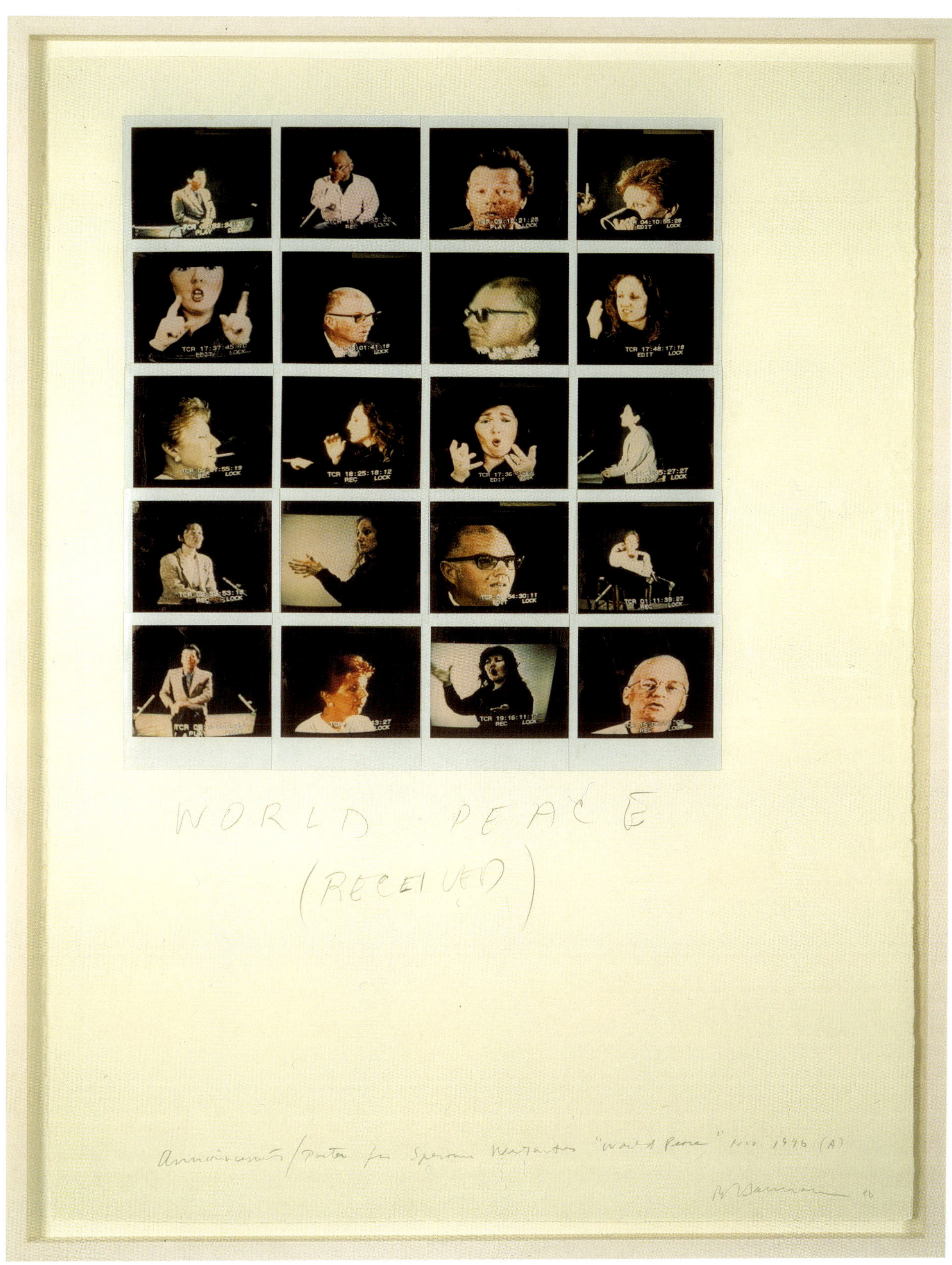

(Fig.103)

Start at left mid-body
level across at one head
Then down to right mid-
body level and back if
possible — next full figure and
head only.

End of the world — get Lloyd Mains? (sp?)
maynes?

you talk to me — male / male
I'll talk to you female / female
(male / female
(female / male —
get ⇒ mei mei — walter
((clown / no clown)?

1. a {I'll talk to you
{you'll talk to me
b {I'll talk to you
{you'll talk to me
2. a (I'll talk to you
b (you'll talk to me
a (you'll talk to me
b (I'll talk to you

(sympathetic (conversational)
+
aggressive (demanding))

World Peace — Bernard/mei mei (Figs.104–5)

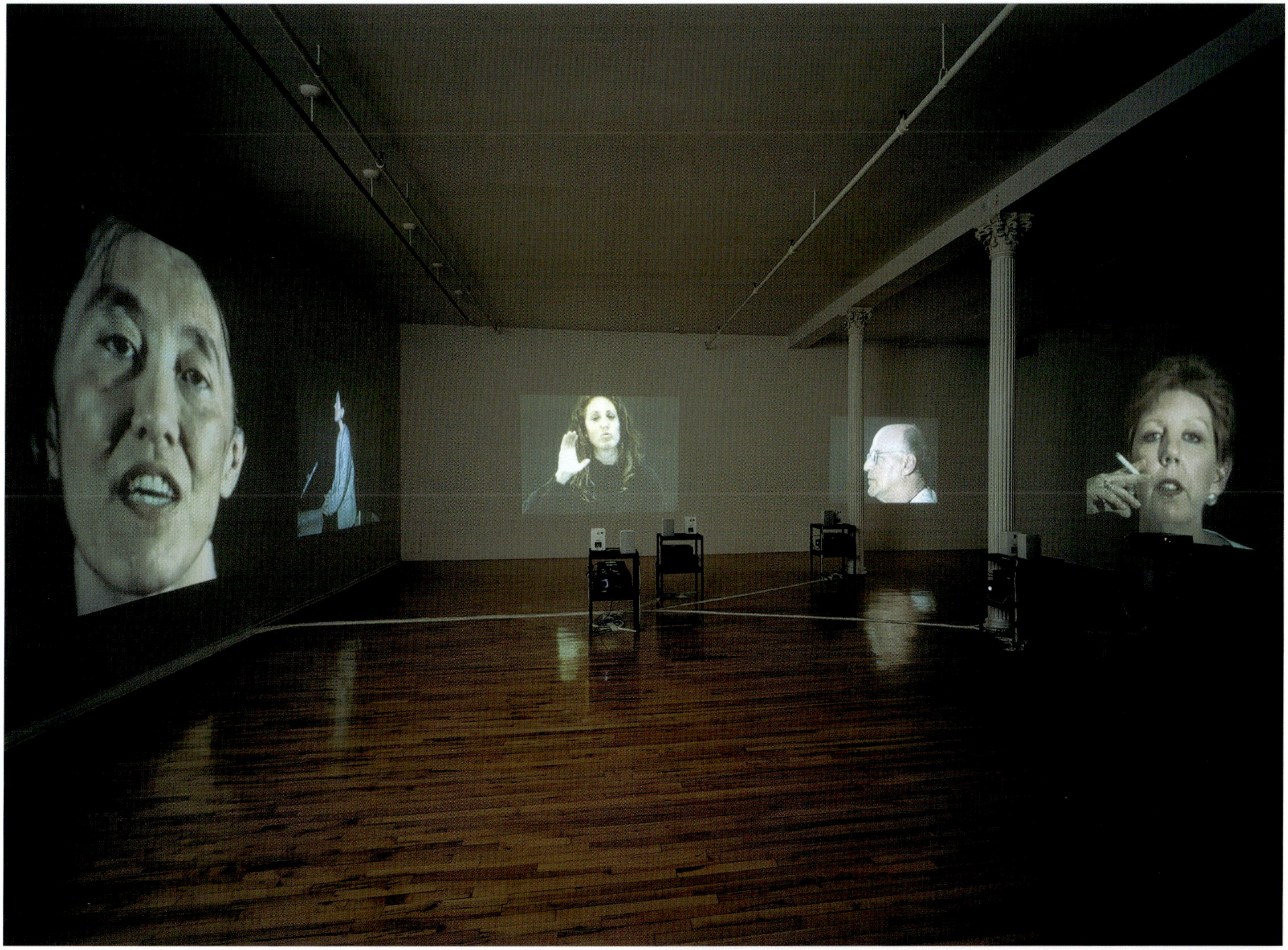

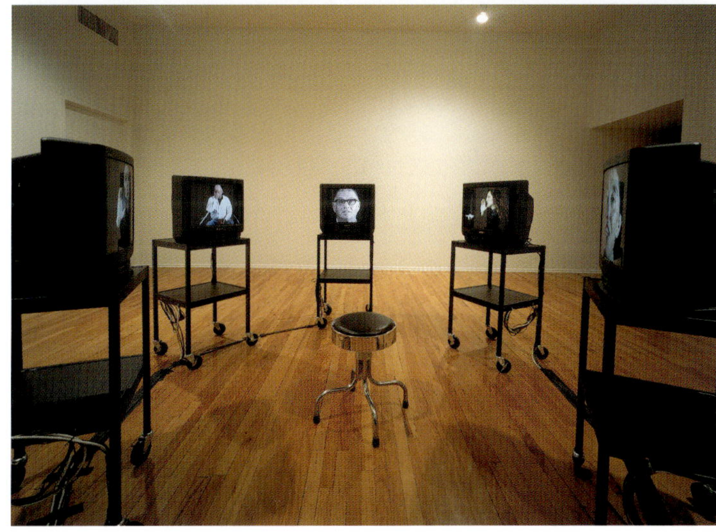

(Figs.106–7)

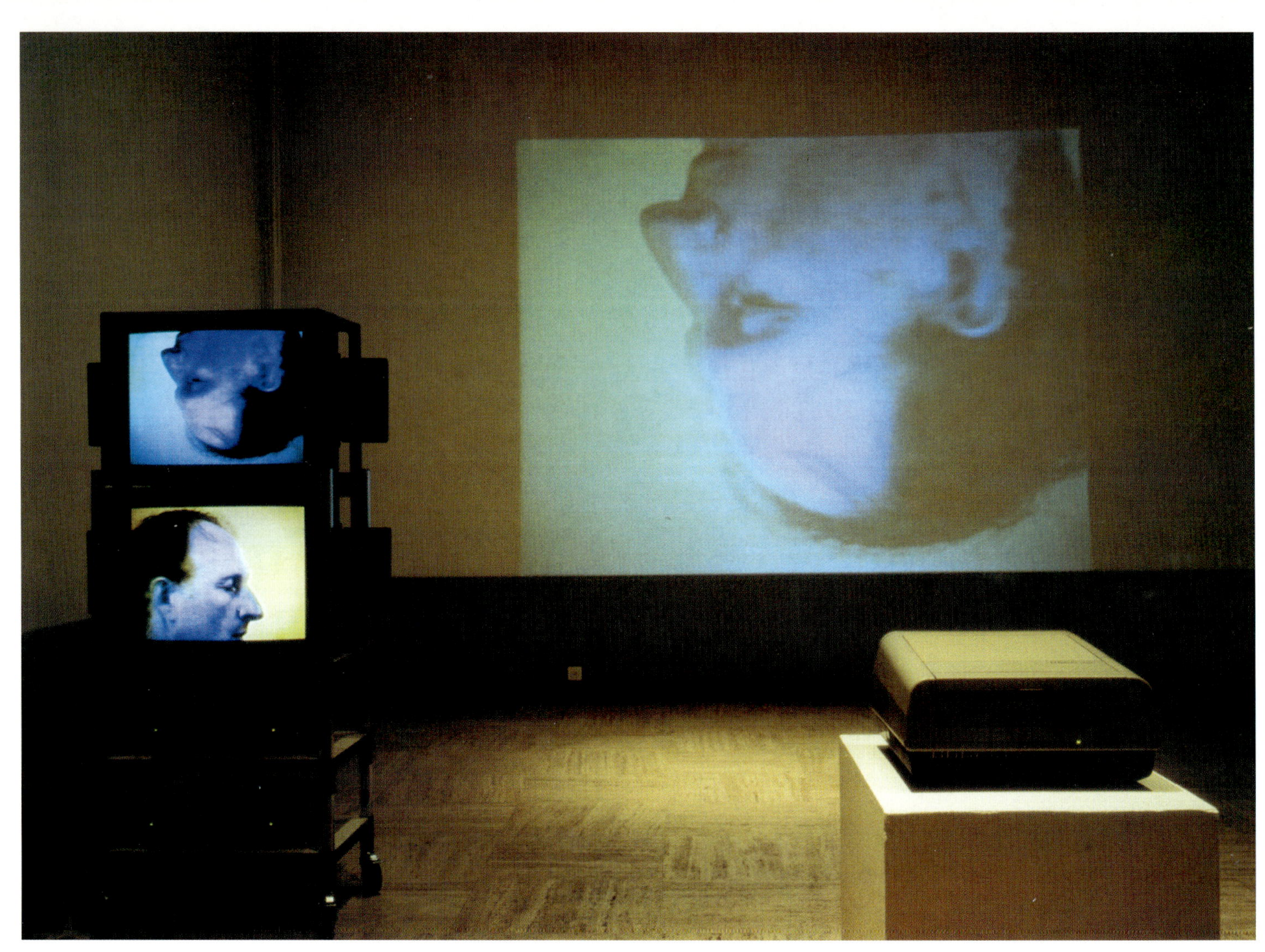

Raw Material — MMMM (Fig.108)

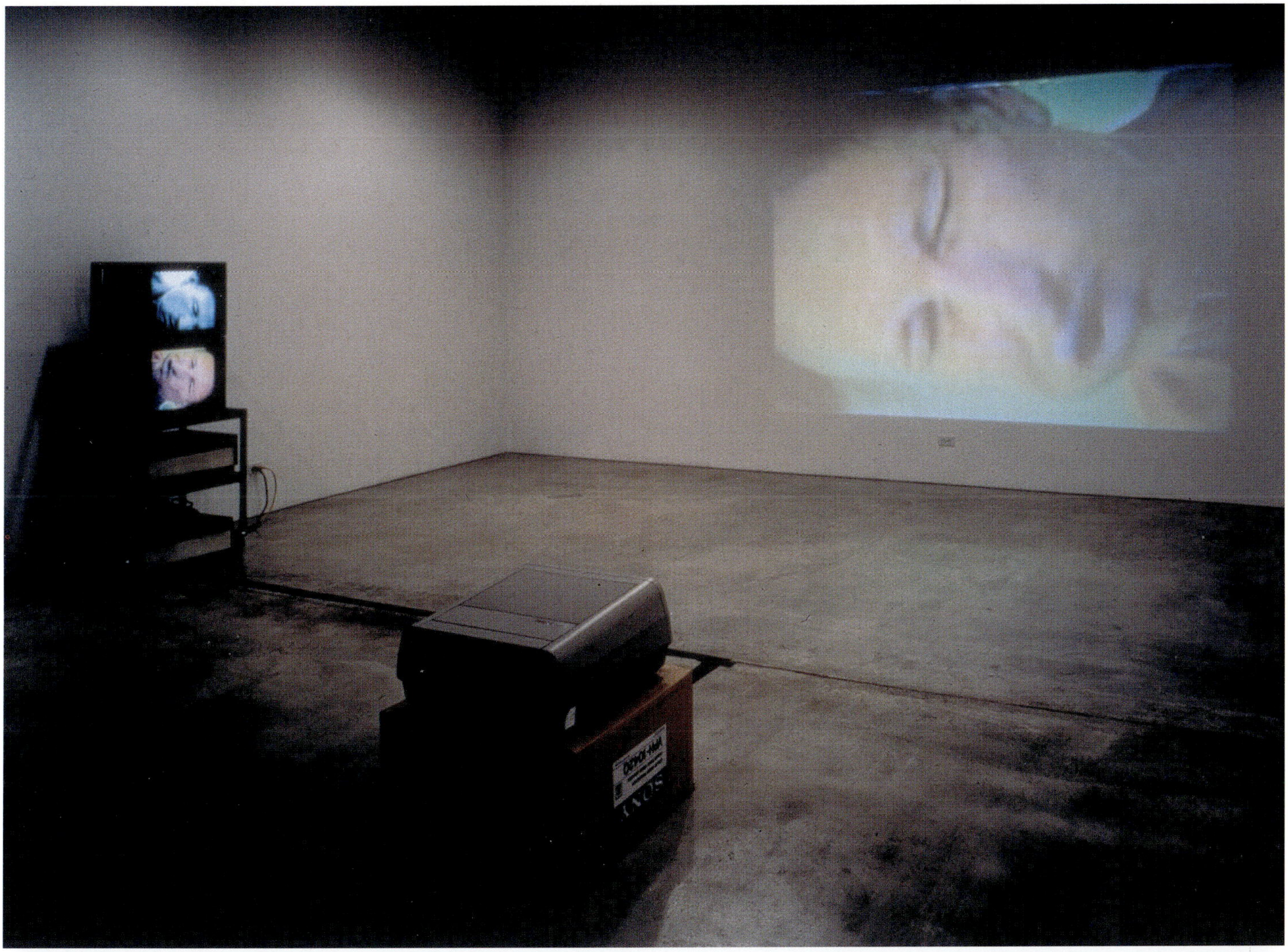

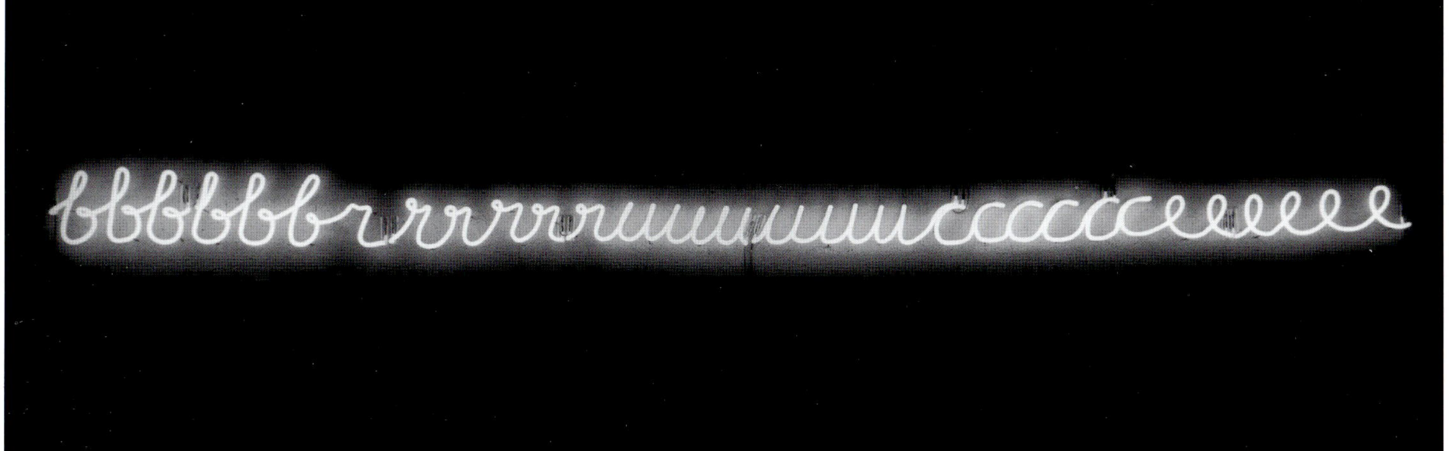

(Figs.109–10)

Raw Materials Preparatory Work Page

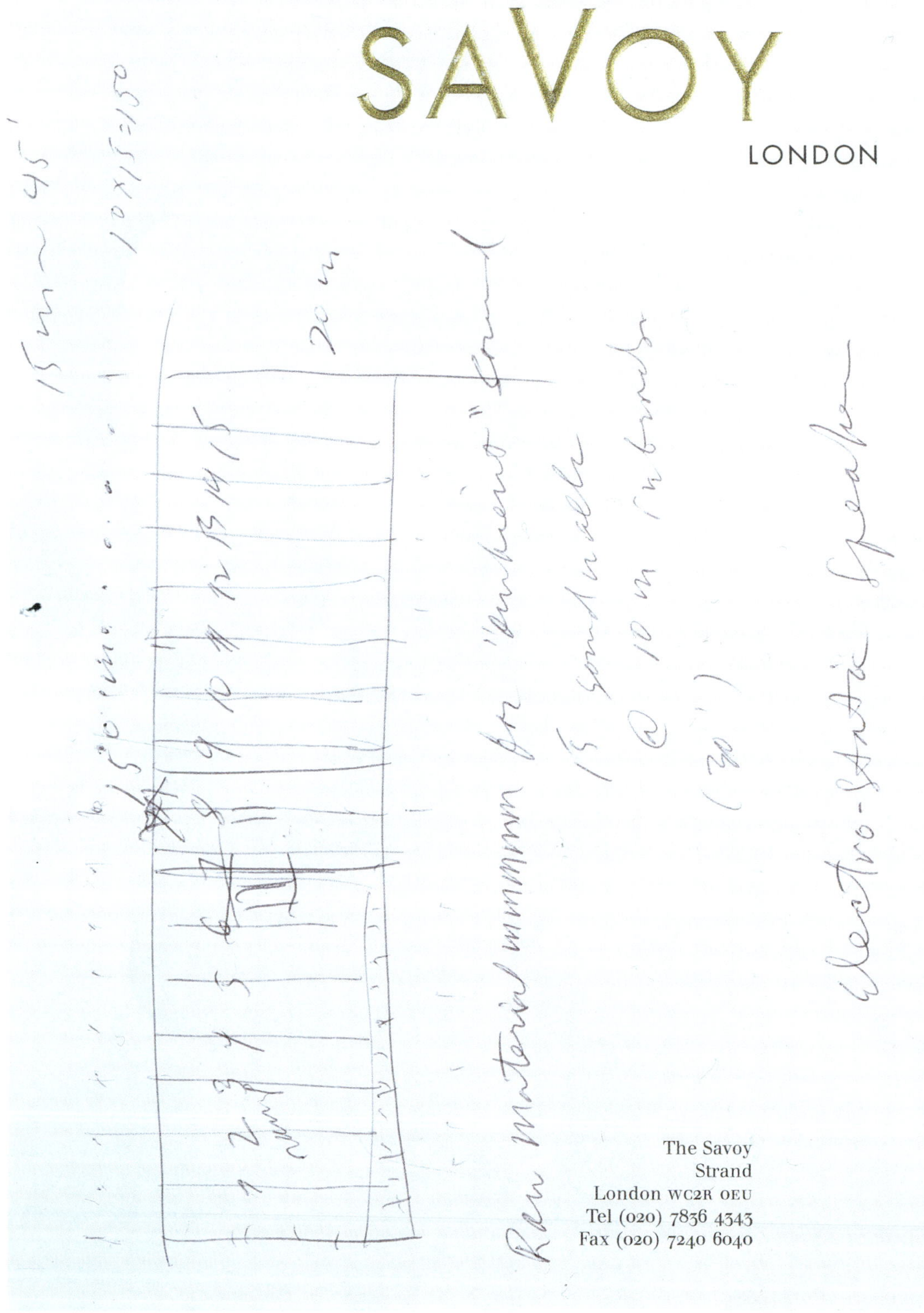

<u>Layout for Raw Materials</u> 6 April 2004 (Fig.111)

B. Corymutes

RAW MATERIAL TEXT LIST 5/24/04

ENTRANCE TO TH

1. THANK YOU, THANK YOU
2. YOU MAY NOT WANT TO BE HERE — Alex. Alexandra
3. WORK, WORK
4. CLOWN TORTURE - PETE AND REPEAT/DARK AND STORMY NIGHT - MIX
5. WORLD PEACE - BERNARD 6. WORLD PEACE - MEI MEI
7. AMAZING LUMINOUS FOUNTAIN - PORTUGESE
8. FALSE SILENCE
9. RAW MATERIAL - OK, OK, OK

Bridge

10. MASK OF ROCK - under bridge
11. THINK THINK THINK - above bridge

Bridge

12. 100 LIVE AND DIE - ENGLISH 13. 100 LIVE AND DIE - BELGIAN
14. GET OUT OF MY MIND, GET OUT OF THIS ROOM
15. STANDING OR LEFT STANDING
16. NONONO - WALTER 17. NO NO NEW MUSEUM
18. ANTHRO/SOCIO
19. GOOD BOY BAD BOY - JOAN 20. GOOD BOY BAD BOY - TUCKER
21. SHIT IN YOUR HAT - HEAD ON A CHAIR

22. RAW MATERIAL - MMMMM / RAW MATERIAL - BRRR - mix for ambient sound

The pairs numbered (5 and 6), (12 and 13), (16 and 17), (19 and 20) have these different texts played opposite each other, the rest have the same text played on opposite sides of the hall.

Entrance to T.H.

1. Thank you Thank you
2. You May Not Want to Be Here – Alexander
3. work work
4. Pete & Repeat / Dark & Stormy Night
5. No No Nee. No No Museum (Walter) (Vandi)
7. 100 Live + Die
8. False Silence

— Bridge —

9. OK, OK – under Bridge
10. think, think – above Bridge

11. Amazing Luminous Fountain
12. Get out of this room – get out of my mind
13. Standing or Left Standing
14. Mask of Rock
15. Anthro/Socio
16. Good boy Bad Boy – Tucker
17. Good Boy Bad Boy – Joan
18. Shit in Your Hat / Head on a chair
19. World Peace – Bernard.
20. World Peace – Mei Mei

END

21. Raw Material MMMM – Raw Material BRRR, mix for white noise

Layouts for Raw Materials 24 May/28 June and 29 June 2004 (Figs.112–13)

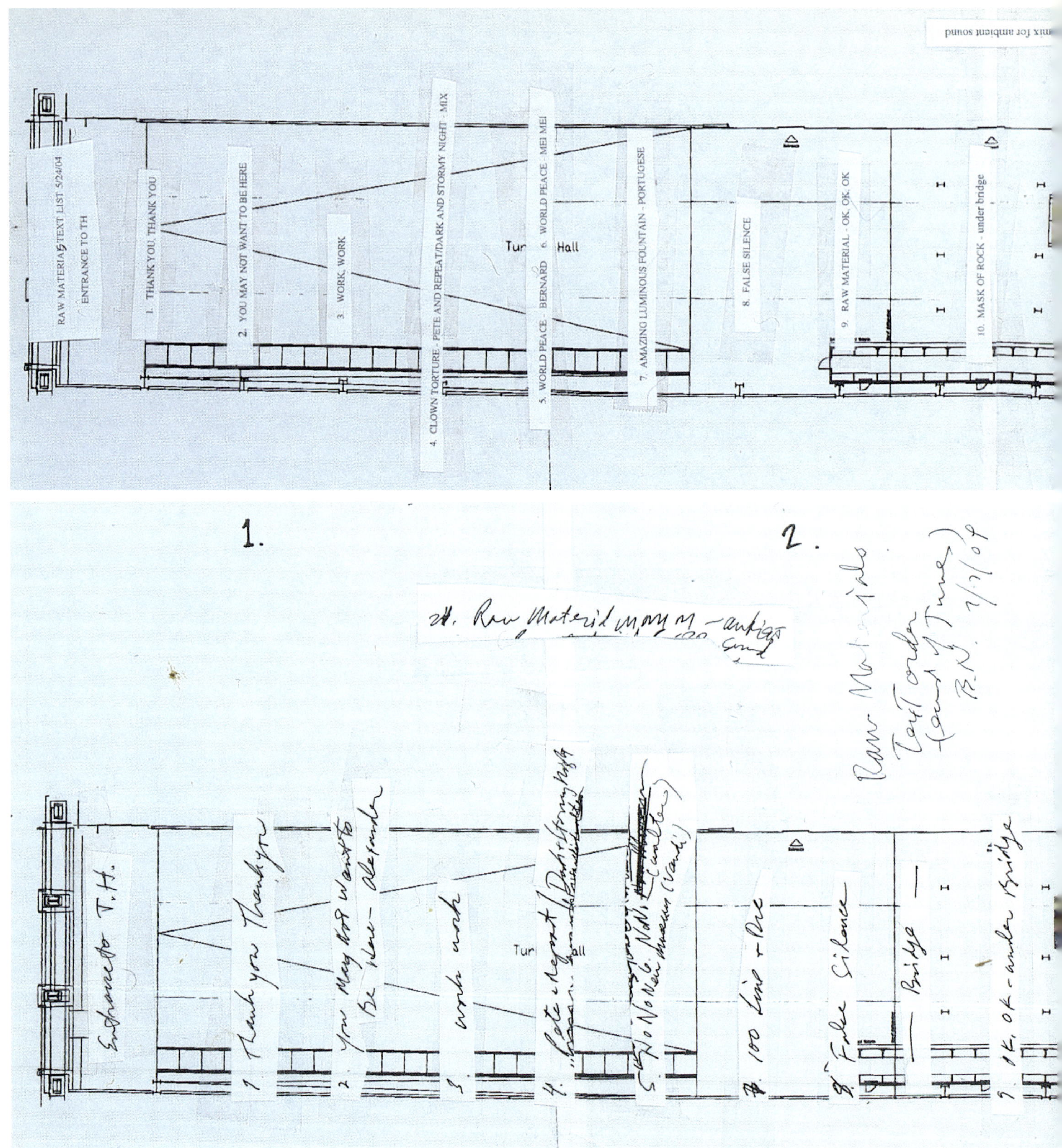

Layouts for Raw Materials 24 May and 7 July 2004 (Figs.114–15)

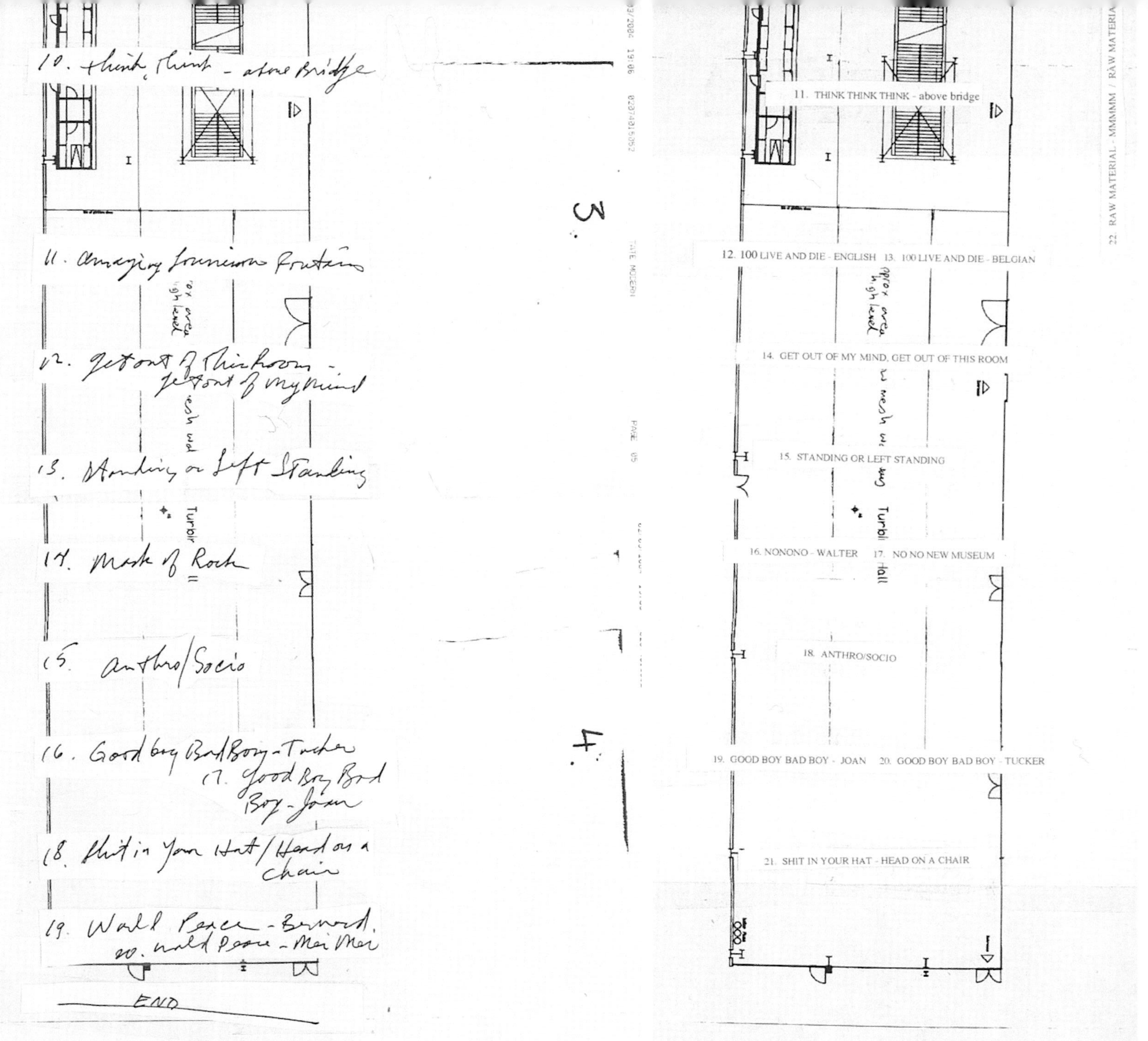
3.
4.
TATE MODERN
PAGE 05
11. THINK THINK THINK - above bridge
12. 100 LIVE AND DIE - ENGLISH 13. 100 LIVE AND DIE - BELGIAN
14. GET OUT OF MY MIND, GET OUT OF THIS ROOM
15. STANDING OR LEFT STANDING
16. NONONO - WALTER 17. NO NO NEW MUSEUM
18. ANTHRO/SOCIO
19. GOOD BOY BAD BOY - JOAN 20. GOOD BOY BAD BOY - TUCKER
21. SHIT IN YOUR HAT - HEAD ON A CHAIR
22. RAW MATERIAL - MMMMM / RAW MATERIA
END

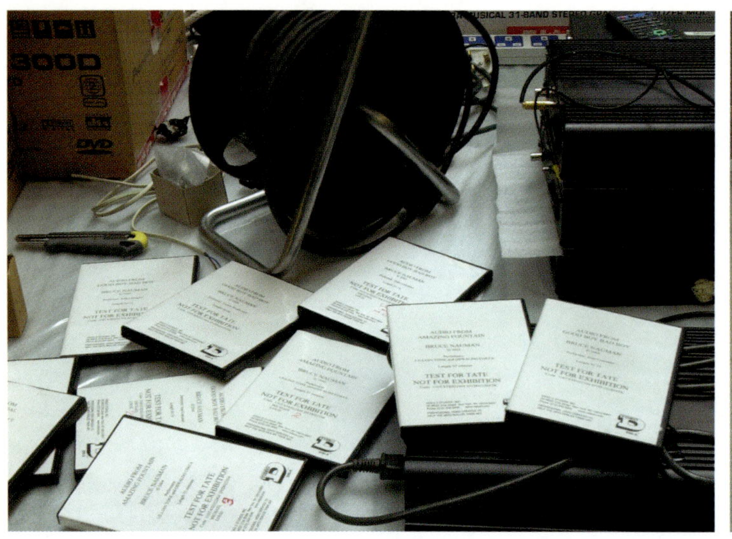

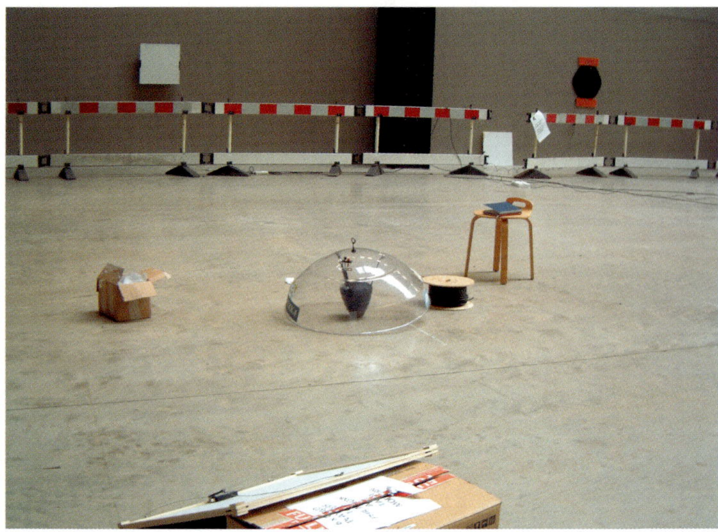

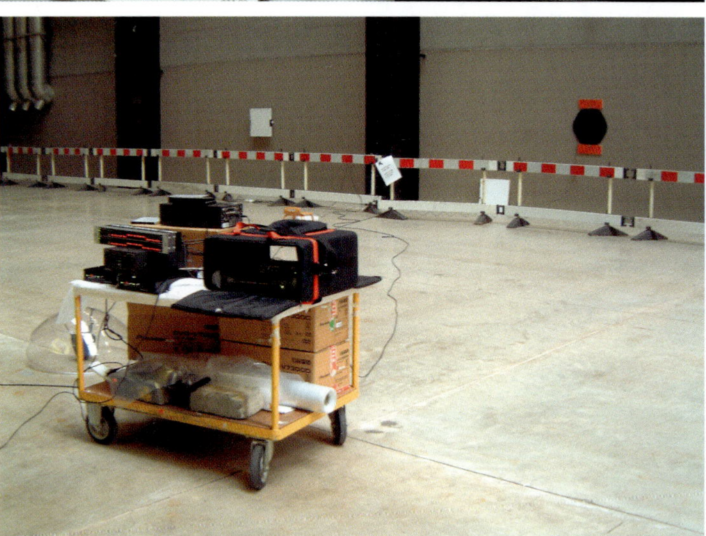

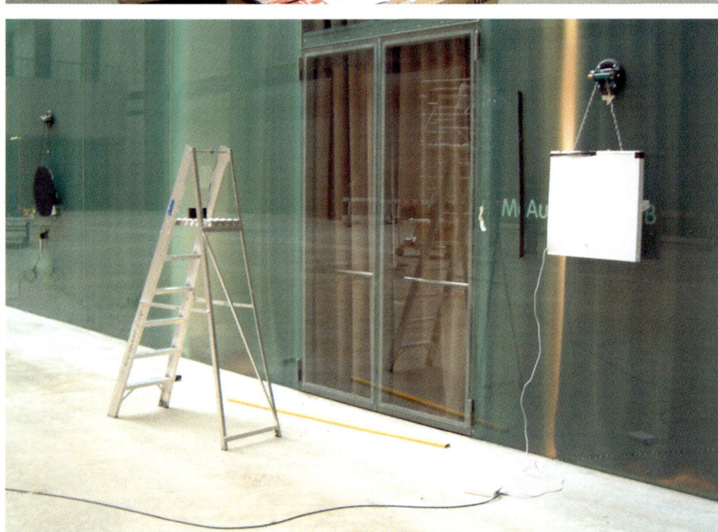

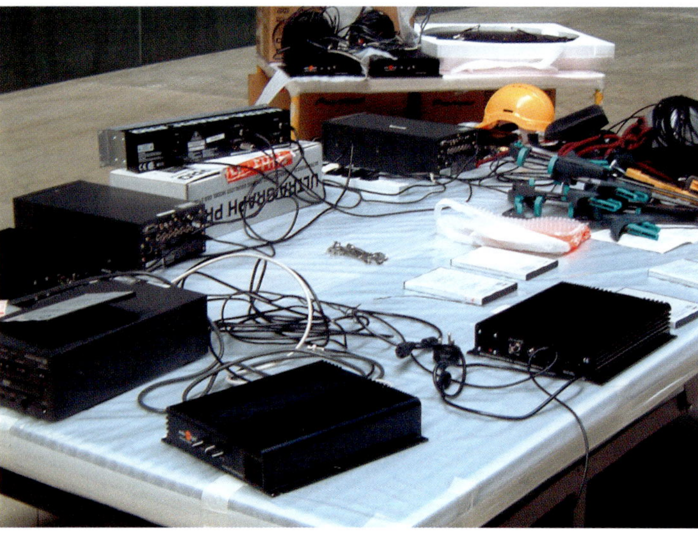

Site visits and tests April 2004 (Figs.116–20)

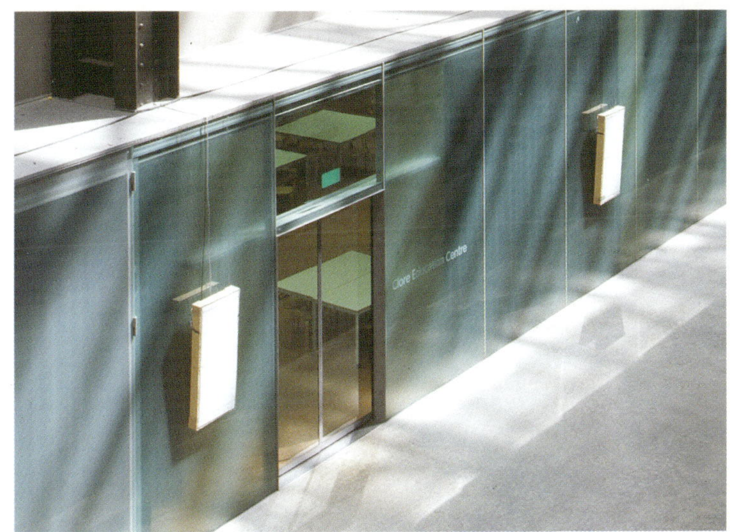

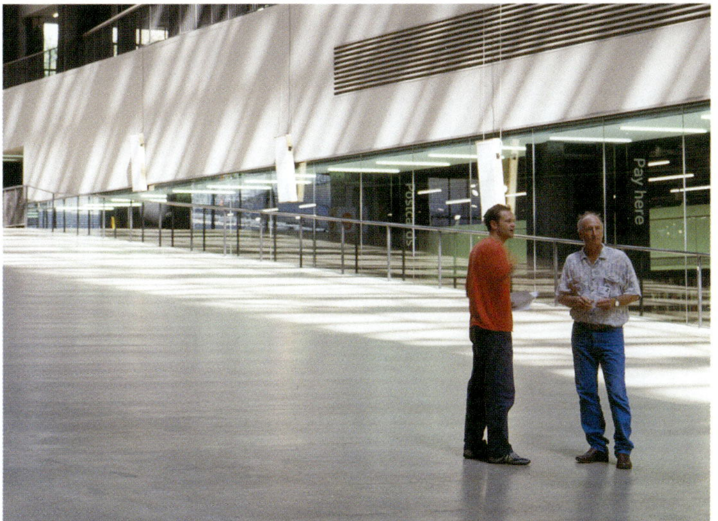

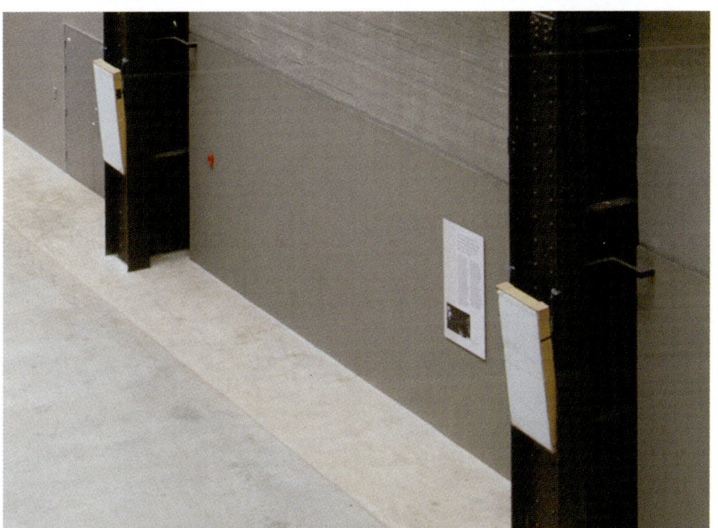

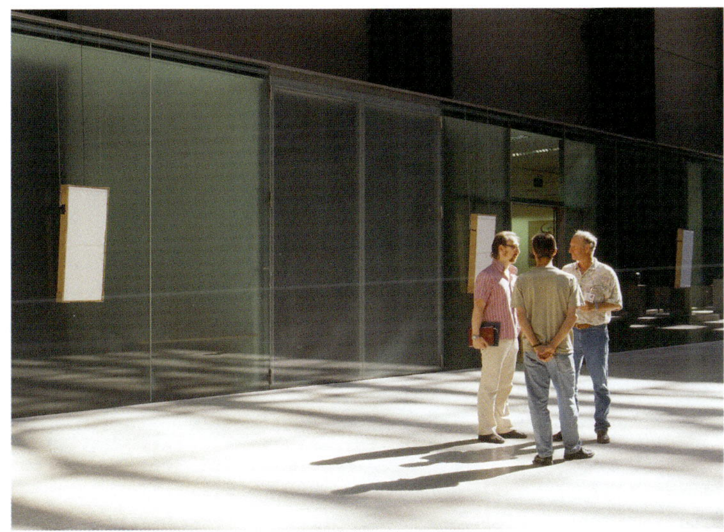

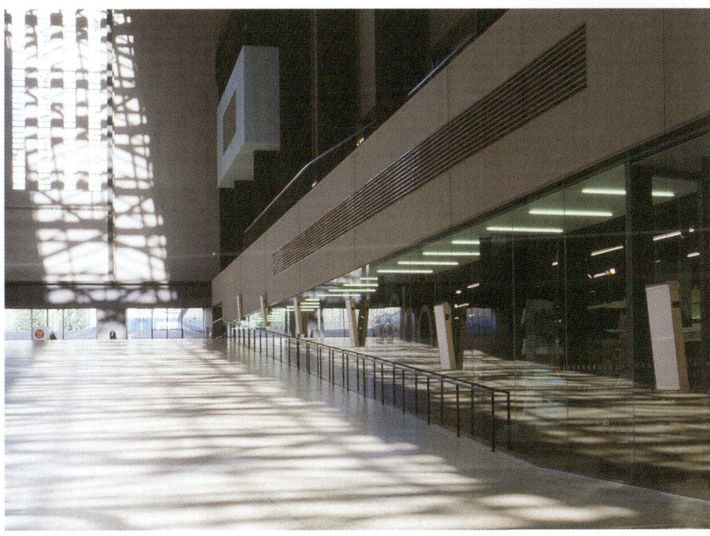

<u>Site visits and tests</u> July 2004 (Figs.121–5)

Speakers:
Myst Systems Electrostatic Speaker 120/40 x 29
Panphonics Audio Element V1.21S in bespoke frame 120/60 x 2
Bent Panphonics Audio Element V1.21S in bespoke frame 120/60 x 1
Bent Panphonics Audio Element V1.21S in bespoke frame 60/60 x 1
SoundTube HP12i BroadBeam Speaker x 4

Playback:
Myst Systems 24 Track Solid-State Audio Playback Module

Routing:
BSS 9088LL Networked Signal Processor Mk1 x 5
BSS 9000 Active Hub
BSS 9012 Remote Control Plate

Amplification:
Cloud CXA850 8 Channel Amp x 5
Cloud CXL40 Live Transformer Module x 40
Cloud CXL800 Module Tray x 5

Racking:
43U Schroff Installation Rack
EMO CM6 Mains Master Switcher
EMO CS6 Mains Slave Switcher

Cabling:
Custom made

Sound design and speakers provided by Sound Directions
System hardware installed and specified by Marquee Audio

Catalogue Entries

Ben Borthwick

The twenty-two audio texts that make up Raw Materials address themes and phrases that stretch back almost forty years over Bruce Nauman's career. This catalogue offers an opportunity to trace their genealogies, demonstrating how meanings in Nauman's work often shift depending on context, and illustrating the wide array of works in which each particular text has arisen. These include individual videos, neon works, text pieces, prints, sculptures, drawings, photographs and sound, light, video and sculptural installations.

There are many tiers of relationships between the texts in Nauman's works. Sometimes an entire text is remapped from one work to another, as with the video and neon versions of Good Boy Bad Boy (figs.82–96); sometimes, as in False Silence and its relatives, a single phrase is isolated or transposed into a different text (figs.50–5); at other times, as evidenced in Self-Portrait as a Fountain, images depict what an earlier text had described (fig.65). Nauman's willingness to recontextualise particular phrases is analogous to his treatment of video footage, sculptural casts and even titles, in which the same source material is used in different works. The smallest change in context or, in the case of language, spelling, can lead to a dramatic shift in meaning, and the creation of ambiguous and anxious spaces.

Nauman, who studied mathematics as an undergraduate, brings an analytical rigour to his investigations of the minutiae and variables of language. A number of these works are linguistic equivalents of mathematical problems, set up to explore their possibilities and limits. 'Many things that you could do would be really boring', he has said, 'so it depends a lot on what you choose, how you set up the problem in the first place. Somehow you have to program it to be interesting.' (Avalanche, no.2, Winter 1971)

These catalogue entries, like the text and image sections that precede them, follow the non-chronological sequence of the installation in the Turbine Hall. Many of the texts were recorded for the first time for Raw Materials. However audio already existed where texts had previously been realised as sound or video pieces. In each case, the work from which either the text was recorded or the audio taken is given as the primary source, even though it may not be the earliest manifestation of the text. Related works in which the text or phrases recur are then listed chronologically. Where these works are included in the catalogue raisonnés of Nauman's work, reference numbers from these books are included, beginning 'CR no.' (Bruce Nauman, exh. cat., Walker Art Center, Minneapolis 1994), 'Drawings no.' (Bruce Nauman: Drawings 1965–1986, exh. cat., Museum für Gegenwartskunst, Basel 1986), or 'Prints no.' (Bruce Nauman: Prints 1970–89, exh. cat., Castelli Graphics, New York, Monk Gallery, New York, and Donald Young Gallery, Chicago 1989).

1 Thank You Thank You
27 Text page
66–7 Image pages

The audio is taken from a video sent by the artist to the collector Ydessa Hendeles. Originally a private 'note' to thank her for her hospitality, it has subsequently been reformatted and exhibited in public.

A single monitor on a cart shows a close-up of the artist's face as he repeatedly shouts the phrase 'thank you'. The original footage has been cut up and reassembled into a ten-minute loop to create an irregular rhythm. As one listens, subtle shifts develop in the intonation, including connotations of pleading, accusation, playfulness and aggression. The words lose shape, playing tricks on the listener, so that 'thank you' appears to morph into its opposite, 'fuck you', and back again. Meaning is slowly evacuated through constant repetition, transforming the phrase into an increasingly ambiguous gesture.

Figs.13–16 Thank You 1992
Laser disc, laser disc player, video monitor, speakers, metal stand (colour, sound), 137 x 76 x 50.8
Ydessa Hendeles Art Foundation

---

2 You May Not Want To Be Here
29 Text page
68–9 Image pages

The text is taken from First Poem Piece 1968, a large metal floor sculpture (figs.18–19). The surface of the sculpture is divided into a grid of eighteen horizontal and seven vertical lines, on which the words are plotted like co-ordinates. The words have been recorded for the first time for Raw Materials, although, in a 1968 drawing, Nauman proposed this text as a sound piece that was never realised. The integration of words with the geometric grid is an early example of Nauman's ongoing fascination with language and mathematics as parallel systems of knowledge that both inform and undermine each other's claims to truth. The related Second Poem Piece 1969 takes a similarly algorithmic approach to the statement: 'You may not want to screw here'.

Nauman explores two sets of linguistic possibilities in this work. Firstly, potential meanings contained in the statement 'You may not want to be here' change dramatically through the systematic omission of words. With each iteration, the statement progressively decomposes as individual words are left out and possible sentence constructions are explored. Secondly, the word 'here' is replaced by its homonym 'hear'. Although this is only evident in the written text, it radically changes the meaning of the words. The text is recited by a child (Alexander Ziffer Diamond), whose frustration with these linguistic ambiguities simultaneously indicates the subtlety and opacity of the way in which language conveys meaning.

Figs.18–19 First Poem Piece 1968
Steel, *c.*1.3 x 152.4 x 152.4
CR no.109
Collection Kröller-Müller, Otterlo

Related works:

Fig.17 Study for First Poem Piece 1968
Pencil on paper, 36.7 x 51.1
Drawings no.72
Collection Kröller-Müller, Otterlo

(Study for First Poem Piece) You may not want to be here ... 1968
Pencil on paper, 50 x 65
Drawings no.73
Collection Martin Visser, Bergeijk

You may not want to be here 1968
Pencil on paper, 47.2 x 61
Drawings no.74
Collection of the artist

You may not want to be here/tape loop – word each second/80 second loop 1968
Pencil on paper, 38 x 67
Drawings no.75
Konrad Fischer, Düsseldorf

Second Poem Piece 1969
Steel, *c.*1.3 x 152.4 x 152.4
Edition of 3
CR no.156
Collection Gian Enzo Sperone, New York

---

3 Work Work
31 Text page
70–1 Image pages

The audio is taken from Work 1994 (figs.20–5). Two stacked monitors each show the same footage of a close-up of Nauman's head jumping into the frame as he repeatedly shouts the word 'work'; the image on the top monitor is inverted. At times the heads appear to collide and envelop each other like a Rorschach image, but the loops are non-synchronous and they immediately fall out of rhythm.

As with Think Think Think (see entry for no.10 below), the repetition imbues the word with contradictory meanings, oscillating between determination, pleading, anxiety, instruction and desperation. This is as much to do with the physical demands of performance as with the linguistic properties of the word itself – the artist becomes increasingly breathless and the word mutates into a grunt that carries both sexual and psychotic overtones. After a short pause he recovers his breath and continues repeating the same cycle. In the background, the slapping sound of the artist jumping and an occasional jingle of metal objects are audible.

Figs.20–5 Work 1994
2 video discs, 2 video disc players, 2 monitors, steel cart (colour, sound), dimensions variable
Froehlich Collection, Stuttgart

---

4 Pete and Repeat/Dark and Stormy Night
32–3 Text pages
72–5 Image pages

These texts are taken from different works in the Clown Torture series. The performer in both videos is Walter Stevens as a red-haired clown in a striped suit who features in many of Nauman's clown works. Pete and Repeat (figs.26–7, 33, 35) is one of four sequences in the multipart Clown Torture installation, which rotates across two projections and four monitors, and also includes 'Clown with Goldfish', 'Clown with Waterbucket' and 'No, No, No, No' (see entry for nos.5/6 below). The clown is depicted in these sequences as an inept character, caught in a humiliating catch-22 from which he seems unable to escape. The final sequence shows a projection of 'Clown Taking a Shit', in which he is seen sitting on a toilet reading a magazine, as if filmed by a surveillance camera. Dark and Stormy Night is from the video installation Clown Torture: Dark and Stormy Night with Laughter 1987 (figs.28–32), which consists of two monitors placed on opposite sides of the room. On one screen Stevens performs the text, both in close-up and standing on one leg pretending that the elevated foot is a campfire against which he warms his hands. The second monitor features Vandi Snyder's laughing jester – this jester also appears in No, No, New Museum 1987 (see entry for nos.5/6 below and fig.36).

Both texts are recited many times and looped in consecutive blocks. They are storytelling games whose hermetic structure forces the narrator to begin the story again as it comes to an end. With each repetition the clown becomes increasingly frustrated by the imperative to start again. Pete and Repeat is an account given in the third person, which exasperates him from the outset, while Dark and Stormy Night, told in the first person, contains characters for which he creates a range of voices that engages him for longer. At the end/beginning of each text, the point at which it feeds back into itself, there is an audible moment of despair as the clown realises he is going to have to repeat the narrative yet again. He tries different deliveries in the vain hope that they will provide an escape route, but he is trapped in the loop. As he becomes increasingly infuriated he departs from the text and adds extra words, but even these fail to disrupt the circular structure. As desperation sets in, the character voices give way to that of the confused narrator who, at one point, snarls the text like a rabid dog.

Figs.26–7 Clown Torture 1987
33, 35 4 colour video monitors, 4 speakers, 4 video tape players, 2 video projectors, 4 video tapes (colour, sound), dimensions variable
CR no.365
Collection The Art Institute of Chicago, Watson F. Blair Prize Fund; W.L. Mead Endowment; Twentieth-Century Purchase Fund; Through prior gift of Joseph Winterbotham; Gift of Lannan Foundation, 1997.162

Figs.28–32 Clown Torture: Dark and Stormy Night with Laughter 1987
2 colour video monitors, 2 video tape players, 2 video tapes (colour, sound), dimensions variable
CR no.366
Collection of Barbara Balkin Cottle and Robert Cottle

5/6 No No No No – New Museum/Walter
34–5 Text pages
76–9 Image pages

These two pieces of audio are taken from different but related works in which a male and a female voice repeat the word 'no' over and over again. The female voice is from No, No, New Museum 1987 (fig.36), which features Vandi Snyder on two monitors as a jester in red and green jumping around as if on an imaginary pogo stick. The work was originally shown in the storefront window of the New Museum, New York, the audio component broadcast at high volume onto the street. The male voice is taken from the installation Clown Torture 1987 (see entry for no.4 above) featuring Walter Stevens as a red-haired clown. The audio used here is from the 'No, No, No, No' sequence in which Stevens is seen having a tantrum on the floor (figs.33, 35).

A possible anagram of 'no no no no' is 'on on on on', a palindrome that could easily act as Nauman's stage directions to the performers. The corresponding values of these two possible words are particularly clear both in the drawing NONO 1984 (fig.37), and during the print-making process, where the image – in this case the word 'no' – is made in reverse, thereby spelling 'on'. These works highlight Nauman's fascination with Wittgenstein's language games, such as the duck/rabbit conundrum, in which a single image can signify two different objects.

The same raw material for No, No, New Museum 1987 was used in Double No 1988 (fig.34), in which two monitors are stacked on top of each other, the top one inverted, and this has led to confusion between the works. Stevens's clown and Snyder's laughing jester both also feature in Clown Torture: Dark and Stormy Night with Laughter 1987 (see entry for no.4 above). Snyder also recites a text in Clown Torture: I'm Sorry and No, No, No, No 1987 in which a pierrot shouts 'no'.

In Raw Materials the two pieces of audio are played concurrently from speakers opposite each other on the north and south walls of the Turbine Hall. Snyder's voice chants the word rhythmically in rapid jabs, each iteration coinciding with the sound of her feet smacking the ground as she ricochets around the room. After two minutes a brief counter-rhythm manifests itself, as if the word is bouncing back against itself.

In stark contrast, Stevens explores the expressive and gestural possibilities of the word 'no' in different accents, extended shouts, operatic arias and screaming streams, liberally interspersed with grunts that run the gamut from admonishment to despair. Occasionally he employs different languages, and the sound of his feet shuffling or stamping against the floor is audible. Three minutes into the twelve-minute cycle the audio loops a short section from the high point of his tantrum.

Fig.36 No, No, New Museum 1987
Colour video monitor, video tape player, video tape (colour, sound), dimensions variable
CR no.371
Private Collection

Figs.26–7, 33, 35 Clown Torture 1987
See entry for no.4 above for details

Related works:

Fig.39 No 1981
Lithograph on Arches Cover paper, 76.2 x 109.2
Edition of 21, plus proofs
Prints no.44
Published by Gemini G.E.L., Los Angeles

Fig.38 NoNo 1983
Neon tubing with clear glass tubing suspension frame, 27.9 x 93.3 x 5.4
CR no.316
Friedrich Christian Flick Collection

NONO 1983
Pencil, charcoal and watercolour on paper, 67.3 x 125.7
Drawings no.415
Private Collection

Fig.37 NONO 1984
Pencil and watercolour on paper, 43.3 x 72.4
Drawings no.460
Collection Robin Wright, San Francisco

Clown Torture: I'm Sorry and No, No, No, No 1987
2 colour video monitors, 2 video tape players, 2 video tapes (colour, sound), dimensions variable
CR no.367
Collection François Pinault, Paris

Fig.34 Double No 1988
2 colour video monitors, 2 video tape players, 2 video tapes (colour, sound), dimensions variable
CR no.381
Froehlich Collection, Stuttgart

---

7 100 Live and Die
36–7 Text pages
80–3 Image pages

This one-hundred-line text was originally recorded in German, followed by Flemish and then English, for successive exhibitions of the installation Chambres d'Amis (Krefeld Piece) 1985. The installation also included the Good Boy Bad Boy 1985 video (fig.95) and Hanged Man 1985 neon – each work occupied a separate room in the Museum Haus Esters, Krefeld (see fig.47). The best-known version of the text is a large neon sign with four vertical columns, each containing twenty-five refrains. The stems in each column alternate with the words 'AND DIE' and 'AND LIVE'. The sign flashes up individual phrases, blocks of text, columns, and then the entire work, according to a complex algorithm (figs.40–5). Many of these phrases or their variants exist as prints and drawings (for instance figs.48–9).

A chorus of six male and female voices recites the one hundred commands in a number of different styles, from an objective reading of the words to an incantatory chant. The three-word commands consist of what Nauman describes as 'lists of human attributes and actions'. The first phrase is 'LIVE AND DIE' followed by its opposite 'LIVE AND LIVE', then 'DIE AND DIE/DIE AND LIVE', then 'SHIT AND DIE/SHIT AND LIVE', and so on. The structure of the work resembles an equation, where all attributes or actions become linguistic integers factored by the binary values LIVE or DIE. These equations should, in theory, cancel each other out, but in certain combinations the value of LIVE or of DIE reacts more powerfully, undermining the precision and logic that initially appears to structure the text. Both the structure and recitation evoke the equally mathematical musical compositions of Steve Reich, where a single refrain mutates with each repetition while never losing its overall structure.

One Hundred Live and Die 1985
Part of Chambres d'Amis (Krefeld Piece) 1985
Audio tape played in a room (language translated to location)
CR no.332
Museum of Contemporary Art, Chicago.
Gerald S. Elliot Collection

Related works:
Shit and Die 1983
Pencil and watercolour, 22.9 x 114.3
Drawings no.420
Collection Leo Castelli, New York (destroyed)

Fig.46 Live And Die 1983
Pencil, pastel, charcoal and watercolour on paper, each 285 x 127 unframed
Drawings no.421
Collection Herbert, Ghent

Figs.40–5 One Hundred Live and Die 1984
Neon tubing with clear glass tubing on metal monolith, 299.7 x 335.9 x 53.3
CR no.324
Collection Benesse Corporation, Naoshima Contemporary Art Museum, Kagawa

Fig.48 Shit and Die 1985
Drypoint on J. Barcham Green Crisbrook paper, 40 x 57.2
Edition of 38, plus proofs
Prints no.51
Published by Gemini G.E.L., Los Angeles

Fig.47 Untitled (Haus Esters Installation) 1985
Graphite and collage on paper, 101.6 x 127
Drawings no.513
Collection of the artist

Fig.49 Live or Die (State I) 1985
Lithograph on Rives BFK White paper, 38.1 x 27.9
Edition of 25, plus proofs
Prints no.52
Co-published by Bruce Nauman and Arber and Son Editions, Alameda, New Mexico

---

8 False Silence
38–9 Text pages
84–7 Image pages

The text is taken from a large architectural installation, first realised in Los Angeles in1975. Nauman recorded the audio using his own voice, but for a recreation in 2000 in the Kunsthalle, Vienna (fig.51) that recording was believed lost and the text was re-recorded by Joan LaBarbara. The original tape has since been found so two versions of the audio now exist. A drawing from 1975 (fig.50) specifies the placement of speakers and dimensions of a narrow, illuminated corridor, which bisects two differently shaped triangular rooms of equal surface area into which it opens. The text incorporates phrases or parts of phrases such as 'You can't help me', 'You can't hurt me' used in other works in a range of media, including neon, print and drawing (figs.52–5).

Joan LaBarbara recites a one-and-a-half-minute text related to bodily and psychological processes. These processes are incomplete, often denying the effect of an action such as 'I inhale, don't exhale'. Its series of short declarations and its non-narrative structure loop seamlessly, so that the listener cannot tell where it begins and ends.

Fig.51 False Silence 1975/2000
Wallboard, audio tape, audio tape player, speakers, corridor: 2011.7 x 38; triangular rooms: 335.3 x 548.6 and 274.3 x 670.6
CR no.242
Solomon R. Guggenheim Museum, New York, Panza Collection (1991; 91.3837)

Related works:
Fig.53 YOU CANT HELP ME 1974
Pencil, blue crayon, black ink and tape, 45 x 187.1
Drawings no.304
Courtesy Sonnabend Gallery, New York

Fig.52 You Cant Help Me (warm white) 1974
Part of Silver Grotto 1974
Neon tubing with clear glass tubing suspension frames, 13.3 x 155.6 x 2.5
CR no.234
Private Collection, Venice

Fig.50 Drawing for False Silence 1975
Pencil and coloured pencil on paper, 76 x 101.5
Drawings no.319
Solomon R. Guggenheim Museum, New York, Panza Collection (1991; 91.3837)

Fig.54 Help Me Hurt Me 1975
Lithograph on Roll Arches paper, 91.4 x 129.6
Edition of 20, plus proofs
Prints no.28
Published by Gemini G.E.L., Los Angeles

No Sweat 1975
Screenprint on Arches 88 paper, 101.6 x 81.3
Edition of 25, plus proofs
Prints no.35
Published by Gemini G.E.L., Los Angeles

Fig.55 Silver Grotto/Yellow Grotto 1975
Screenprint on Arches 88 paper, 76.2 x 211.7
Edition of 20, plus proofs
Prints no.36
Published by Gemini G.E.L., Los Angeles

---

9 OK OK OK

40 Text page
88–9 Image pages

The audio is from Raw Material – OK, OK, OK 1990 (figs.56–7; see also entry for no.21 below) and was the first in a series of single-word videos featuring the artist, although these were preceded by the 'No, No, No, No' series of clown works (see entry for nos.5/6 above). Nauman repeats the word 'OK' in a quick-fire delivery. Occasional dips in the rhythm of the sixteen-second loop are punctuated by a single 'alright'. Along with the insistent repetition of 'OK' there is an irregular background rhythm of creaks and taps, created by the artist spinning round on an office chair (see entry for no.10 for further discussion of diegetic sound in these works). As with other works that repeat a single word or phrase, 'OK' soon loses its definition and could easily be mistaken for 'chaos' or a simple reversal of the letters to 'KO', the boxing abbreviation for 'knock out' (see also entry for nos.5/6 above for word inversion).

Figs.56–7 Raw Material – OK, OK, OK 1990
Video projector, 2 colour video monitors, 2 video tape players, 2 video tapes (colour, sound), dimensions variable
CR no.456
Collection Pamela and Richard Kramlich, San Francisco

Related works:
Raw Material with Continuous Shift – OK, OK, OK 1991
Video projector, 2 colour video monitors, 2 video disc players, 2 video discs (colour, sound), dimensions variable
CR no.473
Collection Selma and Jos Vandermolen, Ghent

Fig.109 Raw Material – BRRR 1990
Fig.108 Raw Material – MMMM 1990
Raw Material with Continuous Shift – BRRR 1991
Raw Material with Continuous Shift – MMMM 1991
See entry for no.21 below for details

---

10 Think Think Think

41 Text page
91 Image page

The audio is taken from Think 1993 (fig.58), which, like Work 1994 (figs.20–5), has two monitors stacked on a cart, but has the lower image inverted. The camera is pointed at a spot of wall just above Nauman's head, which he attempts to jump up into. Sometimes he succeeds in getting his whole head into frame but often he is glimpsed only from the nose up.

The word 'think' is shouted by Nauman repeatedly on a thirty-second loop. As he runs out of breath it morphs into various other words like 'fake', 'thick' and a monosyllabic grunt. This repeated shouting of the word makes it impossible to think, yet as the loop progresses the chant shifts from a bullying demand to a desperate plea. In addition to his voice there are arrhythmic sounds including gasps for breath, feet hitting the floor and the occasional metallic jangle. These initially seem to be random, but as the loop repeats they evolve into a strange polyrhythm that offsets the chant. The rhythms created by Nauman's body in these jumping works should be seen in relation to videos such as No, No, New Museum 1987 (fig.36), Bouncing in the Corner, No.1 1968, Bouncing Two Balls between the Floor and Ceiling with Changing Rhythms 1967–8, Stamping in the Studio 1968, as well as the audio work Jumping, part of the Studio Aids II suite of audio works from which Get Out of My Mind, Get Out of This Room is taken (see entry for no.12 below).

Fig.58 Think 1993
2 video discs, 2 video disc players, 2 monitors, steel cart (colour, sound), dimensions variable
The Museum of Modern Art, New York, Dannheisser Collection

---

11 The True Artist Is An Amazing Luminous Fountain
43 Text page
92–5 Image pages

The audio is from Amazing Fountain 1998 (fig.59), which is in turn a recent Portuguese manifestation of Untitled (The True Artist Is an Amazing Luminous Fountain) 1968. This work is a lengthy text with an exhaustive set of instructions that offers inexhaustible possible realisations of how the statement 'the true artist is an amazing luminous fountain' might be presented around the perimeter of any architectural feature (fig.62). It also provides instructions for how it could be translated into any language. In a related work, Untitled 1969, Nauman presented a pile of blue and gold letters in the corner of a room. Arranged correctly they would spell 'The Artist is a Luminous Fountain' but other possible sentences could obviously be constructed.

The fountain, traditionally associated with knowledge, has been central to sculptural history, from the works of Giovanni Lorenzo Bernini to Marcel Duchamp. This theme has recurred in Nauman's work since 1966. Early photographs and drawings show the artist spouting water from his mouth. The earliest manifestation of this text is a 1966 window screen (fig.61), where it was painted and etched onto rose Mylar and displayed in a window at Nauman's San Francisco studio with a related neon sign (fig.60). The fountain continues to be a point of reference for Nauman, who said that, when invited to produce a work for The Unilever Series, 'I was also working on a fish fountain and I considered hanging a very large number of cast fish at various levels throughout the space either dry or as a vast indoor fountain.'

In this audio, a male voice (Oswaldo Costa) and a female voice (Lillian Tone) repeat two versions of Nauman's statement 'The true artist is an amazing luminous fountain' in Portuguese. Each voice explores the possibilities of pronunciation as the emphasis falls on different words or syllables with each repetition. Nauman has stated that there are two versions because 'there was not a precise translation for "amazing" and the two suggestions were so euphonious that I used them in this way'. The principal meanings of the Portuguese words *assombrosa* and *maravilhosa* are 'haunting' and 'marvellous'. The male and female voices start by alternating, but they slowly begin to overlap and interlock in much the same way that the meanings of the two versions lose their specificity with each repetition. Like many of Nauman's other works, this piece highlights the approximate relationship between language and meaning, in which there is always potential for inexact interpretation or, in this case, translation.

Fig.59 Amazing Fountain 1998 (Portuguese)
Digital video disc player, colour video monitor, digital video disc (colour, sound), dimensions variable
Collection Fundação de Serralves, Porto

Related works:
Fig.65 Self-Portrait as a Fountain 1966 (damaged)
Reprinted in Eleven Color Photographs 1966–7/1970
Colour photograph, *c.*50.2 x 58.4
Edition of 8
CR nos.54, 175
Froehlich Collection, Stuttgart

Fig.61 The True Artist Is an Amazing Luminous Fountain (Window or Wall Shade) 1966
Transparent rose-coloured Mylar, 243.8 x 182.9
CR no.58
Raussmüller Collection, Hallen für neue Kunst, Schaffhausen

The True Artist Is an Amazing Luminous Fountain 1966
Graphite and black ink on paper, 61 x 48.2
Drawings no.17
Sonnabend Gallery, New York

Fig.64 The Artist as a Fountain 1966–7
Black and white photograph, 20.3 x 24.5
CR no.71
Collection of the artist

Fig.60 The True Artist Helps the World by Revealing Mystic Truths (Window or Wall Sign) 1967
Neon tubing with clear glass tubing suspension frame, 149.9 x 139.7 x 5.1
CR no.92
Collection Kröller-Müller, Otterlo

Fig.63 Myself as a Marble Fountain 1967
Ink and wash, 48 x 60.5
Drawings no.49
Collection Emanuel Hoffmann Foundation, permanent loan to the Kunstmuseum Basel

Fig.62 Untitled (The True Artist Is an Amazing Luminous Fountain) 1968
Cut-out letters, dimensions variable
CR no.134
Collection of the artist

Untitled 1969
Cut-out letters, dust, dimensions variable
CR no.159
Collection of the artist

12 Get Out of My Mind, Get Out of This Room
44 Text page
97 Image page

This stereo recording was originally part of a suite of five sound works called Studio Aids II 1968. In 1972, Get Out of My Mind, Get Out of This Room was exhibited separately in a small room with two speakers placed opposite each other at ear level, creating an intensely claustrophobic and intimidating experience. It continues to be presented on its own in this manner, and is the only pure sound work by Nauman included in Raw Materials.

The artist utters the title over and over again in various strained voices – as a stage whisper, a growl, as if suffocating, or through gritted teeth, but it is never clearly spoken. The recording is roughly six minutes long and is of exceptional quality. Strained inhalations and exhalations are clearly audible and integral to the work's sinister mood. Nauman described how 'I said it in a lot of different ways: I changed my voice and distorted it, I yelled it and growled it and grunted it … It was a very powerful piece … it's so angry it scares people.'

Get Out of My Mind, Get Out of This Room 1968
Audio tape played in a room, 6-minute segment, looped to play continuously
CR no.113
Collection Jack Wendler, London

Related works:
Studio Aids II 1968
5 audio tapes, durations vary, each to be repeated consecutively and continuously
CR no.127
Collection Jack Wendler, London

Fig.66 Studio Aids for U.C.L.A. 1967
Pencil on paper, 45 x 37.5
Drawings no.66
Collection Angela Westwater, New York

13 Left or Standing/Standing or Left Standing
46–7 Text pages
98–101 Image pages

The text was first presented as a poster, folded and sent out as the exhibition announcement, then stacked outside Installation with Yellow Lights (Castelli Installation with Yellow Lights) 1971 (figs.69–70). Four false walls that stopped just short of the ceiling created a trapezoidal room within the gallery. The two remaining wedges of space served as corridors with doorways into the main room, which was illuminated by bright yellow fluorescent lighting. When UV light from outside spilled over the top of the walls the viewer experienced a purple afterimage. The disorienting effect both of the light and of standing in a trapezoidal room was further emphasised by three pillars that bisected the Leo Castelli Gallery. In recent installations the pillars are not included and the poster has been replaced by silent videos installed at either entrance to the work, in which the two texts dissolve from one to the other (figs.67–8, 71).

Nauman has made numerous other works involving wallboards and exposed struts, such as Acoustic Pressure Piece 1971 (exhibited at Castelli at the same time), as well as other yellow light installations, most notably Yellow Room (Triangular) 1973, where the disorienting shape of the room is even more accentuated. He explored the idea of brightly lit rooms in a number of works from the period including False Silence 1975 (fig.51) and Changing Light Corridor with Rooms 1971.

A female voice (Robin Hoffman) reads the two related poems. As with so many other components of Raw Materials, the language used in each of the texts is very similar, making it difficult to remember or even recognise the subtle differences. For example, 'His precision and acuity' is replaced by 'His preciseness and accuracy', or the phrase 'clean cuts' by 'small cuts', before the texts diverge more explicitly. In this sense they resemble the slightly differently shaped cubes in Consummate Mask of Rock (see entry for no.14 below). Left or Standing goes on to address those unconscious effects of architecture that are barely discernible yet generate anxiety, specifying time as 'a not long but undeterminate period'. Standing or Left Standing focuses on the physical sensations of such perceptions.

Figs.67–71 Left or Standing, Standing or Left Standing 1971/99
Wallboard, yellow fluorescent lights, 2 monitors, video disc, video disc player, text, dimensions variable
CR no.200
Collection Lannan Foundation, long-term loan to Dia Art Foundation, New York

Related work:
Fig.72 Standing or Left Standing 1999
Pencil, watercolour pencil, glue and masking tape on Waterford paper, 67.3 x 121.6
Collection of the artist

---

14 Consummate Mask of Rock
48–53 Text pages
102–5 Image pages

The original text is a cut-and-paste collage (fig.73) that forms part of a large sculptural installation consisting of sixteen limestone cubes displayed in pairs, one slightly larger than the other, arranged in a square/diamond (fig.75). Viewers are invited to take copies of the text from a stack of posters. Nauman regards this work as a cornerstone of his practice, in which the spatial and linguistic elements are interchangeable, bound by an inextricable if elliptical quality. Drawings such as fig.74 clearly show an algorithmic sequence through which the stone blocks are ordered. The installation has a formal similarity in its relational use of geometric blocks to the Diamond Mind, Forced Perspective and Enforced Perspective series from the same period.

Walter Biggs and Robin Hoffman recite the longest text in Raw Materials. This abstract poem is based on the children's game 'Rock, Paper, Scissors', in which each element has strengths and weaknesses in relation to the other two. When two elements are pitted against each other they either win, lose or draw. Nauman adds complexity to the inherently mathematical basis of this game by including a greatly expanded vocabulary that addresses complex emotional and psychological desires and denials. 'Mask', 'cover', 'need' and 'truth' occur most frequently in the two opening sections and recur regularly throughout the remaining text, often in combination or played off against each other. The terms very quickly cease to be clear cut as the artist compacts them into dense strata of meaning. As with First Poem Piece 1968 (figs.18–19), the addition and omission of particular words in different sentence constructions wring out multiple possibilities from a limited set of means. As the text progresses, terms already introduced are combined or restructured with new terms and strung into increasingly specific statements. By the end, its logic begins to resemble children's nursery rhymes such as 'There was an Old Lady Who Swallowed a Fly', in which a sequence of actions at once causal and incompatible are given an underlying logic, yet here cause and effect have been obscured by many layers of unconscious processes.

Figs.73, 75 Consummate Mask of Rock 1975
Sculpture: 8 limestone cubes (each side 38.1), 8 limestone cubes (each side 35.6), *c.*915 x 915 overall
Text: typewriting, graphite, paper, and tape on paper, 100.3 x 49.5 framed
CR no.238
Private Collection, San Francisco

Related works:
Fig.77 Arrangement of limestone blocks for/ "Consummate Mask of Rock"/eye level/REVERSE/(Castelli) 1975
Pencil on paper, 89 x 114
Drawings no.330
Collection Herbert, Ghent

Fig.76 (Consummate Mask of Rock) 1(18" cubes of granite or limestone/8 x 16" cubes of granite or limestone/ 1 1/2" gap 15'/1 1/2" gap 1975
Pencil on paper, 76.2 x 101.4
Drawings no.331
Collection of the artist

Fig.74 Methods of pairing stone blocks:/16 blocks - 8 large + 8 small (2" diff. on a side/18" and 16"cubes)/ a = large/b = small 1975
Ink on paper, 21 x 27
Drawings no.333
Collection of the artist

Human Companionship, Human Drain 1981
Lithograph on Rives BFK White paper, 76.2 x 55.9
Edition of 50, plus proofs
Prints no.46
Published by the Foundation for Contemporary Performance Arts, Inc., New York

---

15 Anthro/Socio
55 Text page
106–9 Image pages

The large-scale video installation from which this audio is taken consists of three wall-to-ceiling projections and three pairs of stacked monitors, some with the image inverted (fig.78). Each shows a close-up of the shaven-headed performance artist Rinde Eckert chanting in a powerful, almost operatic manner, sometimes extending different syllables yet retaining the simple melody. The statements loop non-synchronously yet interlock. For Raw Materials, Nauman uses only the first stanza 'Feed Me/Eat Me/Anthropology'. The second, 'Help Me/Hurt Me/Sociology', is related to various works including False Silence (see entry for no.8 above) and fig.79.

Eckert features in a number of other works in which three casts of his head are used and modified by Nauman. These include Shadow Puppet Spinning Head, Ten Heads Circle/Up and Down, Ten Heads Circle/In and Out, Rinde Head/Julie Head, Stacked, Back to Back and Rinde Head/Rinde Head, Stacked, Nose to Nose, all from 1990. Three casts of two other heads are also used in these and other works.

Fig.78 Anthro/Socio (Rinde Facing Camera) 1991
6 video disc players, 6 colour monitors, 3 video projectors, 6 video discs (colour, sound), dimensions variable
CR no.466
Ydessa Hendeles Art Foundation

Related works:
Fig.79 Eat Me Feed Me 1990
Oilstick, charcoal, graphite and tape on pieced paper, 112.4 x 161.9
Courtesy Daniel Weinberg Gallery, San Francisco

Fig.80 Anthro/Socio (Rinde Spinning) 1992
3 video projectors, 6 colour video monitors, 6 video disc players, 6 video discs (colour, sound), dimensions variable
CR no.476
Hamburger Kunsthalle, Hamburg

Fig.81 Rinde Spinning 1992
Colour photograph, 38.1 x 57.1
Edition of 45 plus proofs
CR no.478
Collection of the artist

16/17 Good Boy Bad Boy – Tucker/Joan
56–7 Text pages
110–13 Image pages

The video Good Boy Bad Boy 1985 (figs.82–93, 95–6) from which these audio tracks are taken has become one of Nauman's most celebrated works. Two actors – Joan Lancaster and Tucker Smallwood – are talking heads against a black screen, whose array of facial expressions reinforces their tones of voice. They recite twenty-five four-line stanzas relating to the human condition. Texts are read in a range of styles by both actors and loop non-synchronously. Each stanza conjugates a word or phrase such as 'good boy', 'bad girl', 'play', 'evil', using the pronouns 'I/You/We' to explore possible meanings, and ends with a definition of its term such as 'That was good' or 'This is evil'. Phrases often emphasise, specify, oppose or are consequences of previous stanzas. The final sequence is the only negative statement, beginning, 'I don't want to die' and concluding with 'This is fear of death'. There is a strong connection with World Peace, which has a similarly algorithmic structure that investigates possibilities within each set of terms (see entry for nos.19/20 below). In Raw Materials the male and female voices run concurrently from opposite speakers.

This work also has a number of connections with 100 Live and Die which also comprises one hundred lines exploring the human condition and the possibilities of language (see entry for no.7 above). Both exist as large neon sculptures (figs.40–5, 94). The video was first presented with the audio version of 100 Live and Die and the neon Hanged Man in the three-room installation Chambre d'Amis (Krefeld Piece) 1985 at the Museum Haus Esters, Krefeld, and subsequently in a private collector's house (fig.95).

Nauman's use of conjugation to explore the possibilities of language is simultaneously simple and complex. This is how we learn the basics of a foreign language, yet the words he selects incorporate the most fundamental levels of human experience and emotion. A further level of complexity is added by the different tones – objectivity, malice, compassion, pleading and so on – in which the text is read. Nauman's fascination with the impossibility of language to fix meanings is exemplified when the initial conviction each reading lends the text is eroded as successive repetitions destabilise and even contradict the previous recitals.

Figs.82–93 Good Boy Bad Boy 1985
95–6 2 colour video monitors, 2 video tape players, 2 video tapes (colour, sound), dimensions variable
Edition of 40
CR no.337
Published by Castelli-Sonnabend Videotapes and Films, New York, and Donald Young Gallery, Chicago

Related works:
Fig.95 Good Boy Bad Boy 1985
Part of Chambres d'Amis (Krefeld Piece) 1985
2 colour video monitors, 2 video tape players, 2 video tapes (colour, sound)
CR no.332
Museum of Contemporary Art, Chicago, Gerald S. Elliot Collection

Fig.94 Good Boy Bad Boy 1986–7
Neon tubing mounted on metal monolith,
349.3 x 548.6 x 37.5
CR no.370
Daros Collection, Switzerland

---

18 Shit In Your Hat – Head On A Chair
59 Text page
114–15 Image pages

The audio is taken from an installation with a video projection of a female mime, Julie Goelle, following spoken instructions, in front of which a wooden chair is suspended from the ceiling with a wax cast of Juliet Myers's head on the open-seat frame (figs.97–8, 101). The chair was cast and used in the series of three sculptures South America Circle, South America Square and South America Triangle from 1981 dealing with torture in South American regimes. The same mime and a similar cast head feature in the multiple monitor and projection installation Shadow Puppets and Instructed Mime 1990 (fig.100).

Using a limited lexicon of words, a male voice issues a series of inter-related commands. The structure of the text runs through many permutations of four verbs (put, drop, show, shit) and six nouns (hat, table, head, hand, lap, face). What begins as a simple set of commands quickly develops into a manipulative, humiliating and sadistic exercise in power that concludes with the instructions 'Shit in your hat. Show me your hat. Put your hat on your head. Put your head on the table.' Like 100 Live and Die or Good Boy Bad Boy, there is a strongly mathematical structure to this work, where the words are treated as properties organised into strings of equations that throw up unexpected results.

Fig.97–8 Shit in Your Hat – Head on a Chair 1990
101 Chair, wax head, rear-screen projector and screen, video tape (colour, sound), dimensions variable
CR no.460
Colección de Arte Contemporáneo Fundación "la Caixa", Barcelona

Related works:
Fig.100 Shadow Puppets and Instructed Mime 1990
3 wax heads, linen, wood, 4 colour video monitors, 4 video projectors, 6 video tape players, 6 video tapes (colour, sound), dimensions variable
CR no.459
Collection Emanuel Hoffmann Foundation, permanent loan to the Kunstmuseum Basel

Fig.99 Installation Drawing for Shit in Your Hat 1990
Pencil on paper, 27.9 x 35.6
Collection of the artist

19/20 World Peace – Bernard/mei mei
60–1 Text pages
116–19 Image pages

The audio is taken from the five-screen video installation, World Peace (Projected) 1996 (fig.106), featuring five actors reciting the text. Their images switch abruptly, disorienting the simplicity of the relationships between speaker and listener at the core of the text. A related version of the work, World Peace (Received) 1996 (fig.107), uses monitors instead of projections. In Raw Materials the male and female voices run concurrently from opposite speakers.

A man (Bernard Pomerance) and woman (mei mei Berssenbrugge) recite a series of simple phrases around the verbs 'talk' and 'listen'. In the first section, they conjugate these verbs using the singular 'I/You' and plural 'We/They' stems, such as 'I'll talk/ They'll listen', which is then reversed to 'They'll talk/ I'll listen'. In each stanza, the statement is reversed in the following line, before moving on to the next in the sequence. This section pivots in the middle, where the seventh stanza, using 'We/They', and the eighth, using 'They/We', are inversions of each other. This reversal continues through the text so that the fourteenth and final stanza inverts the 'I/You' structure of the first stanza to create a grammatical Rorschach image. Like a round-dance, the text adheres to a structure in which progression through a series leads back to the point of origin. In the second section, Nauman expands the lines, personalising them into phrases such as 'They'll talk to us/We'll listen to them'. This grammatical exploration of these two verbs is confined to a simple cellular structure seen in other works like 100 Live and Die or Good Boy Bad Boy (see entries for nos.7 and 16/17 above).

As with those works, there are strong connections with the work of composers like Steve Reich or Terry Riley who explore modular units of melody. With an economy of means, Nauman simultaneously represents the simplicity and complexity of communication.

Fig.106 World Peace (Projected) 1996
5 video discs, 5 video projectors, 5 video disc players, 5 pairs of auxiliary speakers, 5 amplifiers, remote control, 6 utility carts, maximum room size 914.4 x 1097.3
Bayerische Staatsgemäldesammlungen, Munich – Pinakothek der Moderne, Sammlung Moderne Kunst

Related works:

Fig.107 World Peace (Received) 1996
5 video discs, 5 video disc players, 5 video monitors, 6 utility carts, dimensions variable, maximum room size 914.4 x 1097.3
St Louis Art Museum, Missouri

Fig.102 World Peace (Projected) 1996
Pencil and collaged video prints on paper, 56.5 x 76.5 sheet, 61.6 x 81.3 frame
Collection of the artist

Fig.103 World Peace (Received) 1996
Pencil and collaged polaroids on paper, 56.5 x 76.5 sheet, 61.6 x 81.3 frame
Collection of the artist

Fig.104 Sketch for camera movement/World Peace 1996
Pen on paper, 27.3 x 21.6
Collection of the artist

Fig.105 Notes for End of the World and World Peace 1996
Pen on paper, 27.9 x 21.6
Collection of the artist

---

21 Raw Material – MMMM
63 Text page
120–1 Image pages

The audio is taken from Raw Material – MMMM 1990 (fig.108), part of the Raw Material series, which includes two other works, Raw Material – BRRR 1990 (fig.109) and Raw Material – OK, OK, OK 1990 (see entry for no.9 above). These works have the same visual structure, and focus on an equally simple vocal exercise that recalls Meredith Monk's theory of the choreographed voice. Each exercise also problematises language and speech by evoking stuttering when language becomes locked on a single syllable. This was the first time that Nauman had used himself as the subject of a video since the late 1960s. Nauman hums 'mmmm' on a fifteen-second loop. The melodic drone oscillates and in the background various taps and clicks create an off-kilter rhythm. These can be explained by watching the video, where his head spins around, the sound increasing in intensity as his face spins past the camera. This footage is projected on a screen, and on two monitors, on one of which it is inverted and reversed. Colour effects added to this raw material switch dramatically to emulate what happened when Nauman tried viewing the footage on an upside-down monitor. Each work in the series was reconfigured the following year when these colour switches were replaced by colour fades, as in Raw Material with Continuous Shift – MMMM 1991. Nauman's related neon work (fig.110) provides a link to his long-standing interest in stretching meaning to the limits of coherence.

Fig.108 Raw Material – MMMM 1990
Video projector, 2 colour video monitors, 2 video disc players, 2 video discs (colour, sound), dimensions variable
CR no.455
Musée Cantonal des Beaux-Arts, Lausanne

Related works:

Fig.110 My Name As Though It Were Written on the Surface of the Moon 1968
Neon tubing with clear glass tubing suspension frame, in 8 parts, 30 x 549 x 7
Edition of 3
CR no.117
Stedelijk Museum, Amsterdam

Fig.109 Raw Material – BRRR 1990
Video projector, 2 colour video monitors, 2 video tape players, 2 video tapes (colour, sound), dimensions variable
CR no.454
ZKM, Museum für Neue Kunst, Karlsruhe

Figs.56–7 Raw Material – OK, OK, OK 1990
Raw Material with Continuous Shift – OK, OK, OK 1991
See entry for no.9 above for details

Raw Material with Continuous Shift – MMMM 1991
Video projector, 2 colour video monitors, 2 video disc players, 2 video discs (colour, sound), dimensions variable
CR no.472
Friedrich Christian Flick Collection

Raw Material with Continuous Shift – BRRR 1991
Video projector, 2 colour video monitors, 2 video disc players, 2 video discs (colour, sound), dimensions variable
CR no.471
Collection Kröller-Müller, Otterlo

Biography

Bruce Nauman was born in Fort Wayne, Indiana, in 1941. He received a BS in mathematics and physics from the University of Wisconsin in 1964 and an MFA from the University of California, Davis in 1966. He has also been awarded an Honorary Doctorate from the California Institute of the Arts, Valencia (2000). Nauman's first solo exhibition was held at the Nicholas Wilder Gallery, Los Angeles in 1966, and he has since exhibited widely in galleries and museums across North America and Europe. He has made multiple contributions to Documenta (1968, 1972, 1982) in Kassel, Germany, and to the Whitney Biennial (1984, 1991, 1997) in New York. Nauman's first major exhibition in Britain was held at the Whitechapel Art Gallery in 1987, curated by Nicholas Serota. A large retrospective of his work was organised in 1994 by the Walker Art Center, Minneapolis, and the Hirshhorn Museum and Sculpture Garden, Washington, DC – it also travelled to Madrid, Los Angeles and New York. Bruce Nauman: Image/Text 1966–1996 toured to the Hayward Gallery, London, in 1998. Nauman was awarded the Golden Lion prize at the Venice Biennale in 1999 and, in 2004, the Japan Art Association's Praemium Imperiale Award for sculpture. His room-sized video installation MAPPING THE STUDIO II with color shift, flip, flop & flip/flop (Fat Chance John Cage) 2001 has recently been acquired by Tate. Nauman currently lives and works on a ranch in northern New Mexico, and is represented by Sperone Westwater, New York.

Selected Bibliography

Bruce Nauman, exh. cat., Walker Art Center, Minneapolis 1994. Edited by Joan Simon. Catalogue raisonné and texts by Neal Benezra, Kathy Halbreich, Paul Schimmel and Robert Storr.

Bruce Nauman, exh. cat., Whitechapel Art Gallery, London 1987. Texts by Nicholas Serota, Joan Simon and Jean Christophe Ammann.

Bruce Nauman: Drawings 1965–1986, exh. cat., Museum für Gegenwartskunst, Basel 1986. Catalogue raisonné and texts by Coosje van Bruggen, Dieter Koepplin and Franz Meyer.

Bruce Nauman: Image/Text 1966–1996, exh. cat., Hayward Gallery, London 1998. Essays by Jean-Charles Masséra, Vincent Labaume, François Albera, Gijs van Tuyl and Christine van Assche. Reprinted texts by Marcia Tucker, Willoughby Sharp, Chris Dercon, Joan Simon, Tony Oursler and Michele De Angelus.

Bruce Nauman: Prints 1970–89, exh. cat., Castelli Graphics, New York, Monk Gallery, New York, and Donald Young Gallery, Chicago 1989. Catalogue raisonné and essays by John Yau and interview with Christopher Cordes.

Bruce Nauman: Theatres of Experience, exh. cat., Deutsche Guggenheim, Berlin 2003. Texts by Thomas Krens, Susan Cross and Christine Hoffmann.

Bruce Nauman: Work from 1965 to 1972, exh. cat., Los Angeles County Museum of Art, Los Angeles 1972. Texts by Jane Livingston and Marcia Tucker.

Janet Kraynak (ed.), Please Pay Attention Please: Bruce Nauman's Words, Cambridge, Massachusetts, and London 2003.

Coosje van Bruggen, Bruce Nauman, New York 1988.

Photographic Credits

Cover & figs.13, 14, 16, 78 — Robert Keziere/Ydessa Hendeles Art Foundation; Frontispiece & figs.9–12, 111–16, 121–5 — Marcus Leith and Andrew Dunkley/Tate Photography; Fig.1 — Juliet Myers; Figs.2, 17, 18, 60 — Kröller-Müller Museum, Otterlo; Figs.3, 4, 8, 19, 26, 36, 37, 59, 62, 66–8, 70–2, 74–6, 82–93, 99–103, 106, 107 — Courtesy Sperone Westwater; Fig.5 — Michael Auping; Figs.6, 7, 69 — Rod Tidnam/Tate Photography; Figs.9–12 — Marcus Leith and Andrew Dunkley/Tate Photography; Figs.20–4 — Foto: Uwe H. Seyl, Stuttgart; Fig.25 — David Lambert/Tate Photography; Figs.28–32, 94 — Courtesy Donald Young Gallery, Chicago; Figs.27, 35, 42 — Courtesy Walker Art Center, Minneapolis; Fig.33 — © The Art Institute of Chicago; Fig.34 — Tate Photography; Fig.38 — Courtesy of Friedrich Christian Flick Collection; Figs.39, 48, 54, 55 — © Gemini G.E.L., Los Angeles; Figs.40, 41, 43–5 — Benesse Art Site Naoshima/Benesse Corporation, © Mitsumasa Fujitsuka, © Kojo Murakami; Figs.46, 77 — Courtesy Collection Herbert, Ghent; Figs.47, 64 — Courtesy of the Artist; Fig.49 — Courtesy Robert Arber, Marfa; Fig.50 — © Solomon R. Guggenheim Museum, NY; Fig.51 — © Margherita Spiluttini; Fig.52 — © Giorgio Colombo, Milano; Fig.53 — Courtesy Sonnabend Gallery, NY; Fig.56 — Daniel Weinberg Gallery, photograph courtesy Douglas M. Parker, Los Angeles, CA; Fig.57 — Photograph courtesy SFMOMA; Fig.58 — Leo Castelli Gallery, NY; Fig.61 — Raussmüller Collection; Fig.63 — Photo: Kunstmuseum Basel, Martin Bühler; Fig.65 — Courtesy Froehlich Collection, Stuttgart; Fig.73 — Private Collection; Figs.79, 109 — Courtesy Daniel Weinberg Gallery; Fig.80 — Bridgeman Art Library; Fig.81 — Andrew Dunkley/Tate Photography; Fig.95 — © Attilio Maranzano; Fig.96 — Stefan Altenburger, Zürich; Fig.97, 98, 101 — Fundació "la Caixa"; Figs.99,104, 105 — the Artist; Fig.108 — Photo: J.-C. Ducret, © Musée cantonal des Beaux Arts de Lausanne; Fig.110 — Stedelijk Museum Amsterdam; Figs.117, 120 — Courtesy Hector Pottie